Praise for *The Foxes of Belair*

"Any student or fan of Thoroughbred racing history will be delighted to lay eyes on *The Foxes of Belair*. Meticulously researched and laid out in intimate detail, the story of Gallant Fox and Omaha, father and son winners of the American Triple Crown, is unique in the annals of the sport. Jennifer Kelly provides an exhaustive treatment of their singular feat that will educate both the casual and dedicated follower of racing."—Lenny Shulman, author of *Head to Head: Conversations with a Generation of Horse Racing Legends*

"*The Foxes of Belair: Gallant Fox, Omaha, and the Quest for the Triple Crown* is author Jennifer Kelly's second volume of Triple Crown history, and it's another good one. With meticulous research and an engaging narrative, Kelly brings the intertwined stories of William Woodward and his Belair Stud champions to life. But the title raises an intriguing question: who are the 'foxes'? Gallant Fox, the winner of the Triple Crown in 1930, is an obvious choice, and the 1935 Triple Crown winner Omaha probably is as well. But Kelly's well-told recounting of how Woodward parlayed the purchase of a few inexpensive mares into the dominant racing stable of the 1930s and his influence on racing in the United States and Europe suggest that the Jockey Club chairman was the slyest fox of them all."—Milton C. Toby, author of *Taking Shergar: Thoroughbred Racing's Most Famous Cold Case*

"For anyone whose interest in Thoroughbred racing is piqued by a view back into the history of the sport, here's your new hero: Jennifer Kelly. Her latest work, *The Foxes of Belair: Gallant Fox, Omaha, and the Quest for the Triple Crown* is as good as it gets. Turning these pages, I found myself standing next to 'Sunny Jim' Fitzsimmons and William Woodward, eavesdropping as they gave their jockey his instructions, cheering as their horses neared the finish line. Replete with classic figures of American racing like Man o' War and Citation, Earl Sande and Willie Saunders, Jimmy Breslin and W. C. Vreeland, Kelly's concise history will captivate you from cover to cover just like her previous work, *Sir Barton and the Making of the Triple Crown*."—John Perrotta, WGAW

"Spanning more than two centuries of racing lore, *The Foxes of Belair* traces international currents that created a unique father and son legacy. Illuminating the long view and fine details, Jennifer S. Kelly celebrates the power of intention, perseverance, and passion for the sport of kings."—Dorothy Ours, author of *Battleship: A Daring Heiress, a Teenage Jockey, and America's Horse*

The Foxes of Belair

The Foxes
of Belair

Gallant Fox, Omaha, and the Quest for the Triple Crown

JENNIFER S. KELLY

UNIVERSITY PRESS OF KENTUCKY

Scholarly publisher for the Commonwealth,
serving Bellarmine University, Berea College, Centre
College of Kentucky, Eastern Kentucky University,
The Filson Historical Society, Georgetown College,
Kentucky Historical Society, Kentucky State University,
Morehead State University, Murray State University,
Northern Kentucky University, Spalding University,
Transylvania University, University of Kentucky,
University of Louisville, University of Pikeville, and
Western Kentucky University.
All rights reserved.

Editorial and Sales Offices: The University Press of Kentucky
663 South Limestone Street, Lexington, Kentucky 40508-4008
www.kentuckypress.com

Library of Congress Cataloging-in-Publication Data

Names: Kelly, Jennifer S., 1977– author.
Title: The foxes of Belair : Gallant Fox, Omaha, and the quest for the
    Triple Crown / Jennifer S. Kelly.
Description: Lexington : The University Press of Kentucky, [2023] | Series:
    Horses in history | Includes bibliographical references and index.
Identifiers: LCCN 2022048811 | ISBN 9780813197371 (hardcover) | ISBN
    9780813197388 (pdf) | ISBN 9780813197395 (epub)
Subjects: LCSH: Horse racing—United States—History—20th century. |
    Race horses—Breeding—United States—History—20th century. |
    Woodward, William, 1876–1953. | Belair Stud (Bowie, Md.) | Gallant
    Fox (Horse), 1927–1954. | Omaha (Horse), 1932–1959. | Triple Crown
    (U.S. horse racing) | Horse breeders—Maryland—Biography.
Classification: LCC SF335.U5 K45 2023 | DDC 798.400973—
    dc23/eng/20221118
LC record available at https://lccn.loc.gov/2022048811

Member of the Association
of University Presses

For Jackson and Beckett, who make this
life brighter.

For Gallant Fox and Omaha, sire and son, whose
greatness is both immortal and immeasurable.

Contents

Prologue

The Battle Joined

The crowd sees the horses before they hear them, rounding that final turn into the long straight. All along the sweeping grandstand, faces crane toward the action as the wire looms in the distance, growing closer with each hoofbeat.

Arms pumping, legs reaching, shards of grass and earth flying, the herd meets the thunderous cacophony of shouts, spectators urging on their favorites with voices straining to their limits. As the horses roar by, the gathered crowd, resplendent in their marvelous fashions, stand impervious to the soaked grass beneath their feet. Their focus is the spectacle before them, the scant seconds of battle ticking by as the undulating herd moves on.

Over the soft turf, bathed in the tentative sunshine of a clearing day, two horses fly ahead of the rest, long, languid strides pushing them faster and farther than the faltering lot behind them. After nearly two miles, sixteen furlongs of patient endurance, they fly side by side toward the inevitable finish, noses apart. The men on their backs stretch themselves forward as if they are mere extensions of the machines beneath them, sinew and bone, fixed on one goal: first under the line.

With the wire imminent, the sleek dark filly pulls ahead of her competitor, body and soul bent toward widening her advantage. The other, a powerful golden colt, calls upon the same deep reserves that had brought him to this point time and again. Beneath twin spires, over venerated ground, down long straightaways, he had produced

1

the turn of foot needed for this final push, his great stride swallowing ground to find victory and a crown. Years of training, of planning, of hoping were down to this.

As they near the finish, a hundred thousand pairs of eyes fix on the spot, anticipating the sight of the end. Who will show first? Will it be Omaha, the Triple Crown winner who crossed an ocean to vie for this prize? Or will it be Quashed, the homegrown filly who had proven her determination over the longest of courses? Will it be white with red or black with white? The pair come down to the wire as one, inseparable, the battle joined again and again. *How can this end?* It feels like they will always be in flight.

Just when it looks as though he might take the advantage, that she might give up ground, she fights back and he tries again. The crescendo of sound abates as the crowd watches the denouement, an eerie quiet greeting the finale. The two horses finish in perfect synchronicity, a climax that is at once immortal and fleeting. At the final jump, it is not the click of a shutter that determines their fates, but the blink of an eye, the adjudication of a man. Dark and sleek or golden and powerful? Hopes realized or dreams denied?

Against the backdrop of the grandstand of Royal Ascot, the drama between Omaha and Quashed played out. The third Triple Crown winner's very presence was owed to the ambitions of the man who had crafted his pedigree, thrilled at his victories, and dreamed of his success. William Woodward had everything a man of his time could want: a family, a fortune, and societal status that opened doors. Yet he pursued one passion: breeding and owning a horse capable of winning on the sport of horse racing's biggest days. Omaha's turn on the Ascot heath was indicative of the heights that Woodward aspired to, ambitions that both drove the man and changed the sport. His decades on racetracks both English and American would see racing's evolution from a game played by sportsmen to an industry spanning a continent, with a crown at its center and a door wide open to the world.

All because a boy had a dream and a man had the means to realize it.

1

A New King in Town

On a brisk December day in 1925, the smooth black hull of the *Minnetonka* sliced through the gray waters of New York Harbor while workers milled about on the dock, awaiting its arrival.[1] With only days until the Christmas holiday, this homecoming seemed business as usual, but among the passengers on this ship's decks was a horse who would usher in a new era in racing, standing in his specially appointed stall awaiting his first breaths of New World air.

As the ship slid into place, Arthur B. Hancock, the master of not one but two formidable breeding operations, watched dockside, awaiting the precious equine cargo inside. From his special stall, the stallion emerged into the open air as his new owner watched; the groom who had crossed an ocean with his charge led the brown horse to a ramp. The stallion's hooves resonated on the wood as he took in the new world around him. His head high, the horse stopped for a moment, bombarded by the new sights and smells. *America.* His human companion pulled on the lead shank, prompting the horse to continue downward toward the dock and a waiting railcar. The men paused, their gazes drawn to the tall stallion, their eyes fixed on the white star in the center of his forehead and the fleck of white on his muzzle. Nearby, the man who had signed the check, himself newly disembarked from his cross-ocean journey on the *Mauritania,* oversaw this precious cargo's transfer from ship to shore.

Under Hancock's watchful eye, Sir Gallahad, winner of the French Two Thousand Guineas and the Lincolnshire Handicap, conqueror of French champion Épinard, stepped off the New York

Sir Gallahad III at Claiborne Farm, 1937. Keeneland Library Meadors Collection.

dock and into a railcar sitting atop a barge, a spare structure that would float them from dock to shore.[2] His destination? Claiborne Farm, Paris, Kentucky.

In the late afternoon chill of December 1925, the arrival of Sir Gallahad signaled the dawn of a new age in the sport, the age of the syndicated stallion and the Triple Crown.[3]

Sir Gallahad's purchase and import to the United States came at a time when Claiborne Farm needed another good sire to bolster its roster of stallions. So necessary and valuable was the new stallion to Hancock and his partners in the sale that the horseman sailed to France to inspect Sir Gallahad at owner Jefferson Davis Cohn's Haras du Bois-Roussel near Alençon. After making the deal to bring the stallion to the United States, Hancock oversaw Sir Gallahad's boarding on the *Minnetonka* and then sailed on the speedier *Mauritania* to meet him there in New York. Hancock understood the importance of this purchase not only for his farms, Claiborne and Ellerslie, but also for American breeding in general. As the second generation of a family that would outlast more than one dynasty in racing, Hancock understood what made Sir Gallahad the right horse to add to Claiborne's list of stallions.

Arthur Hancock had learned his discernment of breeding stock from his father, Captain Richard Hancock. The elder Hancock, a thrice-injured Confederate soldier, became a Thoroughbred breeder when he married Thomasia Harris and then inherited her family's estate Ellerslie, outside of Charlottesville, Virginia. In 1871, Hancock accompanied his friend Thomas W. Doswell on a trip to Pimlico to watch Eolus, Doswell's own stakes winner, race. Taken by the colt's conformation and temperament, Hancock knew that Eolus could help him create a Thoroughbred breeding program at Ellerslie, but Doswell was asking too much for the horse. Finally, six years later, Eolus had changed owners and Hancock tracked the horse to Maryland. The determined horseman offered to trade his own Scathelock, a half brother to Eolus, for Eolus himself. The stallion helped Hancock establish Ellerslie as an eminent Virginia breeding operation, producing horses like Knight of Ellerslie, winner of the 1884 Preakness Stakes.

His father's successor, Arthur Boyd Hancock married Nancy Tucker Clay in 1908, and, two years later, inherited the thirteen hundred acres that would ultimately become Claiborne Farm.[4] The hiatus in New York racing after antigambling legislation effectively shut the sport down prompted an exodus of horses and owners from racing. Some opted to move to Europe while others left the sport altogether, including owner and breeder James R. Keene. Initially, Keene had leased the stallion Celt, long considered the second best of the crop of 1905 behind his stablemate Colin, to Hancock to stand stud for two seasons at Ellerslie.[5] However, Keene would not extend the lease past 1912, opting instead to sell Celt along with the rest of his breeding and racing stock. Keene died in early 1913. He had sold his Castleton Farm in 1911 and the remainder of his breeding and racing stock went on the auction block eight months after his death.[6] Hancock bought Celt at the Keene dispersal sale at Madison Square Garden on September 2, 1913. The master of Ellerslie

Arthur B. Hancock of Claiborne Farm. Keeneland Library Cook
Collection.

and Claiborne paid $20,000 for the stallion and brought him back to Virginia.

Celt was indicative of the type of stallion that Hancock sought over and over: good racehorses coupled with quality bloodlines that were just below the top tier and, thus, were good prospects at affordable prices.[7] As a stallion, Celt's time was marked by a low ebb in breeding in America, owing to the suspension of racing in New York and the slow recovery within the industry as a result. Regardless, Celt marked himself as a quality sire even with his limited access to good mares; he sired a total of thirty stakes winners, including Belmont Futurity winner Dunboyne and Coaching Club American Oaks winner Polka Dot.[8] His foals tended to show speed and quality early, mostly at sprint distances.[9] In his final season at stud, Celt covered a mare named Fairy Ray and produced a lovely chestnut filly named Marguerite. She would become the best known and most productive extension of Celt's quality after his early death at age fourteen in 1919.

After Celt's purchase, Hancock then ventured to England in 1915 to find a stallion to complement what Celt already brought to Ellerslie, knowing that he needed one with an exceptional pedigree and respectable form on the racetrack.[10] British breeding stock was still considered among the best in the world and a number of Americans were in the market for English bloodstock to add variety into the country's breeding lines. The fledgling British Bloodstock Agency spotlighted Wrack, who had wins both on the flat and over jumps, as a candidate. Wrack fit the profile of what Hancock was looking for: good form on the track and a great pedigree to pass on in the breeding shed.[11] His sire, Robert le Diable, had won the Doncaster Cup and the Duke of York Stakes; and his dam, Samphire, was a product of Isinglass, 1893 English Triple Crown winner, and Chelandry, winner of the 1897 One Thousand Guineas.[12] Wrack came from the best mare line of his breeder, Lord Rosebery, and the horse's gameness made him one of his breeder's favorites.[13] All of this added up to a pedigree deep in classic winners at the bargain price of $10,000.[14] At a time when New York's racing scene was still in recovery and the possibility of war loomed over the world, Arthur Hancock was thinking ahead. He understood that these sturdy mid-priced sires would be his bread and butter, allowing him to produce enough horses to become the successor to prolific breeder John E. Madden of Kentucky's Hamburg Place.

Both Celt and Wrack became leading sires in the country during their years at Claiborne and Ellerslie. Since sires were ranked based on money won by their progeny, Hancock's job was to see that his sires had full books of mares to cover each season. By 1921, Celt was ranked the top sire in the United States and was in the top ten for five of his seven seasons; Wrack did not climb quite that high, but he was second on the list in 1922 and in the top ten over his long stud career.[15]

What the prolific breeding of sires like Celt and Wrack did for Hancock was allow him to step away from Ellerslie, which had been the family's primary residence for many years, and devote more attention to the fledgling property at Claiborne Farm. While Ellerslie was in Albemarle County, Virginia, outside of Charlottesville, Claiborne was more centrally located for the breeding industry in Paris, Kentucky, about twenty miles east of Lexington. When Wrack came to America to stand stud, Hancock installed him at Claiborne, not Ellerslie. Hancock was all in for breeding in Kentucky, where his stallions would be more accessible. Claiborne would soon stand out as one of the preeminent studs in the country.

Hancock continued to depend on Europe for more stallions to reinvigorate his breeding lines at both of his breeding establishments. He brought in sires that belonged to other owners, such as War Cloud, who sired the Coaching Club American Oaks winner Nimba; Omar Khayyam, 1917 Kentucky Derby winner; and Stimulus, winner of the 1922 Pimlico Futurity and a close second in the Belmont Futurity that same year.[16] Neither War Cloud nor Omar Khayyam proved to be sires of import, but Stimulus, owned by Marshall Field III, became a top ten sire in the 1930s and also led the juvenile sire list and the broodmare sire list. Claiborne's record of standing sires with consistent crops of progeny both on and off the track created the reputation that the Hancock family enjoys to this day, one which other breeders and owners banked on whenever they sent their own horses to the farm.[17] Photos of Sir Gallahad winning the Lincolnshire Handicap in *Sporting and Dramatic News* caught Hancock's attention, prompting him to reach out to the British Bloodstock Agency to inquire about purchasing the French horse.[18] If the stallion was as good at stud as he was on the racetrack, he would make a dynamic addition to the farm's roster. Hancock was willing to bet that this son of Teddy and Plucky Liege had what he needed, but he needed the money to make it happen.

Leaning on his reputation for finding stallions of value, Hancock brought together several men who had their own horses at Claiborne and formed a syndicate to purchase another European stallion to diversify Hancock's sire roster. Shareholders in the syndicate would have the right to breed their mares to the stallion and keep the foals that resulted from the covers. No doubt the men recruited for this syndicate would have been familiar with what Jefferson Davis Cohn's Sir Gallahad had accomplished in both France and England. Part of the same crop as Épinard, the French-bred colt had raced at a variety of distances and demonstrated the right balance of speed and stamina to win at the highest level. Sir Gallahad had also defeated Épinard in a match race, but, because he was more of a miler than a distance horse, that put him below Épinard in the estimation of the French breeding establishment. In America, where shorter races were run more often than the longer distances favored by Europeans, his speed was far more of an advantage. Arthur Hancock traveled to France in November 1925 to negotiate with Cohn on behalf of the syndicate and made a deal to bring Sir Gallahad to the United States for a reported $125,000.[19]

Of all of the sires that the master of Ellerslie and Claiborne had brought in, Sir Gallahad, or Sir Gallahad III as he was known in the United States, was by far the biggest investment he had made.[20] Syndicates of this type were not new; bloodstock agent William Allison had put one together to bring the stallion Tracery back to England in 1923.[21] Not even Hancock, with his dual studs and prolific production of horses, could foot the bill for such a high-class stallion.[22] To secure this new addition for Claiborne's book of stallions, Hancock needed money men. He recruited three prominent owners and breeders to partner with him on the massive investment required to bring the stallion to America.

Marshall Field III, grandson of the founder of the same-named department store, grew up in England, where he attended both Eton and Cambridge before starting his career, not in his grandfather's department stores but as a bookkeeper for a brokerage house. He joined the Army as the United States entered World War I. After the war, he went into banking and then expanded his investments in other areas. Like August Belmont II and other figures in the sport of horse racing in this era, Field played polo and then turned to racing and breeding as well. In addition to his American interests, he also had an English stable, where he engaged Captain Cecil Boyd-Rochfort as his trainer. Field kept several mares at Claiborne, getting the Kentucky Oaks winner Nimba from War Cloud before that stallion's untimely death.[23]

Robert Fairbairn, a Nabisco executive and former president of the National Horse Show, was new to breeding Thoroughbreds, but not to horses: he bred Clydesdales and Standardbreds and had established Fairholme Farm in Kentucky. His successes on the racetrack were to come, but he knew that the chance to breed to a champion like Sir Gallahad III could yield good horses for his nascent stable.[24] While both Fairbairn and Field had much to gain from their investment, the syndicate had another partner who would reap benefits that not even he could have imagined.

William Woodward had moved away from standing stallions and foaling broodmares at his Belair Stud in Maryland; instead, he housed his weanlings and yearlings there as he decided which he wanted to keep for racing and which he would sell. He had started breeding nearly two decades earlier and had purchased several mares from France in 1914, all sired by the undefeated French champion Ajax. From that same consignment of horses Jefferson Davis Cohn had purchased Teddy, also sired by Ajax.[25] World War I changed the continent's racing calendar, so Teddy raced first in Spain and next in France, winning six of his eight races before he was retired to stud. Cohn bred Teddy to Plucky Liege, daughter of English classic winner Spearmint and dam of multiple stakes winners. Their mating produced Sir Gallahad III. Woodward, fond of Ajax's influence on his progeny, happily contributed to the effort to bring Sir Gallahad III, son of Teddy and grandson of Ajax, to America. Woodward kept his mares at Claiborne and had already purchased a number of horses from Hancock, including a Celt filly that raced once in the white and red silks of Belair before Woodward retired her to broodmare life.[26] Becoming a part of the Sir Gallahad III syndicate was another chance for Woodward to grow Belair's racing and breeding stock. The stallion would bring him more than just a good pedigree to pair his broodmares with. This investment would yield him opportunities and victories akin to those he had dreamed of as a boy.

When Sir Gallahad III stepped off the van and took his place in the stallion barn at Claiborne Farm, this quartet of owners and breeders could not have anticipated how one horse would revolutionize the sport as they knew it. Indeed, the new stallion "was destined to exercise a more potent influence upon the American breeding fabric than any other stallion imported for many years."[27] Their purchase set the stage for Sir Barton's pioneering Triple Crown win to go from a novel concept to a celebrated tradition within a few short years, thanks to the vision of a breeder and owner who wanted to see his colors bring home these classics of American horse racing.

2

Familial Ambition

The railcar that had carried Sir Gallahad III from New York to Paris, Kentucky, was supplied by one of the members of the syndicate that Arthur Hancock had put together, William Woodward.[1] After nearly twenty years of breeding at his Belair Stud in Maryland, Woodward had his share of experience with stallions and brood-mares. As he continued his efforts to produce a champion, he knew that the new stallion could be a game changer and was more than happy to put his money into finding out.

Woodward's willingness to finance Hancock's endeavor was another step forward for the banker and breeder as he pursued his goal: a horse capable of winning on racing's biggest days. From Epsom to Ascot, from Belmont to Pimlico, William Woodward's pursuit of the sport's greatest prizes, including the Epsom Derby, was possible because of the fortune he had amassed and the determination that dated back to his earliest years.

In 1665, the governor of New York, Richard Nicolls, in his first year of command, made it a priority that his colony include something essential to many an Englishman: a racetrack. Laid out over what is now known as Hempstead Plain in modern-day Nassau County, the grass course stands as the first known formal course in what became the United States of America.[2] Then, the breeding of racehorses was still in its infancy, with many horses imported from England to the colonies for the sporting endeavors of their owners. Two centuries later, Americans like Pierre Lorillard were sending their American-bred horses to England to race with the best that Europe had to offer. One of those horses was a colt named Iroquois.

Bred in Pennsylvania by Aristides Welch, the brown colt was by Leamington, an English stakes winner who had been imported to the United States in 1865. In addition to Iroquois, Leamington sired Harold, 1879 Preakness Stakes winner; Longfellow, Saratoga Cup winner and a sire of Kentucky Derby, Preakness, and Travers winners; and Aristides, the winner of the first Kentucky Derby in 1875.[3] Pierre Lorillard III, grandson of the founder of Lorillard Tobacco Company, admired Leamington so much that he purchased all of Welch's yearlings by the English stallion, including the young Iroquois. On the heels of his success with another Welch-bred horse, Parole, Lorillard sent Iroquois to England. Though Iroquois was not a big horse, only fifteen hands, 2½ inches, he found great success over the English turf, winning four races at age two.[4] At three, though, Iroquois became a history maker.

In the 1881 Two Thousand Guineas at Newmarket, Iroquois had been entered as a rabbit for his stablemate Barrett, but ended up finishing second instead; the one-mile distance was not enough ground for the son of Leamington to run at his best. At Epsom, though, the mile-and-a-half Derby was ideal for Iroquois, who stormed home late to win the storied classic by a length over Guineas winner Peregrine. The New York Stock Exchange even stopped trading as word of the victory circulated.[5] Four months later, Iroquois won the St. Leger at Doncaster, a 1¾-mile test that was another of the sophomore classics in England. Had Iroquois won the Guineas, the Lorillard colt would have been crowned the "triple event" winner, the fourth winner of the English Triple Crown.[6]

When the news of Iroquois's win at Epsom came down in America, Lorillard received the ample congratulations of his fellow sportsmen. His success in England left an impression on other American owners, like James R. Keene, whose Foxhall would win the Ascot Gold Cup the following year. Iroquois's and Foxhall's wins in two of

England's biggest races became an inspiration for generations of Americans who aspired to race their horses there.

A few years after Iroquois's win, the future master of Belair would sit down to breakfast with his parents and sister and hear his father, who followed the equine sports with the expected vigor of a late nineteenth-century gentleman, relate that Pierre Lorillard was the first American to win the Epsom Derby. "The remark made an impression on me," an adult Woodward would remember years later, "and I made up my mind (not knowing if I could ever own a race horse or hardly what a race horse was) to be the second American to win the Derby."[7]

With that, a dream was born.

Much like his contemporaries with the names Vanderbilt and Whitney, William Woodward was a member of a family of means. Born April 7, 1876, the only son of William Woodward Jr. and wife, Sarah Abigail Rodman, the younger Woodward was the last of the couple's children. He was named simply William Woodward rather than William Woodward III. He and his three sisters descended from a family that settled in Maryland in the early eighteenth century, making Anne Arundel County their home.[8] After some success in their native state, William Jr. and his brother James had moved to New York to pursue their business interests after the Civil War.[9] William Jr. had worked in the boot and shoe wholesale business with his uncle, also named William Woodward, who owned a cotton goods business with his nephew W. H. Baldwin Jr. in Baltimore.[10] In New York, William Jr. opened his own cotton brokerage and eventually became a partner in Smith and Dunning. Later, they would reorganize as Stillman and Woodward and shift from speculation to supplying cotton mills.[11] The elder Woodward also was a founding member of the Cotton Exchange in New York, and he parlayed that influence into other arenas, like banking and real estate. With that success came wealth, including a home at Eleven West Fifty-First Street in Manhattan, a summer home in Newport, Rhode Island,

William Woodward. Keeneland Library Cook Collection.

and a steam yacht, *Wanda*.[12] William Jr. also loved his carriage and horses and attending the races at Jerome Park, his young son accompanying him on the long rides from their Manhattan home out to the elegant racetrack.

As an older man, William Woodward would remember attending the races each Decoration Day, May 30, with his father; the two would venture out to Jerome Park as it began its summer meet. "We would arrive in time for lunch," the future breeder and owner remembered, "and on the way out there would be numerous drags with their fine teams which would be going along with us. It made a gala sight and a pleasant holiday."[13] William Woodward Jr. took his son to see Sir Dixon win the Belmont Stakes at Jerome Park in 1888, another memory that Woodward would cite whenever he talked about the origins of his fascination with the sport of kings. The next year, William Woodward Jr. would be dead.

On March 20, 1889, William Jr. was on the floor of the Cotton Exchange as usual and, from all indications, appeared to be in good health at age fifty-three. That evening, he boarded a streetcar bound for his brother James's residence on Twenty-Eighth Street when he suffered an apoplexy, a sudden loss of consciousness, and died within a few minutes.[14] Three weeks shy of his thirteenth birthday, William, his sister Edith, and his mother, Sarah Rodman Woodward, were bereft of their father and husband.[15] In his brother's absence, James stepped in to act as his nephew's second father, ensuring that the young William would have the education and connections necessary to be successful. James would also prove influential in encouraging the younger Woodward's interest in all things equine.

James Thomas Woodward, William Woodward Jr.'s younger brother by about nine months, was born September 27, 1837, to Henry Williams Woodward and Mary Edge Webb. Educated alongside his brother in a country school near his family's farm, Edgewood, and then in Baltimore, James worked for the dry goods merchant Duval, Rogers, and Company. He accompanied William Jr. on his journey to New York after the Civil War ended.[16] While

William Jr. found success in the cotton business, James started his career with the importing house of Ross, Campbell, and Company and moved up through that company with his eye on becoming a banker.[17] In 1873, James became a director in Hanover National Bank, and three years later, this man of "universal respect and confidence" was elected the president of Hanover National Bank.[18] As president, James Woodward grew the bank's deposits; was elected president of the Clearing House Association, an organization that cleared transactions between banks; and was a personal friend of President Grover Cleveland, serving as a delegate at the Democratic National Convention in 1884.[19] A lifelong bachelor, James did not have any children; instead, he took his nephew under his wing. When he purchased Belair, a 371-acre estate located outside of Bowie, Maryland, in 1898, the Hanover president had a homestead in his native state that would enable him to indulge his love of the outdoors, including fox hunting, riding, and fishing.[20] Young William would visit his uncle at Belair, where he quickly became a favorite of Andrew Jackson, a former slave and jockey who oversaw the equine side of the estate. William's time at Belair cultivated his love of horses, but his pursuit of racing was relegated to simply following the sport as his education became the top priority.

Neither James nor William Jr. had attended college. They had gotten much of their education in a rural school near the family's farm and then attended school in Baltimore before the Civil War. The Hanover president made sure William had the best education possible, sending him first to Groton, the same Massachusetts boarding school that boasts such alumni as President Franklin Delano Roosevelt and Harry Payne Whitney, noted Thoroughbred breeder and owner of Regret, who became the first filly to win the Kentucky Derby in 1915.[21] After Groton came Harvard, where young William Woodward studied law, played football, managed the varsity crew team, and was a member of multiple social clubs, including Hasty Pudding, Porcellian, and Zeta Psi.[22] A good student and a popular figure on campus, he was elected chairman of the Class of 1898 and then entered Harvard Law, passing the bar in 1901. Rather than practice law, Woodward was tapped by Joseph Hodges Choate, ambassador to the United Kingdom, to serve as his private secretary.[23] A fellow Harvard graduate, Choate was a lawyer in New York whose career included antitrust cases against Standard Oil Company; a challenge of the Chinese Exclusion Act of 1882 before the Supreme Court, where he argued on behalf of detained Chinese laborers; and the prosecution of members of the Tweed Ring in New York City. His work in the courtroom and longtime support of the Republican Party caught the attention of President William McKinley, who appointed Choate to the post of ambassador to the Court of St. James in the final years of Queen Victoria's reign.[24]

By June 1901, when William Woodward arrived in England to work with Choate, Queen Victoria had died and her son Albert Edward had ascended the throne as Edward VII. The new king, an avid fan of horse racing, won the Epsom Derby in 1896 with Persimmon, the English Triple Crown with Diamond Jubilee in 1900, and the Grand National with Ambush II that same year. The young American fit right in with the new monarch and other luminaries invested in the sport, and he attended the races at Newmarket and Ascot with Edward VII. Even Choate remarked on this friendship, writing to his wife that "the King and W. Woodward and Wadsworth have all gone to Newmarket. How anybody can stand such frequent races passes my comprehension."[25] As a young, unmarried man fresh out of law school, William Woodward was exposed to all things British during his tenure as Choate's executive secretary. He picked up an aristocratic habit of dress and comportment, dressed impeccably, and conducted himself with reserve and dignity.[26] His time at English racetracks exposed him to the practices of racing in that country and also piqued his interest in pedigrees, which he started studying with the same vigor that he had applied to his law studies. His frequent visits to the races informed his approach to racing his own horses years later: he preferred to breed and own horses that raced at classic distances, privileging stamina over speed.[27] That childhood desire to win the Epsom Derby would have to wait for another year, though. His tenure as Choate's secretary complete, the young lawyer returned to New York in April 1903.[28]

The next year, the young Woodward married the socialite Elizabeth Ogden Cryder, better known as Elsie. Born in 1882, Elsie was one of the famed set of triplets born to tea importer Duncan Cryder and his wife, Elizabeth Callender Ogden.[29] The family had moved to France following a scandal in which Cryder's brother William was indicted for perjury and embezzlement from the same bank where Duncan served as a director. After eight years in Europe, the family returned to the United States in 1899.[30] When the triplets made their debut at a dinner given by their parents at the Cryders' home at Forty-Three West Ninth Street in December 1900, they officially became part of the "400," the exclusive list of those considered members of New York society.[31] That same year, Elsie recalled later, she met the twenty-four-year-old Harvard Law student at a horse show; it was a case of purported "love at first sight" for the socialite and the future master of Belair.[32] The couple reconnected after William's return, got engaged in May 1904, and married on October 24 at Grace Church in Manhattan. They resided with Woodward's mother, Sarah, at Eleven West Fifty-First Street, where they welcomed their first child, Edith, in 1905.[33] After moving to James Woodward's home on East Fifty-Sixth Street, the couple added three more daughters: Elizabeth, Sarah, and Ethel.

While William was building his family with Elsie, he also nurtured his ambitions to build equine families. His time in England had whetted the young Woodward's appetite for realizing the goals he had set for himself as a child, and his uncle James's Belair estate was the perfect place to learn and build toward his goal of winning an Epsom Derby. The success his friend August Belmont II enjoyed as a breeder and owner in both the United States and England may have played a role as well. Like Belmont, Woodward valued horses that could run classic distances, and he bred toward that end, seeking a horse that could win at the Epsom Derby's distance of 1½ miles.[34] First, though, he would need some mares and a stallion to build his breeding stock.

When Woodward heard that one of Governor Oden Bowie's sons was selling some of the late breeder's mares, he bought three for $100 each, the first of many bloodstock purchases to come, and then, per his uncle James's request, he built stalls for them at Belair.[35] With his first mares came his first stallion purchase. Andrew Jackson, the Belair equine foreman, also had worked as a jockey for Governor Bowie and knew the local Thoroughbred scene.[36] Jackson knew of the stallion Captain Hancock, named for the master of Ellerslie, standing nearby, and advised William that the horse could be purchased. Woodward inspected the stallion, which he later described as "a bag of bones, but he had four legs and the necessary anatomy to serve my mares, and I bought him for $60."[37] So, for a grand total of $360, William Woodward started his career as a Thoroughbred breeder.

From the pairing of Captain Hancock and one of the Bowie mares, Charemma, came the filly Aile d'Or ("wings of gold" in French) that was foaled at Belair in 1906. The aspiring owner took his homebred filly, that had been trained on the backroads around Belair by both Andrew Jackson and Woodward himself, to the Southern Maryland Fair at Upper Marlboro in August 1909. In her first race, Aile d'Or, a three-year-old filly who had never faced a barrier or run on a track, finished third, but, in her second try, she won by a nose.[38] For William Woodward, the victory for this daughter of his $360 investment foreshadowed what was to come. Despite her piecemeal preparation and inexperience, Aile d'Or became "the first success of Belair Stud."[39]

With Aile d'Or's victory, William Woodward was in the breeding business, and Belair became a part of the Maryland Thoroughbred scene. The young banker still had a long way to go to reach the lofty goal he had set for himself all those years earlier. The Southern Maryland Fair was not quite the resplendent greens of Ascot or the vaunted oval at Saratoga, yet it was the first step toward history.

James had welcomed William's return from England with a position as vice president at Hanover Bank as he continued his efforts to ensure his nephew's success.[40] James encouraged the young Harvard graduate to go into banking rather than the law. Under his uncle's tutelage, William had attended the best schools, Groton and Harvard; had spent time in England working for Joseph Choate; and had become an integral part of the bank that James had presided over for three decades. For James, William was the only immediate family remaining. William Jr. had passed away two decades earlier, and his niece, William's sister Edith, was unmarried when she died in 1898 at age twenty-five.[41] James had purchased Belair and set about improving the dilapidated estate. He updated the mansion and built stables, creating a space that was ideal for the horses that he rode and hunted with.[42] The elder Woodward had built a fortune and a life that enabled him to enjoy his work and his play, and, when his life was done, he would pass that on to the next generation. On April 10, 1910, the seventy-two-year-old elder Woodward passed away at his home on East Fifty-Sixth Street in Manhattan.[43]

A week later, William Woodward filed his uncle's will with the Surrogate's Court in New York. James Thomas Woodward left trusts to his other nieces and nephews, a "slight remembrance" to William Jr.'s widow, Sarah, and $10,000 to Elsie Cryder Woodward. He left money to St. Thomas's Church, St. Luke's Hospital, and New York Hospital, which was to name a bed for Mary E. Woodward, mother of James and William Jr. But the bulk of the estate—the townhouse on Fifty-Sixth Street, the Cloisters in Newport, Rhode Island, and Belair in Prince George's County, Maryland—went to William Woodward. In all, James T. Woodward's estate was estimated at $5 million, giving William even more resources for pursuing his dreams of a victory on racing's biggest stages.[44]

His uncle's passing vacated the position of president of Hanover National Bank, which Woodward was elected to fill a month later.[45] Alongside his business interests, William took over James's stewardship of Belair, which had grown from 371 acres in 1898 to almost fourteen hundred acres when the elder Woodward died in 1910. In the years following his uncle's passing, William added another six hundred acres, bringing Belair up to two thousand acres by the mid-dle of the decade.[46] With the inheritance from his uncle added to the fortune he received upon his father's passing in 1889, William Woodward had the resources not only to spoil his family but also to fund his goal of breeding horses bound for the racetrack. Historic Belair was the perfect spot to build his empire and add to the estate's long history of equine excellence in Maryland.

That initial investment of three $100 mares and the $60 stallion, Captain Hancock, had produced Aile d'Or. From there, Woodward expanded his breeding stock, bringing Belair Stud into the industry through the horses he produced for others. New York's Hart–Agnew laws had forced racetrack operators to shut down for almost two years, from 1911 through 1913, damaging the state's racing industry. As a result, some owners opted to disperse their bloodstock, un-willing or unable to wait for any potential resolution to the situation. One of those, William S. Fanshawe, sold his thirty-one mares, year-lings, and foals at a September 1911 sale; however, the center of his Silver Brook Farm, the stallion Heno, did not meet his reserve.[47] Instead, Arthur Hancock of Ellerslie Stud in Virginia leased the stal-lion in 1912, and then, between 1912 and 1915, Woodward was able to buy Heno for $100 and bring him to Belair to stand.[48]

As the Hart–Agnew laws had affected racing in New York, the first World War prompted European breeders to sell some of their bloodstock, which gave Americans like Woodward the opportunity to bring new blood into the country. In 1914, the master of Belair spotted an announcement in the *New York Times* that Edmond Blanc, the French businessman and politician who also bred and owned Thoroughbreds, was selling several broodmares in Paris the next day. The list included five mares by Ajax, Blanc's Prix de Jockey Club and Grand Prix de Paris champion. Sired by Flying Fox, the 1899 English Triple Crown winner, Ajax was rapidly proving to be a stallion of import, which attracted the attention of breeders like the master of Belair. The only problem was, how could Woodward, who was at his summer home in Newport, Rhode Island, buy these mares a whole ocean away? His friend Philip Allen Clark, a financier who leased Belair horses for racing, suggested that Woodward contact George Blumenthal, of Les Frères Lazard, an investment firm with offices in New York and Paris, and have Blumenthal cable his partner Michael Lazard to bid on Woodward's behalf.[49] The transaction was successful: Woodward had set a budget of no more than $7,500 for the lot, but Lazard was able to procure them for $3,750, a bargain price for horses with a pedigree that Woodward valued.

Unfortunately, the five mares—Mousse de Bois, Parthenis, La Delivrance, La Belle Aventure, and La Flambee—could not be transported to the United States immediately; the French government, in an effort to protect the country's bloodstock, would not allow the mares to be exported.[50] Thus, they remained on the Normandy farm of French breeder Jules Jariel, while the wartime moratorium on bloodstock imports remained in place. It would be four years before Woodward would add those mares to his band at Belair.[51] When they did arrive, they were in such terrible shape that he did not breed them immediately, giving them time to acclimate and recover from their stay in war-torn France. With those mares were a two-year-old and two yearlings, the result of covers that Woodward had authorized during their time on Jariel's farm. The two-year-old was the filly La Rablée, who would later finish second in the 1919 Coaching Club American Oaks. Of the two yearlings, the colt Sarmatian did not race, but would become a sire for Woodward; he appeared in the pedigree of Granville, a Belmont and Travers Stakes winner who would be voted 1936's Horse of the Year. The other yearling was a filly out of La Flambee that Woodward would name Flambette; she would go on to play more than one role for her new owner.

With the addition of the Ajax mares and others, William Woodward had evolved from small-time breeder, to one with enough stature to purchase horses from one of Europe's elite breeding establishments, signaling that the nascent Belair Stud was destined to be a player in American racing. About this time, Woodward made a connection with another elite breeder, Arthur B. Hancock. The master of both Claiborne Farm in Kentucky and Ellerslie in Virginia, Hancock was active at sales, buying and selling bloodstock regularly. He happened to purchase a mare whose pedigree Woodward admired. The master of Belair wrote to Hancock to ask if he would be willing to sell the unnamed mare. Hancock agreed and sold her to Woodward for the same price that he paid. After the transaction, the two men met in person for the first time and struck up a friendship and a business relationship that would last for the rest of their lives.[52]

From 1910, when he inherited Belair from his uncle James, to 1923, Woodward concentrated on building the breeding side of his interests in horse racing. He bought mares from both domestic and international breeders, sold the colts he produced, and kept the fillies to add to his broodmare band. His activities on that front were enough to merit membership in the Jockey Club. Nominated by Joseph Widener, Woodward's pending membership was put to a vote at a September 1917 meeting, and the master of Belair was welcomed into the exclusive group of turfmen.[53] In addition to the Jockey Club, Woodward was a member of clubs like the Knickerbocker, the Harvard, and the Metropolitan. He also belonged to the Coaching Club, which promoted four-in-hand driving and was the namesake of the Coaching Club American Oaks at Belmont Park.[54] Outside of his equine pursuits, his business interests were considerable, from his status as president of Hanover National Bank to his appointment as one of the original directors of the Federal Reserve Bank of New York in 1914, a position he held for five years.[55] With all of his commitments, his recreation time was limited, and his ability to race the horses he produced was limited as well. Those he did not sell he leased to P. A. Clark, who also had a successful stable.

Clark's successes included Dunboyne, a colt bred by Arthur Hancock, who defeated future Triple Crown winner Sir Barton in the 1918 Futurity at Belmont Park; Polka Dot, winner of the 1919 Coaching Club American Oaks, also bred by Hancock; and Nancy Lee, a filly bred at Belair Stud and leased from William Woodward.[56] At two, Nancy Lee won the Demoiselle Stakes at Empire

City and beat a field of eight colts in the United States Hotel Stakes at Saratoga. At three, she won the Kentucky Oaks and then finished second in the Coaching Club American Oaks behind stablemate Flambette, also leased by Clark from Belair Stud.[57] In addition to Nancy Lee, Clark campaigned Lion d'Or, sired by Heno during his time at Belair out of Woodward's touchstone mare Aile d'Or, for the colt's two-year season before selling him to Thomas Healey and Walter Jennings the next year.[58]

In 1919, Hancock and Woodward continued their partnership with the transfer of half interest in stallions Wrack, Rock View, and Jim Gaffney to Belair Stud and the purchase of British stallion Ambassador, all of whom stood at Claiborne Farm.[59] Though Heno would remain at Belair until his death in 1920, the farm was in transition from the latter part of the 1910s into the early 1920s. Realizing that Belair did not have the variety of stallions or the expert labor necessary to achieve the goals he had set for himself, Woodward opted to send his broodmares to Claiborne Farm to be covered by one of Hancock's stallions and then give birth there.[60] Once the foals were weaned from their dams, they were transported to Belair, where Woodward would then sort out those he wanted to sell and those he would keep. Belair Stud became a regular consigner at the Saratoga yearling sales, with several colts and fillies going to buyers like famed Sam Hildreth, legendary owner and gambler E. R. Bradley, fellow Marylander Ral Parr, and businessman Robert L. Gerry. William Woodward's yearlings were sired by Heno, Wrack, Ambassador, and others, and out of Belair mares like Aile d'Or, Naughty Lady, and Mousse de Bois. He was a student of pedigrees, having learned from his time in England and his ties with Arthur Hancock, August Belmont II, and others. All that remained for the master of Belair, now in his forties, was to realize the last part of those goals he had set for himself all those years ago: to race the horses he bred and win the classics that he valued.

Given his position as president of Hanover National Bank among his many other responsibilities, Woodward had been hesitant about how the bank's board would regard his involvement with racing. Vices like gambling and alcohol were the targets of growing political movements in that era, and his involvement in the sport might violate the sensibilities of the men he worked with at institutions like the National Reserve and the New York Clearing House. He had addressed the idea of racing under his own name with the board of directors at Hanover, and they had approved; the board in general had, as Woodward himself put it, "a sporting tinge to it."[61] Yet Woodward had eschewed racing from 1917 onward, concerned about "our American ideas" regarding a gentleman in his position owning and racing horses. Breeding Thoroughbreds was an acceptable pursuit for the time being; Belair also produced sheep, cattle, fowl, and pigs as well as horses suitable for the Coaching Club. Woodward showed off his skills with the four-in-hand on a 1916 trip with August Belmont II and Frank Sturgis, fellow members of the Jockey Club.[62] By the early 1920s, after he had transformed and expanded the Belair estate into more than just another home for his family, William Woodward's role in the sport of horse racing in the United States entered another phase. When John Sanford resigned his post as steward for the Jockey Club, the master of Belair was elected to take his place, effectively becoming part of the board of directors for the organization that ran horse racing in the United States. With that promotion, Woodward stepped into the spotlight in the sport, preparing to devote even more of his energy and passion to the pursuit that had inspired him as a young man. A decade after antigambling laws had almost ended organized horse racing in the United States, the sport was about to experience an evolution that would create racing as modern fans know it today, and William Woodward would be there to help guide the Jockey Club through it all.

By 1923, William and Elsie were twenty years into their marriage, their family complete after adding son William Woodward Jr., also known as Billy, to their four daughters in 1920. Woodward was a member of the Jockey Club and a proven breeder of good horses with a strong band of broodmares he had acquired in both the

United States and Europe. After a decade of growing the breeding business at Belair, William Woodward decided to add another role to his résumé: owner. He registered his colors, white with red polka dots and a red cap, purchased from the estate of the late Lord Zetland, who had won the Derby and St. Leger in 1850 with Voltigeur; he then hired trainer James H. "Jack" McCormack, who also handled P. A. Clark's horses, for his Belair Stud stable.[63] With his focus on classic Thoroughbreds, William Woodward set his sights on "these historic stakes [which] give so much pleasure, far more than those stakes which do not carry the great traditions."[64] He wanted to win the races that represented the sport he had invested his time and money in, stakes imbued with the history and prestige that he and his peers valued. This was not about money; the master of Belair wanted his name on the list of the sport's most valued prizes.

At the age of forty-seven, the adult Woodward, now six feet tall with broad shoulders, bold blue eyes, and a sweeping mustache, was a far cry from the boy that had witnessed Sir Dixon win the Belmont Stakes at Jerome Park thirty-five years earlier.[65] He had taken the first steps on his path toward realizing the goal he had set for himself decades earlier at the breakfast table with his late father. His passion was evident in the way that he had studied pedigrees, purchased mares, and built Belair into a place where Thoroughbreds could take their first steps toward immortality. Alongside this passion were the deep pockets and determination necessary to create a legacy. From his pursuits would arise names that would be etched in immortality alongside the sport's greats.

3

Here Comes the Sun

Jack McCormack was a veteran horseman and trainer of champions when he took on the Belair string as William Woodward dove into the ownership side of the sport. In addition to training horses for P. A. Clark, who had leased horses like Nancy Lee and Flambette from Belair, McCormack had trained for James Butler, a New York grocer who owned Empire City Race Track in New York and Laurel Park in Maryland, and Jefferson Livingston, who founded ketchup manufacturer Snider Preserve Company.[1] With such horses as Travers Stakes winners Hermis and Spur and Kentucky Oaks winner Lillian Shaw on his résumé, McCormack looked like a good choice for Woodward's blossoming stable.[2] A $100 fee and an application later, "Belair Stud" was registered with the Jockey Club in April 1922, a year before the date that Woodward himself gives for the first start in his colors.[3] That same year, Woodward also was elected a steward of the Jockey Club, a position that gave him a supervisory role on racetracks in addition to his status as an owner and a breeder. After two decades of breeding, the president of Hanover National Bank was now laying the foundation for an even larger role in the sport he loved.

A February article in the *Daily Racing Form* listed Nancy Lee, Violet Blue, Chewink, Skirmish, and a two-year-old Celt filly named Marguerite as part of Clark's stable for 1922. Later that same year, in past performances and form charts, all except Nancy Lee appear at least once as entrants for Belair Stud, not P. A. Clark. In February 1923, the *Form* listed Belair's roster as ten two-year-olds and the

three-year-olds Brumellini, Violet Blue, and Skirmish, all of whom
had raced the year before for P. A. Clark's stable.[4] According to
Thomas M. Bancroft Jr.'s family memoir *The Red Polka Dots,* the
first official starter for Belair Stud was Priscilla Ruley, a daughter of
Ambassador out of the Trap Rock mare The Reef. The two-year-old
filly ran in the stable's first race on June 4, 1923, a 4½-furlong sprint;
Exalted Ruler won while Priscilla Ruley finished fifth in the field of
eight.[5] Bonnie Omar and Aga Khan, both two-year-old colts by
1917 Kentucky Derby winner Omar Khayyam, represented Belair as
well; Aga Khan placed in five stakes, including finishing second to
the undefeated Sarazen in the Champagne.[6] In that first year, Belair
Stud accounted for $6,750 in purses, with no winners and eight
in-the-money finishes. Although small purses accounted for some of
the lackluster totals, that first season was certainly not quite the performance that Woodward had envisioned. After this "thoroughly
unsuccessful" beginning, the master of Belair needed to change
something to improve his stable's fortunes.[7]

His first step was to hire James "Sunny Jim" Fitzsimmons to
train the Belair horses in December 1923. From McCormack's Belmont Park headquarters to the backside of Aqueduct Racetrack, seventeen horses were transferred to the new trainer's care.[8] This was
the beginning of a beautiful—and historic—friendship.

In the late nineteenth century, tracks like Jerome Park and Brighton
Beach dotted the New York City landscape; these venues were popular with tourists who flocked to the region's parks and beaches. Capi-
talizing on the sport's burgeoning popularity, men such as August
Belmont II, Leonard Jerome, and James R. Keene came together to
build more in the area. Out Ocean Avenue in Brooklyn, near Manhattan Beach, Jerome, William K. Vanderbilt, and a coalition of
sportsmen purchased 112 acres near the village of Sheepshead Bay.[9]
The area was a destination for New Yorkers during the summer
months, the amusements of Coney Island and the Atlantic Ocean
just a train ride away. On this acreage, they wanted to build a series

of tracks to capitalize on the influx of vacationers and other tourists that populated this area of New York City, envisioning that Brighton Beach, which opened first in 1879, and Gravesend, which opened last in 1886, would become a destination for horsemen and fans alike.[10]

On those 112 acres that Jerome and Vanderbilt and others, operating as the Coney Island Jockey Club, purchased for the new racetrack was the home of James Edward Fitzsimmons, son of George Fitzsimmons and Catherine Murphy. James was the grandson of Irish immigrants who, like so many in the mid-nineteenth century, had left Ireland during the tragic potato famine to come to the New World, where they settled in this farming and fishing area of Long Island.[11] The family lived in a frame house in the Irishtown section of Sheepshead Bay, on land that had been owned by the Lorillards, the family of the very sportsman whose Epsom Derby win with Iroquois would jog the imagination of a young William Woodward a few years hence.[12] As the track went up around them, the Fitzsimmons family was allowed to stay in their home, located in what would become the infield, until the landscaping phase of the construction process would force them to vacate. Thus, whenever young James Fitzsimmons, age five, stepped out of his family's home, he could walk out onto the dirt track that would become home to events like the Suburban Handicap, the Sheepshead Bay Stakes, and the Futurity Stakes, races that are still part of the New York stakes schedule.[13]

Each day, as the workers progressed through the phases of building the grandstand and other spots around the track, a man named Jim Claire would follow the crews around the site, collecting debris in a wagon for disposal. Workhorses, broad backed and strong, pulled the wagon, and, each day, Claire would leave them in the Fitzsimmons's barn overnight. Young James would ride the horses into their stalls and then would groom and water them, a treat for the young boy fascinated by all animals, especially horses.[14]

When the racetrack was complete, the family moved to another house in Irishtown. With seven children to feed, each member would take a series of odd jobs, young James included. He helped his father with the daily job of picking up the wares George would sell, driving their wagon to the market and back alongside his father. Because of the family's financial struggles, James attended school intermittently, between seasons and gigs; given his family's economic situation, he spent much of his youth working rather than learning. He took any job where he could interact with animals, from minding milk cows as they grazed to sweeping floors in a blacksmith's shop.[15]

One of his jobs included delivering milk to the stable kitchens at the very track built over the homestead where he was born. Around the barns of Sheepshead Bay Race Track, a ten-year-old James would deliver cans of milk to the different cooks preparing meals for the backside workers. While the young Fitzsimmons was going about his deliveries, he would look at the horses and attempt to finagle himself a job working there. Finally, the cook for the Brennan Brothers Stable said he could use James's help, and thus, on March 4, 1885, James Fitzsimmons got his start in racing by mucking out stalls, washing dishes, and galloping the occasional horse for the Brennan brothers.[16]

When the Brennans took their stable west, young James, nearly thirteen, had to scramble to find new employment at Sheepshead Bay. Hardy Campbell, trainer for a division of the Dwyer brothers' stable, took the slight Fitzsimmons on as an exercise boy. The young man was barely over eighty pounds but had picked up enough riding experience with his previous employer to exercise horses for the famed brothers, who together operated Gravesend Race Track.[17] Their stable was also one of the finest in the country; working for them was a huge opportunity for the young Fitzsimmons.

The Dwyer brothers had made their fortune by turning their father's butcher shop into a lucrative wholesale meat business, which gave them the means to take the plunge into racing.[18] One of their customers happened to be August Belmont II, who later sold them their first good horse, a colt named Rhadamanthus. This purchase was indicative of the Dwyer brothers' formula for success: buy horses that had already proven their quality, turn them over to capable horsemen, and then reap the rewards.[19] Between 1876 and 1890, their stable campaigned a number of champions, including Hanover, 1887 Belmont Stakes winner who also won the Withers and the Brooklyn Derby, which was later renamed for the brothers; Hindoo, winner of the 1881 Kentucky Derby and Travers Stakes; and Miss Woodford, a Hall of Fame filly who won the Alabama Stakes, the Ladies Handicap, and the Monmouth Cup—twice.[20]

Two years later, Fitzsimmons, fifteen and still a scant eighty-five pounds, got an assignment that would change his life: Hardy Campbell asked him to ride Newburg for Phil and Mike Dwyer in a six-furlong race on August 17, 1889. "To this day, I can't tell you much about that race," Fitzsimmons said decades later, "except that it was six furlongs and I finished fourth."[21] A year later, the young man struck out on his own, working as a freelance rider on the so-called outlaw circuit, tracks that operated outside of the purview of the Jockey Club. His first stop was Gloucester in New Jersey, across the river from Philadelphia.[22] There, a sixteen-year-old Fitzsimmons notched his first victory as a jockey on September 13, 1890, riding a horse named Crispin: "I was winning from here to that seven-eighths pole over there, but I suddenly got anxious and commenced to whip. I whipped and whipped, and I guess I won by a sixteenth of a mile."[23] It was a one-mile selling race with a $250 purse, and, while it might not have been the Kentucky Derby or another big-name stakes race, it remained one of Fitzsimmons's clearest memories of those early days.[24]

But a jockey's life was not sustainable for Fitzsimmons, who married his wife, Jennie, at age seventeen and then started a family that ultimately totaled five sons and a daughter. He rode around the "Frying Pan Circuit," racetracks in Pennsylvania, New Jersey, and New York with names like Iron Hill and Guttenberg, and at the original Aqueduct, which opened as an outlaw track on September 27, 1894. He even rode as far west as Covington and Roby, Indiana, but his growing weight started to tell on the lanky Fitzsimmons, who dialed back his riding and turned to training in 1898. He rode his horses when he could make weight, but the shift from riding to conditioning horses was a natural progression that many a former jockey had undertaken, from Andy Schuttinger to Johnny Longden.[25] He was still working the outlaw circuit, scraping by and sending money home to Jennie and their growing family when he could. The life of a man who simultaneously worked as a jockey, trainer, and owner was precarious, though, and he would take opportunities to make a few dollars where he could. He rode the mounts he could pick up but stayed away from unsavory tasks like pulling horses.

While he spent only a decade as a jockey before going on to train for seventy years, that time in the saddle took its toll on James Fitzsimmons, one that became increasingly visible as the years went on. At Alexander Island in Virginia, a man named Murphy offered him $100 if he would ride Luray in a race the next day. The only problem was the filly was slated to carry 108 pounds and Fitzsimmons was hovering around 118 pounds himself. "If you can make 105," her trainer Bill Mosley said, "we got a chance to win a $100 bet." To a married man with a family, $100 was a fortune. Fitzsimmons sweated in a Turkish bath, slept under three blankets, ran in the hot sun after working horses, and then baked in front of a brick kiln. The day of the race, he weighed in at 105 pounds, sure enough, and won the race, Luray putting a nose in front at the wire. He split $160 with Mosley, but that win came at great cost.[26] That kind of weight reduction, even for just ten years of the nine decades that Fitzsimmons lived, led to arthritis and a stooped posture. It did not stop the former jockey from becoming his era's greatest trainer.

But the up-and-down finances of a racetracker almost did. Jennie Fitzsimmons, tired of living the vagabond life, persuaded her stepmother to get her husband a job with the Philadelphia Traction Company, a streetcar line owned by Peter Widener, father of Joseph Widener, himself on the cusp of becoming one of the most prominent Thoroughbred owners of the early twentieth century.[27] Mrs. Fitzsimmons was fed up with the itinerant life of a racetracker and had her

husband all but straightened out when he encountered Hughie
Hodges, a harness racing man. Hodges told Fitzsimmons that Colonel Edward de Veaux Morrell was looking for an exercise rider and
jockey for a small set of horses. Provided Fitzsimmons could make the
weight, he had the job; James got right to work taking the extra weight
off his lanky frame. After years of riding on outlaw tracks, Fitzsimmons was not licensed by the Jockey Club, which would have been
necessary for him to ride for his new boss, who preferred to race his
horses on those familiar New York tracks. With Morell's help, James
Fitzsimmons got off the outlaw list and received a license from the
Jockey Club. Within a year, though, his weight again prompted him
to retire from riding. He rode his final race in the 1901 Tidal Stakes
at Sheepshead Bay, the place where it all started, aboard Agnes D.,
whom he also trained. Coincidentally, Agnes D. also had provided
Fitzsimmons with his first win as a licensed trainer on August 7, 1900,
the filly leading from start to finish in a six-furlong maiden race at
Brighton Beach.[28] James Fitzsimmons, trainer, was on his way.

He stayed with Morrell until 1906 and then hung out his shin-
gle as a public trainer at Aqueduct but life was still a struggle. The
family lived with his sister Nora in their parents' home in Sheepshead Bay, so at least he was home even if his financial situation had
not improved.[29] He had a few clients, like Christie Sullivan, who was
a part of the Tammany Hall gang; Roxie Angerola, betting commis-
sioner for a few of Sullivan's compatriots at Tammany; and William
A. Stanton.[30] Then the Hart–Agnew laws in New York restricted
gambling there as early as 1908, and strict enforcement of the laws
led to racing's curtailment in 1911 to 1912. The loss of the sport on
his home turf forced Fitzsimmons to move elsewhere to ply his trade,
so he traveled from Canada to Maryland to Florida while he and
many others waited for events to play out in New York. In 1913,
James, Jennie, and their four children returned to New York for
good; but, like everyone else forced to pull up stakes and settle elsewhere while racing there was shut down, he now had to start over
again. He cast back in and waited for the fish to bite.[31]

He did have some clients, like Joseph E. Davis, financier and president of the Island Creek Coal Company; Herbert L. Pratt of Standard Oil Company; and Howard Maxwell, vice president of the Atlas Portland Cement Company.[32] But none of them were invested in the sport at the Whitney and Widener level; each had only about five or six horses at a time.[33] These clients were not enough to build a career on, but they were the kind of owners that enabled trainers to hone their skills, to gain just enough notice to attract the attention of the bigger fish. In 1914, Fitzsimmons snared one. James Francis Johnson, who was in the sugar business and was also a Wall Street speculator, had plunged into racing enthusiastically. He hired the now forty-year-old trainer to head up one division of his racing stable, which would total upwards of fifty horses at its zenith. He offered to send Trojan, the Quincy Stable's hope for the 1914 Futurity, to his new trainer, but Fitzsimmons recommended leaving the horse with his original trainer Steve Lawlor to maximize the colt's form.[34] Trojan won, and Lawlor reaped the trainer's cut of the $16,000 purse. Fitzsimmons maintained his reputation as an honest man, sunny even with "his disposition that ever makes for a smile"; the moniker "Sunny Jim" accompanied him into print as early as 1918, thanks to George Daley of the *New York Evening World*.[35] The nickname came from a character featured in advertisements for Force cereal, a popular wheat cereal of that era, and the moniker would become the trainer's signature, immortalized along with the man himself in the National Museum of Racing and Hall of Fame.[36] Racing, though, has a way of testing even the sunniest of personalities.

In 1919, Fitzsimmons traveled to Claiborne Farm to purchase horses for Johnson's Quincy Stable; he picked out several yearlings, including one with a pedigree that attracted plenty of notice: a colt by Fair Play, out of Mahubah, by Rock Sand.[37] The yearling, whom Johnson would name Playfellow, was a full brother to Man o' War. Fitzsimmons would claim years later that he had bid on Man o' War on his boss's behalf in August Belmont II's dispersal in a Saratoga paddock in 1918. Because Johnson was not present, the trainer did

James Edward "Sunny Jim" Fitzsimmons. Keeneland Library Cook Collection.

not feel comfortable bidding beyond a certain amount, and thus the greatest horse of the first half of the twentieth century went to Samuel Riddle.[38] Playfellow was a second chance, so Fitzsimmons bought the yearling as part of a package deal for $40,000; it was another transaction built on the eternal hope that lightning might strike twice.[39]

However, this time, it did not. Slow to develop, Playfellow finally managed to put it all together in his three-year-old season, winning one-mile allowance races three days apart, the second one at 1:36⅘, which was fast enough to raise eyebrows. Sure, he was no Man o' War, but the big red champion had ignited a fervor for the next one of his kind, and Playfellow's pedigree plus his performances made him attractive. Three owners put in bids of $100,000 for the colt: John Day, inquiring on behalf of Commander J. K. L. Ross, who had campaigned Sir Barton; Gifford Cochran, who would later own Flying Ebony, 1925 Kentucky Derby winner; and Rancocas Stable, owned by oil magnate Harry Sinclair. Founder of Sinclair Oil, the West Virginia native had thrown himself into racing in the same way that Johnson had, except for his pocketbook: his went much deeper. The industrialist had also purchased Rancocas Farm from the estate of Pierre Lorillard, the very same sportsman who had owned the land on which Sheepshead Bay Race Track was built and the owner of Iroquois, the 1881 Epsom Derby winner who had inspired a young William Woodward.[40] Sinclair, who was on a buying spree in 1921, spent upward of $200,000 to stock his stable. Playfellow was another headline-grabbing purchase at $125,000, but, later that year, the colt would attract headlines for an altogether different reason.[41]

His first two starts in the Rancocas colors were duds, which led Sinclair to ask Johnson to take the colt back. He alleged that Johnson had misrepresented the colt before the sale, failing to share that the full brother to Man o' War was both a windsucker and a cribber.[42] Windsucking, or aerophagia, and cribbing were bad habits; one involved sucking in large amounts of air through the mouth rather than the nose and the other nibbling on a manger or a door while sucking in air.[43] Such habits were thought to be contagious, so horses that exhibited either were undesirable in any barn, especially one as high profile as Sinclair's. Johnson, incensed by the allegations of fraud, reminded the press that Sinclair's trainer, Sam Hildreth, had inspected the colt before the purchase. How convenient, Johnson posited, that these issues were discovered *after* the colt had been purchased and raced for Sinclair. Johnson's refusal to rescind the purchase led to a lawsuit that had not one, but two trials. The first ended in a hung jury. The second led to a verdict in favor of Sinclair, much to the surprise of observers who had judged that the facts played in Johnson's favor.[44] Johnson was ordered to return the money Sinclair had paid for the colt and then take Playfellow back.

Fitzsimmons had had his integrity questioned, which rankled even this man with the sunniest of dispositions. He averred that Playfellow had been in good condition when he left his care and was sent over to Hildreth. Fitzsimmons knew that Hildreth did not work his horses the same way he did; if Playfellow had not run well, Hildreth needed to condition the colt more. However, Snapper Garrison, former jockey turned trainer, testified that he had been in Fitzsimmons's barn, no employees in sight, and had witnessed Playfellow cribbing.[45] This was not possible, Fitzsimmons testified, because he always had at least one watchman on hand at all hours of the day. The trainer held no grudges, and, once he got Playfellow back, he did his best to train the purple-pedigreed colt, then four years old. But the time off had done Playfellow no favors and he never did realize the potential inherent in those bloodlines.[46]

Even as Johnson and Fitzsimmons were dealing with the Playfellow case, the trainer was preparing the Quincy Stable's horses for the races, which, like many things in show business, must go on. In 1922, Captain Alcock, a son of Ogden, one of the era's most prominent sires, won the Suburban Handicap and the Pimlico Cup, where he defeated Kentucky Derby winners Paul Jones and Exterminator for Quincy Stable.[47] The following year, soured on the whole thing, Johnson had only twenty-three horses in training. By the end of the year, Fitzsimmons saw the writing on the wall and faced the uncertainty of what was next if Johnson got out altogether.

And then the Sage of Sheepshead Bay met the master of Belair.

In November 1923, William Woodward, age forty-seven, had everything he needed: a wife, four daughters, a son, a yacht, a home in New York City, a home in Newport, Rhode Island, and a sprawling estate in Maryland where he was executing his passion project, Belair Stud. That project needed the right trainer, though. The operation needed someone skilled and experienced, patient and respected. William Woodward needed "Sunny Jim" Fitzsimmons.

The austere Victorian approached the genial horseman in the paddock at Pimlico on a Saturday afternoon. Woodward was leaving just as the trainer was coming in; the two were acquainted enough to nod hello in passing but had never really met. The banker approached the trainer and, in just a few moments, changed their lives and the history of the sport.

Jimmy Breslin's portrait of Fitzsimmons relayed their terse conversation as follows:

> "Fitz, I'd like to speak to you," he said. "Would you like to train my horses?"
>
> "Love it."
>
> "Fine. Supposing you come out to my farm tomorrow, and we'll talk about it."[48]

Fitzsimmons rode out to Belair the next day. Woodward offered him a contract. The trainer declined it, saying he did not believe in them. That was it. Other than a few horses owned by clients like Howard Maxwell and Herbert Pratt, which Fitzsimmons wanted to keep, the deal was sealed.[49] Sunny Jim applied for more stalls at Aqueduct; he was going to need them as the Belair horses would join his stable imminently.[50] After thirty-eight years, after sleeping in haylofts and starving to make weight, after struggling through years on outlaw tracks and scraping by as a public trainer, James Edward Fitzsimmons had the door to a new world opened to him by William Woodward.

"Sunny Jim" Fitzsimmons did not need long to realize success with the Belair horses. In his first season with Woodward, the barn at Aqueduct had twenty-seven horses, seventeen of them from Belair, including Priscilla Ruley, Spearpoint, and Aga Khan.[51] Both Priscilla Ruley and Aga Khan had been good at two, but, at three, they found another level. Priscilla Ruley went from winning a few small purses at two to winning the Gazelle Stakes, the Miss Woodford Handicap, and the Alabama Stakes in 1924. She then went on to defeat Princess Doreen, winner of the Kentucky Oaks and the Coaching Club American Oaks, before going on to beat the boys in races like the Saratoga Handicap over the next three seasons.[52] Priscilla Ruley would add a victory in the Jerome Handicap over Mad Play, owned by Harry Sinclair's Rancocas Stable and trained by Sam Hildreth. Two years after the Playfellow suit all but drove his former boss out of racing, Fitzsimmons had bested a Sinclair horse in his first year of training for his new boss.

Alongside Priscilla Ruley was Aga Khan, sired by 1917 Kentucky Derby winner Omar Khayyam out of the Radium mare Lady Carnot. Cited as an early Derby contender himself, he never made it to Churchill Downs for the Run for the Roses, which was won that year by the immortal Black Gold. Instead, Aga Khan made the rounds of Maryland and New York; he finished third behind Mad Play in the Belmont Stakes and won the Pierrepont Handicap, the Lawrence Realization, and the Pimlico Autumn Handicap.[53] The three-year-old accounted for much of the stable's $109,936 in purses won in 1924. In just one year, Belair's fortunes had completely turned around. Woodward had bred his share of stakes winners before 1924, but his colors had not been seen in any of those winner's circles. That all changed when he brought on "Sunny Jim" Fitzsimmons. From then on, the white with red polka dots became a common sight on the biggest of stages, a combination of Woodward's breeding acumen and Fitzsimmons's ample patience and expertise as a horseman.

Not even their combined talents could make every horse Woodward bred or purchased a horse that would carry the Belair colors. Sired by Spearmint, the 1906 Epsom Derby winner, Spearpoint had been imported from England, but had not withstood training. Instead of sending the three-year-old colt to stud at Belair, Woodward donated Spearpoint to the Jockey Club's Breeding Bureau in upstate New York, where he could sire horses for other equestrian pursuits.[54] Such programs, like the United States Army Remount Service, allowed greater access to pedigrees that might not have been available to people outside of the racing industry.[55] As a steward of the Jockey Club, Woodward was familiar with the program and would support it with such gifts more than once in his time as a breeder.

Fitzsimmons's success with the Belair horses led him to pick up another high-profile client in 1926 when Gladys Mills Phipps and her brother Ogden Mills started Wheatley Stable and asked the Sage of Sheepshead Bay to train their horses. The stable started with ten yearlings purchased from the pair's friend Harry Payne Whitney, homebreds that included horses like Dice, who was undefeated in five starts before dying prematurely at age two; Diavolo, winner of the 1929 Saratoga Cup and Jockey Club Gold Cup; and Distraction, 1928 Wood Memorial winner.[56] Like his partnership with William Woodward, Fitzsimmons's relationship with Wheatley Stable would last the rest of his career.

As Fitzsimmons worked with the top-class stock that Wheatley and Belair sent to his Aqueduct headquarters, he had people like George "Fish" Tappen and Bill Dallimore by his side. Tappen was the son of a Sheepshead Bay restauranteur whose namesake seafood restaurant became one of New York's most famous eateries until its demise in 1950.[57] Fitzsimmons and Tappen bonded over horses in their earliest years, when a young Jimmy would swing by and visit with George and the two horses he minded for a saloon owner.[58] Over the course of their lifelong friendship, Tappen served as valet when Fitzsimmons was riding, rode and trained on his own, and then became his friend's assistant trainer; he worked with Sunny Jim until his death in 1952.[59] Farrier Bill Dallimore had also been part of Fitzsimmons's barn since the last years of the nineteenth century, when Fitzsimmons was still splitting his time between riding and training.[60] By the late 1920s, "Sunny Jim" Fitzsimmons, flanked by longtime friends like Tappen and Dallimore, ran one of the best operations in the country. The fifty-year-old trainer had found success after years of struggling through the physical demands of riding, the financial uncertainties of the outlaw circuit, and the vagaries of racing luck.

The master of Belair brought Fitzsimmons along with him as he chose the horses he wanted to race in his colors and those he wanted to sell. The two would ride around Belair looking at the weanlings in the estate's broad paddocks, deciding their fates: a trip through the sales ring or a stall at Aqueduct? In 1928, as spring blossomed around them, the two men hung over a paddock fence at the grand Maryland estate, looking at a bay colt with a narrow blaze that cascaded down from the center of his forehead to sweep over his left nostril. His owner talked about naming him Gallant Fox. The trainer looked at his nostrils, concerned that they were too narrow for the type of running he envisioned for the son of Marguerite, one of Woodward's favorite mares. "We just have to take him and see what he can do," Fitzsimmons said of the yearling colt.[61]

If anyone was going to make something of that colt or any other horse bred by Belair, it was going to be James Edward Fitzsimmons. With that colt and many more, the son of Irish immigrants realized the dreams that began during those nights he slept in a hayloft in the Dwyer brothers' barn. Together, the master of Belair and the Sage of Sheepshead Bay built a juggernaut that would dominate a decade and make the white with red polka dots among the most recognizable colors ever in the sport of horse racing in America.

4

The Queen Bears an Heir

In 1752, the preferred currency of the international shipping trade was the Spanish pistole, a coin made of gold that might also be called a doubloon, colloquially known as the currency of pirates. One pistole could buy a cow; five hundred could furnish a mansion.[1] A purse of twenty-five hundred pistoles would bring horses from Virginia and Maryland together in a race that would ignite a ban on Maryland horses racing in Virginia and that would help make an imported mare a foundational part of American horse racing.

William Byrd III, proprietor of a vast Virginia empire, liked the diversions of games, especially gambling on them. He had just imported a horse named Tryal from England and wanted to show off his new toy. Byrd proposed a winner-take-all race for five hundred pistoles per entry; with the entries from his takers, including Benjamin Tasker Jr., the purse increased to twenty-five hundred pistoles, a mind-boggling sum in a time when a race might yield thirty pistoles. Tasker brought his imported mare Selima, a daughter of foundational sire the Godolphin Arabian, to face four others, including Tryal, in a four-mile race on December 5, 1752. Selima, who was at the height of her racing powers at age seven, beat them all, her second win in only her second start. She brought home that extraordinary purse and then went on to follow up her historic victory with an even more historic broodmare career.

Selima lived out her life at Maryland's Belair estate, where Tasker lived as the caretaker for his nephew Benjamin Ogle, son of Governor Samuel Ogle. There, this daughter of the Godolphin Arabian foaled colts and fillies who would go on to make their own impact on the racetrack and in breeding. Her descendants include Lexington, the nineteenth century's most influential sire; Foxhall, the 1882 Ascot Gold Cup winner; and Hanover, the damsire of America's first Triple Crown winner, Sir Barton. Selima's name continues in her status as a foundational mare in American racing, and also as the namesake of a present-day stakes race at Laurel Park, a race suggested by the twentieth-century owner of Belair, William Woodward.[2]

The legacy of breeding champions that Selima established for Belair would not be the farm's only contribution to horse racing history. In addition to this extraordinary mare and her notable lineage, Woodward and his stud operation would continue Belair's influence on the American Triple Crown with another successful broodmare, a beautiful chestnut with a tiny splash of white on her forehead, Marguerite.

When World War I began in 1914, Americans ventured to Europe, seeking to buy English and French bloodstock from breeders and owners who were faced with a continent at war. Among those who sought new stock was Frederick Johnson, owner of 1917 Kentucky Derby winner Omar Khayyam.[3] Johnson contacted the British Bloodstock Agency seeking a suitable broodmare to add to his breeding stock. For $500, the mare Fairy Ray came to the United States; her new owner found her to be dissatisfactory and bred her to his Cock o' the Walk rather than sending her to a more notable sire.[4] When Johnson sold his racing and breeding stock in 1918, Fairy Ray was part of that consignment, her Cock o' the Walk colt by her side as she was sold to Captain Phil Walker.

Arthur Hancock saw the potential in Fairy Ray's pedigree even if Johnson had found her looks to be subpar. Fairy Ray was by the English sire Radium, who won the 2¼-mile Jockey Club Cup twice and the 2½-mile Doncaster Cup as well.[5] On her dam's side, the mare counted St. Marguerite, the granddam of English Triple Crown winner Rock Sand, among her ancestors.[6] Fairy Ray's pedigree was loaded with classic winners, and, owing to Johnson's dissatisfaction, she was a bargain. Shortly after the sale, Hancock approached Captain Walker and asked to buy the mare and her colt. Though Walker had just purchased both, he agreed to a coin flip to decide who would get Fairy Ray. If Walker won, he kept both horses; if Hancock won, Fairy Ray and her colt, later named Top Sergeant, would be his.

Hancock won.

Fairy Ray became part of the Ellerslie broodmare band while Top Sergeant was sold as a yearling for $600.[7] Hancock bred his newest acquisition to Celt in 1919 and she delivered a chestnut filly in 1920. This filly was part of Celt's last crop, her pedigree one of classic and distance horses on both sides. Arthur Hancock brought her to Saratoga in 1921, part of a lot of twenty-seven yearlings from both Ellerslie and Claiborne that he sold on August 12, 1921.

William Woodward saw Fairy Ray's chestnut filly at the sale and took a liking to her. Unable to stay for the auction himself, Woodward asked Fasig-Tipton's managing director E. J. Tranter to bid in his stead. The gavel fell at $4,700.[8] She was not the highest priced yearling in Hancock's lot, but she would turn out to be the most accomplished of them all.

Woodward named his Celt–Fairy Ray filly Marguerite and sent her to Belair trainer Jack McCormack, who prepared her to race. The filly was a light chestnut, standing over sixteen hands, "powerful at all points—broad, big-bodied, powerful and rugged in appearance," according to an account from *Horse & Horseman*.[9] For her two-year-old debut, McCormack brought her to Belmont Park for the Daisy Purse on May 27, 1921. She carried 109 pounds with jockey Harold Thurber aboard and finished last of eight, her form so inconsequential that she merited no mention in the race's form chart.[10] Her workouts to that point had shown promise so that last-place finish implied that she must have had some trouble over the 4½ furlongs.[11] Marguerite remained in training for the rest of 1921 and into 1922;

her name was on the list of nominations for a number of well-known stakes races, including the Belmont Stakes, but she had no more starts after that first race.[12] Her only race had left her with an injury she could not overcome, a troublesome hip that was aggravated whenever she trained. She did not race again at two and then was put back into training at three. However, the hip continued to trouble her, and Woodward opted to retire the filly rather than continue any efforts to race her.[13] Marguerite had never been long for the track in the first place, so her progeny would do the racing for her, starting with her first foal, Petee-Wrack.[14]

For Marguerite's first cover, Woodward bred her to Wrack, Hancock's former jumper and flat racer who had also sired Blazes, Careful, and a yearling filly out of Woodward's Flambette, who was to be named Flambino.[15] The resulting foal was a bay colt named Petee-Wrack. Though Marguerite's first son was fourteenth in the 1928 Kentucky Derby, he went on to win the Travers Stakes and then several handicaps in 1929 and 1930.[16] Petee-Wrack would become a fair sire, having some success as a sire of jumpers, including Brother John, winner of the American version of the Grand National.[17] Petee-Wrack was the first of nine foals in Marguerite's lifetime, two by Wrack and the rest by Sir Gallahad III.

After Marguerite foaled the unraced Anastasia by Wrack in 1926, William Woodward decided to send her to Claiborne's newest sire, the one that he had helped bring to the United States, Sir Gallahad III. In terms of pedigree, the French stallion could run a mile and a quarter but showed his best at shorter distances, while Marguerite had classic distance champions on both sides of her bloodlines. On March 23, 1927, Marguerite foaled a leggy bay colt with a streak of white splashing down his face. Combining elements of the names of his sire Sir Gallahad III and his great-great-grandsire Flying Fox, Woodward would name him Gallant Fox.[18]

He first saw the newborn Gallant Fox in May 1927 and reported that he was "very much impressed with him. . . . He had the so-called 'look of eagles' and one could see a very fine skeleton in spite

Marguerite with young Gallant Fox at Claiborne Farm. Keeneland
Library Sutcliffe Collection.

of his well-covered frame. His well-shaped legs, their cleanness, his
very deep and beautifully placed shoulder, and his fork were to me
his outstanding points."[19]

Unlike Petee-Wrack, Gallant Fox's half brother, Marguerite's
second colt did not seem as "heavy-footed," giving Woodward cause
to think that this son of Sir Gallahad III "would have many of the
requisites necessary for success."[20] He also had a walleye, a condition
in which a horse's iris has no pigment and is, therefore, surrounded
by a light ring.[21] Woodward saw the unique eye as an advantage, jok-
ing that it would intimidate other horses on the track.[22]

Once the Fox was weaned, he was sent to Belair Stud in October
1927, where Woodward put him in a barn away from the half dozen
or so other weanlings on the farm. There they would all stay, growing and running around the estate's ample paddocks, until the following year. By the time Gallant Fox came along, Woodward sent
yearlings not only to the sales at Saratoga but also to England "with
the object of contesting the best stakes and if possible win[ning]
some of them."[23] He was ready to pursue that childhood ambition to

win the Epsom Derby, and now he had the other three-year-old English classics like the St. Leger and the Two Thousand Guineas in his sights.

His friend and fellow syndicate member Marshall Field III had started his English stable after World War I, when he engaged trainer Captain Cecil Boyd-Rochfort, a lifelong horseman and decorated World War I veteran.[24] The son of Major Rochfort Hamilton Boyd-Rochfort, a high sheriff in Ireland, Boyd-Rochfort was born on the family's estate in County Westmeath. He was educated at Eton and then worked as an assistant trainer or racing manager for several stables until the outbreak of World War I. After serving with the Scots Guards and winning the Croix de Guerre, he returned to his position with Sir Ernest Cassel, working as the stable's racing manager until Cassel's death in 1921. Boyd-Rochfort then purchased his training yard, Freemason's Lodge, at Newmarket and began what would become a successful career, training for Americans like Field and Joseph Widener and also for Lord Derby, Sir Ivor Churchill, and, later, the royal stables of King George V and Queen Elizabeth II.[25] A partnership with Boyd-Rochfort had the potential to be fruitful as the master of Belair expanded his racing interest in pursuit of England's grandest prizes.

Field's success and a meeting with Boyd-Rochfort in 1927 prompted Woodward to send yearlings to the trainer's Freemason Lodge in Newmarket starting in 1928. Additionally, the master of Belair sent several broodmares to the Boyd-Rochfort farm in Ireland, where they were bred to English and Irish stallions and foaled potential racers for Belair.[26] As Gallant Fox and others from the 1927 crop went through their inspections by Woodward and Fitzsimmons, two were selected for the trip to Newmarket, others were designated for the sales ring at Saratoga, and one was selected to join Fitzsimmons at Aqueduct. That one was Gallant Fox.

Woodward elected to keep Gallant Fox stateside, believing him to be more of a miler; he sent The Scout, who shared a sire with Gallant Fox, and Fair Game to England to be the first Belair yearlings to race over the English turf.[27] The master of Belair also took the rare step of insuring the son of his favorite mare for $10,000.[28] Under the care of his groom William Hall, Gallant Fox grew into "a big colt, [who had] broadened considerably. . . . He was particularly broad in the rump, and that was one reason why I did not send him to England to race."[29] Gallant Fox joined Fitzsimmons's barn at Aqueduct in August 1928.

As a yearling in training, the Fox showed that he had the speed but also that he needed ground to get into stride; he would work out with other horses and outrun them, but not without needing a sixteenth of a mile or so to get his legs moving.[30] While most colts are aggressive and fractious at this young age, the Fox was pleasant and enjoyed the humans working with him. He also tended to be curious, wanting to know everything that was going on around him, a personality quirk that showed up in his earliest starts.[31] Marguerite's newest colt, the first of her seven with Sir Gallahad III, showed something special to Woodward and Fitzsimmons, but they needed to find ways to keep the Fox's mind on his task and trick him out of his apparent laziness. The colt would slow down once he passed other horses, as though he knew how to win by just enough to save something for the next time.[32] Gallant Fox was allowed to grow and develop at his own pace, and Fitzsimmons set his first start for June 24, 1929.

The legacy of Selima, the mare who helped establish two centuries of Thoroughbred excellence at Belair Stud, found itself resurrected in Marguerite and the champion foals she produced for the man who loved her best, William Woodward. First, she brought Petee-Wrack, a multiple stakes winner who would later appear in other champion pedigrees. Then she birthed the likes of Fighting Fox, who would sire Crafty Admiral, the damsire of 1978 Triple Crown winner Affirmed. However, of her nine foals, including the multiple stakes winners that she delivered before and after him, the best was Gallant Fox, a walleyed wonder who would go on to wow the world, a Man o' War-esque meteor that would streak across the heavens while wearing a crown.

5

A Bumpy Road

William C. Vreeland knew horses. His beat had been the racetracks of New York for decades, his face well-known among Gotham backsides. Other names came and went but Vreeland remained as eternal as the ground they all worked on. One February day in 1929, Vreeland followed "Sunny Jim" Fitzsimmons around his barn, previewing the collection of Thoroughbreds that would carry the red polka dots that year. "For two years," Vreeland observed, "his [Woodward's] colors were only occasionally in front. Now his juveniles were most promising."[1] One of those young horses was a colt named Gallant Fox.

"A bay colt, with a white strip down his face and a white off hind leg," this son of Sir Gallahad III "stands over a lot of ground, but is well coupled."[2] Before the Fox had even started a race, he had already attracted the attention of more than his owner and trainer. This was a juvenile that was more than simply promising: he had all of the ingredients to make him a bigger star than his half brother Petee-Wrack.

Of course, at age two, he was still learning.

His first start was to be a five-furlong allowance race for two-year-olds at Fitzsimmons's home base of Aqueduct. It was a Monday, a quiet day of mostly allowance and maiden races over a fast track, with ideal summer weather for a day of racing. Aqueduct did not yet use a starting gate so Gallant Fox's first experience would be a standing start alongside nine other two-year-olds, including stablemate

Peto. The Fox stood toward the outside, and, when the starter sprang the barrier, he did not break with the field but, instead, dashed off to a delayed start. As Woodward himself recalled, "Gallant Fox was looking around the country . . . and was left about seven or eight lengths" behind the field.[3] Five furlongs does not provide many chances for a horse to catch up when so disadvantaged. At the wire, Gallant Fox was third, a half-length behind Peto in second and a full length behind the winner, Desert Light. Despite the defeat, he showed a nice turn of foot: he closed fast, from eighth after the first quarter of a mile to third. With more distance, Gallant Fox's finishing kick would have carried him past the others, which promised better results with more experience.

Five days later, the Fox was back at the starting line for his second start, the Tremont Stakes. The six-furlong race dated back to 1887, with horses like Man o' War on its list of winners. Under allowance conditions, horses with better records, like Sarazen II and Mokatam, were to carry 125 pounds, while Gallant Fox, with only one race under his belt, was assigned 110 pounds. The advantage of less weight was countered by the heaviness of a green horse. In a field of thirteen, the Fox was caught flat-footed at the start again, leaving him fifteen lengths behind the leaders. Over the six furlongs, he was only able to improve his position from eleventh to eighth; the crowded field impeded his ability to find a running position that would allow him to gain more ground. The loss, the worst finish of his racing career, could be chalked up to the colt's innate curiosity.[4] "He was so interested in the others," Fitzsimmons said of the Fox's try in the Tremont, "that he forgot to leave the barrier until he saw them running down the track away from him, when he started after them and did pass five of them but only finished eighth."[5]

With two bad starts under his belt, it was clear that Gallant Fox needed to get off to a faster start, especially since it took him time to get into full stride. If Fitzsimmons could get him to start more quickly, Gallant Fox would be more of a factor than he had been in these early starts. More races would hone that, and, if all went well and the two-year-old learned quickly, Gallant Fox could take all of that natural talent and make it shine.

Woodward's ambitions for his colt led him to skip Empire City's summer meet in favor of a trip to Saratoga, the grand summer playground of horse racing.[6] Most of the sport's legends had run at the Spa in their careers: Sysonby, Colin, Regret, Sir Barton, Man o' War, and more. It was a place to see and be seen. Woodward brought Gallant Fox there for the track's series of tests for two-year-olds, knowing that this was where many a champion started down the path to glory. Rich prizes awaited—that is, if they could get him to break on his toes and run his race.

At 5½ furlongs, the Flash Stakes was another of those races where speed would be a friend to those who could find it and find it early. On Saratoga's opening day, the Flash preceded the feature, the Saratoga Handicap, as twenty thousand fans greeted the new season under an idyllic sky.[7] Thirteen horses pranced to the barrier, including Prometheus, the favorite, and Sarazen II, who had beaten Gallant Fox in the Tremont. The maidens all carried 112 pounds, meaning that Sarazen II gave the Belair colt eighteen pounds, a clear advantage for Woodward's Fox.

Although Gallant Fox again broke slowly in the Flash, he was more on top of his task than in his previous starts. Jockey Jimmy Burke was content to sit in the middle of the field until the far turn, when he took his mount to the outside, running wide as they entered the stretch. On the straightaway, though, that mighty closing kick propelled him toward the lead, his sights set on the front-running Caruso. The red polka dots blew past the leader, who had seemed to have the race in hand, and pulled away to win by two lengths.[8] With that, Gallant Fox joined the likes of Fair Play, Sysonby, Old Rosebud, and Hamburg, who had also won this Saratoga fixture. The Fox had broken his maiden and shown a preview of what fans would see as he grew into his role as a racehorse.

Next came the six-furlong United States Hotel Stakes on August 3, just five days later. Another of Saratoga's fixtures for two-year-olds, the race counted greats like Man o' War and Old Rosebud among its winners, rarefied air that Woodward hoped his Gallant Fox would join. No longer a maiden, the Fox would have to carry 122 pounds, the same weight as Caruso. The rest of the field, most of them maidens, would carry as much as ten pounds less. As it turned out, weight did not matter; the two top weights were the race's top two finishers, but not in the order that Woodward and Fitzsimmons might have hoped.

Again, Gallant Fox broke slowly, but caught up enough on the backstretch to sit just off pacesetter Hi-Jack. Caruso sat behind those two, biding his time, as the Fox began to make his move to pass Hi-Jack. On that final turn, he took the lead, stretching it out to as much as two lengths, looking every bit like he had the race in hand. Then Gallant Fox seemed to slow down, even idle a bit like he was looking around.[9] Behind him, jockey Mack Garner let Caruso loose in the stretch and this son of good sire Polymelian bore down on Gallant Fox and passed him to hit the wire first.[10] Caruso took home $14,000 for his win. The Fox came away with splints.

Horses have splint bones surrounding their cannon bones in their lower forelegs. They start at the knee and taper downward to the fetlock, akin to an ankle in a human. In young horses, especially Thoroughbreds in training like Gallant Fox, these can get sore from overuse, with rest the best treatment for such an ailment.[11] Fitzsimmons gave Woodward's colt a five-week break, and kept his experienced eye ever watchful on this son of Sir Gallahad III. If he trained well, Gallant Fox would race again in 1929. If he did not, he might not see the racetrack again until the next year. As Woodward himself mused, "He [Gallant Fox] was still very much of an overgrown baby in spite of the things that he was doing, and a let-up and consequent accumulation of strength would surely do him some good."[12]

When a young horse starts to show potential, inevitably he attracts the attention of not only the average racegoer standing by the rail but also those who want to have that horse for themselves, who want to watch him run in their colors and have their names etched in history. Such aspirations led to historic moments, like John E. Madden's legendary sale of Hamburg to Marcus Daly for $40,001, seed money that allowed Madden to found Hamburg Place. William Woodward fielded the same inquiries from those who wanted to have Gallant Fox for their own. He turned them all down. "I hope to win the Belmont with him," the owner of Belair Stud told Algernon Daingerfield, assistant secretary of the Jockey Club.[13] Woodward was aiming for the American classics, which he held in the same esteem as the English classics. He had plans for his prized colt.

Bypassing the rest of Saratoga's juvenile stakes, Fitzsimmons sent Gallant Fox back to New York to prepare for the famed Futurity at Belmont. The Futurity was one of the richest races in the United States, its $138,000 purse larger than that of any of the Triple Crown classics. Its prestige was not simply monetary: winners of this race were among the first, nearly three decades later, to be inducted into the National Museum of Racing and Hall of Fame, including Colin, Domino, Man o' War, and more. To prepare for this, Fitzsimmons put Gallant Fox in the Futurity Trial, a six-furlong allowance race set for September 10, four days before the Futurity. Aboard again was Danny McAuliffe, who had ridden the Fox in the Tremont, the same jockey that W. C. Vreeland of the *Brooklyn Daily Eagle* had accused of "time and again demonstrat[ing] that he can make more errors of riding judgment during the progress of a race than any other jockey of his years in the saddle."[14] Given McAuliffe's ride in the Futurity Trial, Vreeland's assessment seemed on the mark.

The Widener Chute, home to the Futurity and the Futurity Trial, was a seven-furlong straightaway cut through both the main and training tracks at Belmont Park. Photographs from the Futurity show horses running along both rails; since there were no turns to navigate, horses did not have to hug the inner rail to run the shortest path. Interference forced Gallant Fox from the middle path within the field of twelve to the near outside, losing ground in the process. Polygamous held the lead throughout, but the Fox swerved in and found a good place to run, finishing second by a scant neck. In his memoir about his horse's career, Woodward remarked that McAuliffe had not gotten along with his mount, which perhaps accounted for this defeat; but this was also the Fox's first race back after his break, which could account for that performance.[15] If anything, the Futurity Trial was a chance to knock off any rust before the big test on Saturday.

The field for the seven-furlong Futurity, a massive seventeen, was the toughest that Gallant Fox had faced to that point. Harry Payne Whitney had his two well-bred stakes winners, Whichone, winner of the Saratoga Special, and Boojum, who had taken the Hopeful Stakes on the last day of Saratoga's 1929 meet. Gallant Knight, Audley Farm's stakes winner in Maryland; Hi-Jack, who took the Sanford Stakes at Saratoga; and Caruso, the Fox's conqueror in the United States Hotel Stakes, were all entered to try for that rich purse.[16] Gallant Fox would deal with stiff competition and a large field of other two-year-olds, an unpredictable combination.

At the Widener Chute's starting line, Whichone stood by the rail, Gallant Fox farther outside in post twelve. Whitney's other horse, Boojum, and George Widener's Hi-Jack were between them.[17] At the start, Boojum showed first, the cavalry charge of horses behind him trying to keep pace. Gallant Fox stayed close to the front runners, sandwiched between horses, unable to shake his competitors. Even though he broke from the inside post, Whichone eluded any crowding and found running room, taking over second until Boojum swerved and lost momentum four furlongs in.[18] As his stablemate faltered, Whichone took the lead, with Gallant Fox in second but several lanes out from the Whitney colt's position on the rail. Behind them, Hi-Jack bore down on the front runners, passing Gallant Fox as Whichone began to pull away. At the wire, the field was spread out, across the track and along the rail. Whichone won

Gallant Fox wins the Junior Championship Stakes at Aqueduct, September 28, 1929. Keeneland Library Cook Collection.

by a margin of three lengths, and Hi-Jack nosed out Gallant Fox, who finished a nose ahead of Boojum. However, the margins do not tell the story. Woodward's colt found himself running alone, not close enough to other horses to see the margins between them. That was the Fox's Achilles heel: if he saw no competition, he would wait for other horses to join him before he would pick up his pace again. It was enough of a concern that Fitzsimmons started advising jockeys to keep Gallant Fox in company so that he would not slow down and possibly cost him a race.[19]

The Futurity, Gallant Fox's sixth start at age two, came fewer than ninety days after his first start in late June. Woodward and Fitzsimmons decided that the Junior Champion Stakes on September 28 would be the Fox's last start of 1929.[20] Other good juveniles would have more starts that year, but the master of Belair, satisfied that his son of Sir Gallahad III had progressed enough in his short career, felt that he was best saved for the big stakes that would come at age three.[21] At Fitzsimmons's home base of Aqueduct, the Fox faced three others at the barrier.

The one-mile Junior Champion Stakes made the ideal final start for 1929. Most of the elite three-year-old stakes were at longer distances, so a race beyond the usual six or seven furlongs gave the Fox a chance to stretch out and experience that extra yardage.[22] Joining him for this race were Desert Light, the colt who beat him in his first start, and Sir Johren, who finished behind Boojum in the Futurity. The Fox seemed a lock on this race, a closer who could finish with a rush. The extra distance would be a boon, even if he got away slowly.

While sportswriters did not comment on Gallant Fox's start, Woodward reported that his colt got away from the barrier "none too well," which left him boxed in and forced to hang out behind the other three horses until the far turn.[23] Desert Light took the lead from Sir Johren in the backstretch, extending his lead to four lengths as the field swept around the far turn. Jockey Johnny Maiben gave Gallant Fox his cue then, moving the colt in toward the rail as other horses went wide on that last turn.[24] In the stretch, Maiben drove Gallant Fox to the front, that now-familiar closing speed turned on as they approached Desert Light. With a furlong left, he swept by the former front runner to win the one-mile stakes by two lengths.[25] "Gallant Fox romped home," wrote W. C. Vreeland, "and henceforth with a capable jockey must be reckoned with in races over a route."[26] After the complaints about Danny McAuliffe's rides on the Fox in races like the Futurity Trial, Vreeland did have a point. Those valuable three-year-old races ahead would come with longer distances and stiffer competition. The Fox was not a horse that would run for just anyone: he was too smart for that. Fitzsimmons and Woodward needed to find the right jockey and they needed to do it soon.

With the new year looming, the answer was not Burke or Maiben or McAuliffe, but a handy guy named Sande.

A month after Gallant Fox concluded his season with a win in the Junior Championship Stakes, economic troubles were brewing on the horizon. The boom that had marked much of the 1920s had slid into a recession that summer, and, on two black days in late October, that downturn became the Great Depression. The severe economic crisis would last a decade, and its alleviation would require significant changes to government policy. Though the sport could not escape the effects of this financial calamity, horse racing would play a role in helping the country through this difficult time.

6

The Fox Comes Around

Now when I want to win
Gimme a handy
Guy like Sande
Bootin' them hosses in!
—Damon Runyon, "Saratoga Chips," August 13, 1922

For a jockey, Earl Sande was taller than most: at five feet, six inches, he found himself fighting his own body for his livelihood on a regular basis.[1] Sharing an era with Hall of Fame jockeys like Laverne Fator, Clarence Kummer, and Linus McAtee, Sande's status as a multiple Triple Crown classic winner and three-time leading rider made him one of the most famous names in racing in the 1920s. His consistent visits to the winner's circle for the sport's biggest races led famed raconteur and racing enthusiast Damon Runyon to extol the Handy Guy's virtues in verse on more than one occasion.

Born in Groton, South Dakota, Earl Harold Sande grew up in American Falls, Idaho, and found his natural talent for riding horses early. At twelve, he bought a filly and took her around the local fair circuit. He caught the eye of Burr Scott and then Doc Pardee, both of whom took the young man under their wing and around the western bush track circuits, where Sande learned his trade.[2] Still a teenager, he decided to try the next level up, moving his tack east to the Fair Grounds in New Orleans in late 1917. He rode in his first official race on January 5, 1918, and then got his first win twenty days later.[3] By the time he was twenty-one, he was at the top of his industry. He rode Sir Barton to victories in the Saratoga Handicap and a world record performance in the Merchants and Citizens Handicap, and piloted Man o' War in the 1920 Miller Stakes after the colt's regular rider Clarence Kummer was injured in a spill. For Harry Sinclair and Rancocas Stables, he won the 1921 Belmont Stakes on Grey Lag and then the Kentucky Derby and the Belmont Stakes on Zev in 1923. He married his first wife, Marion, niece of trainer Sam Hildreth, that same year and then guided Zev to victory in an international match race against Epsom Derby winner Papyrus. A year later, Sande's career as a jockey was in jeopardy.

On August 5, 1924, Sande was riding Spurt, a two-year-old colt owned by James Butler, in a claiming race at Saratoga. Sitting sixth in a field of nine, Spurt was on the rail when another horse swerved into him, knocking the colt off his feet. Sande was thrown from the saddle, leaving both horse and rider in the path of the rest of the field. The horses behind them could not avoid the fallen Spurt, causing each to crash to the track. The two-year-olds managed to struggle to their feet, but their jockeys, including Sande, lay unconscious as stable hands scrambled to move them to safety. Sande was rushed to the hospital with serious injuries, including multiple fractures in his left femur.[4] He was out of the saddle for eight months, fans fearing that Sande would never ride again. Despite complications from his injuries and a gallbladder surgery, he returned in 1925 and slowly regained momentum with wins on Flying Ebony in the Kentucky Derby and then Mad Play in the Belmont Stakes.[5] The handy guy was back, but the lingering effects of his injuries and other health issues complicated his ability to make weight.

Weary of fighting his body, Sande retired from riding in 1928 and turned to training and owning Thoroughbreds instead. The problem is, owning and training horses to race can be an expensive proposition, especially if the winner's circle is elusive. Sande found that out the hard way; debt forced the famed jockey to sell off all but one of his horses by the end of 1929.[6] In early 1930, Sande was living

Jockey Earl Sande in the Belair silks. Keeneland Library Cook
Collection.

in New York and exercising horses for his previous employer, Joseph Widener, as he prepared for a comeback in the new year.[7] He had offers from several owners, but had not yet committed to one, still on the lookout for that right horse.[8] If he was going to return to the saddle, he needed it to be on some winners.

After Gallant Fox's inconsistent two-year-old season, William Woodward was determined to find the right jockey to ride his prized colt in the year's rich three-year-old races. His colt had wintered well, growing and progressing as he went from two to three, and the master of Belair knew the right person on his back would help Gallant Fox reach the potential hinted at in his two-year-old races. Years later, Fitzsimmons recalled the conversation with William Woodward for writer Jimmy Breslin:

"Fitz," he said, "wouldn't it be good if we got a regular rider for this horse?"

"Yes, it would," Mr. Fitz agreed. "Who would you like it to be?"

"Who would you like?"

"The fella that can do the best job."[9]

That fella? Earl Sande.[10]

Woodward reached out to Sande, who was riding a few mounts at Havre de Grace in Maryland, trying to set up a meeting with the famed rider. Sande offered to meet with the master of Belair when he was back in New York, and the two sat down for a long conversation. The veteran jockey was not immediately sold on Woodward's proposition, but listened as Woodward laid out what his horse was capable of: "he would outrun anything that was around and could move once or twice in a race, and that we felt him to be a high class colt, just the kind that he, Sande, should be looking for on which to make his comeback."[11] Sande agreed to ride the Fox in his first two races at least, their verbal agreement enough to seal the deal.[12] When Gallant Fox returned to the racetrack, the great Earl Sande would be on his back, wearing the red polka dots of Belair.

In late January, Tom Kearney named Whichone the winter book favorite for the 1930 Kentucky Derby. At 4–1, his odds were the shortest of a long list of potential contenders; his stablemate Boojum and Gallant Fox were tied for second choice at 10–1.[13] The Whitney colt had been rated the best two-year-old of 1929; he had won $135,455 in purses and victories in the Saratoga Special and the Champagne Stakes in addition to his Futurity win. But rumors about injuries had followed both colts since their turn in the Futurity, and Whitney himself admitted that a tendon in one of Boojum's legs and Whichone's knees had been nagging issues.[14] When trainer Tom Healey went to Whitney's Brookdale Farm to see his charges, he saw Whichone's two enlarged knees and knew that the colt would need time to respond to treatment. It was uncertain when the two would be ready to return, and Whitney and Healey made no promises about their 1930 campaigns.

Gallant Fox did not escape Kearney's notice, especially after winning the one-mile Junior Champion Stakes in a standout time of 1:38. Couple that with his breeding for distance and Gallant Fox certainly merited backing in the Kentucky Derby winter book. His stock rose even higher when both Whichone and Boojum were taken out of contention in early February, as Whitney opted to save his colts for stakes races later in the spring.[15] With their exit, Gallant Fox was at the head of what prognosticators considered a wide-open field for the 1930 Kentucky Derby.

As the weeks leading up to the Run for the Roses ticked by, the Fox's name was often cited as the logical choice to win the race. His come-from-behind finishes in the shorter route races and his easy win at a mile could both be signs that longer races like the Kentucky Derby would be his specialty.[16] After spending the winter at Belair Stud in Maryland, Gallant Fox joined the Fitzsimmons barn at Aqueduct in late February and stretched his legs in a two-mile gallop on March 4.[17] Two weeks later, he was worked a mile with stablemates Diavolo and Flying Gal, showing, according to W. C. Vreeland, that the Fox "in appearance and in point of physical condition measures up to his place of being one of the favorites for the Derby."[18] Over the winter, the Fox had developed into a striking and potent colt measuring sixteen hands and weighing about twelve hundred pounds.[19] Meanwhile the master of Belair arrived in New York to inspect his horses and found his colt working well and ready to race. His first start would come in the Wood Memorial on April 26.

The field was small, with only four others joining Gallant Fox at Jamaica Race Course in Queens. Other potential Derby starters had already made their season debuts, with Sarazen II taking the Paumonok Handicap on the track's opening day and Desert Light finishing second in the Calverton Handicap.[20] With the Fox making his own 1930 debut, interest in the race was high, especially since Desert Light, Spinach, and Crack Brigade were all set to start as well. "Dollars to dimes that the [Derby] winner is now quartered on Long Island or racing in Maryland," John Lewy predicted as he assessed the chances of the horses carded for the Wood Memorial.[21] Indeed the Fox's name appeared at the top of the list for this Derby prep race, selected over and over as the best bet to finish first in this test.

Wearing number one on his saddlecloth, Gallant Fox was the first to emerge, leading the parade of starters to the barrier at Jamaica Race Course. At the sight of Earl Sande on the back of the Belair starter, "cheering and applause commenced and swelled in volume as he passed down in front of the crowded stand and lawn."[22] They stood at the barrier for five minutes, the start delayed by Gallant Fox's antics; he broke through three times in his eagerness to get going. Sande had plenty of horse underneath him: W. C. Vreeland even observed the Fox pawing at the dirt with his right front foot in his haste to race already. At the break, though, it was Crack Brigade who darted out to the front, with Desert Light falling in behind him. Sande held Gallant Fox behind both, looking boxed in on the rail for this first part of the race.[23]

As they entered that final turn, Sande turned the Fox on, took him out from the rail, and gave him the cue to turn on the speed. Gallant Fox bullied his way past Desert Light and set his sights on Crack Brigade, his stride efficient and smooth, building momentum as they straightened out of that final bend into the stretch.[24] He and Crack Brigade raced on even terms for a sixteenth of a mile, but soon

Gallant Fox and Earl Sande lead Crack Brigade and Desert Light in the Wood Memorial at Jamaica Race Course, April 26, 1930. Keeneland Library Cook Collection.

the former front-runner gave way to the big horse as Sande drove Gallant Fox under a hand ride.[25] By the time they hit the wire, the Belair colt was four lengths in front, a sweeping and impressive victory two weeks before the Preakness Stakes.[26] With that, Gallant Fox became the 4–1 favorite for the Kentucky Derby, just three weeks away.[27] A once wide-open race now was down to the son of Sir Gallahad III and a long list of others who might challenge him. First, though, he needed to ship to Pimlico and take on the Preakness Stakes before he could start smelling the roses.

For modern fans, the fact that the Preakness preceded the Kentucky Derby from 1923 to 1931 is simply a part of the history of the Triple Crown, a reminder of the achievement's evolution since Sir Barton won the first one in 1919. Before 1918, the Preakness had been a minor stakes race, while the Kentucky Derby was in the midst of a renaissance that would soon bring it to iconic status as one of the quintessential American sporting events on the calendar. When the Maryland Jockey Club elected to triple the Preakness's purse in 1918, that bump in value started the race on the trajectory toward its present place as the middle jewel of the Triple Crown. Sir Barton's Kentucky Derby–Preakness Stakes double in 1919—which then became the first Triple Crown when he added the Belmont Stakes— came on the heels of another boost in purse money, and his dual wins further boosted the reputations of both races. Until 1922, the schedule for both races had not overlapped, as the Derby was run the first day of the Churchill Downs meet and the Preakness went off on the last day of the Pimlico meet. A shift in Churchill Downs's starting date in 1922 saw both races scheduled for the same day; that coincidence touched off laments from owners and turf writers that horses could not run in both. The need to cooperate led the Maryland Jockey Club to shift the Preakness Stakes back from its original spot on the last day of Pimlico's spring meet to a week earlier so that the Derby could be run on the second Saturday of May as it had been for a number of years.[28] In 1930, the Preakness Stakes was on Friday, May 9, with the Kentucky Derby scheduled for eight days later, May 17.

On April 30, "Sunny Jim" Fitzsimmons put his horse on a train for Baltimore and the Preakness Stakes.[29] Assistant trainer George Tappen met the Fox's train and reported his safe arrival at Pimlico, less than forty miles north of Belair Stud.[30] Earl Sande checked in with Tappen and took Gallant Fox for a workout on May 2. Their presence on the track attracted the attention of other horsemen, who stopped to watch the Preakness and Derby favorite do his work.[31] Also competing for consideration as Derby favorite alongside Gallant Fox was High Foot. Based at the Fair Grounds in New Orleans and owned by Richard and Patrick Nash of Chicago, the son of Prince Pal had won two of three starts that spring already and had bypassed the Louisiana Derby in favor of coming north to Louisville to prepare for the Kentucky Derby.[32] Forgoing the Preakness Stakes,

High Foot left Gallant Fox on his own to demonstrate why he was the Derby's true favorite.

Speaking of the Derby favorite, some horses look great working out in the morning and then may not show that same turn of foot in their races in the afternoon. Others, who may not stand out among the crowds of horses jogging and breezing in those early hours, give little indication of what they can do when the afternoon comes. In the lead-up to the Preakness Stakes, two weeks after his win in the Wood Memorial, Gallant Fox showed a habit that often caused his owner and trainer consternation: the tendency to only give just enough, a habit perceived as loafing by some observers. Once he was clear of horses, he would start "looking around the country," as his owner put it, and slow down as if he wanted to wait for a competitor to catch up to him so he could start running again.[33] In reality, though, "if he got off by himself, he'd kinda loaf a bit," Joe Pierce, one exercise rider for the Fox, remembered. "If he had a workhorse to go along with him, he'd put out a little more. But I wouldn't say he was a lazy horse. He just liked company."[34] Fitzsimmons would often send two or three horses in relays with him, using stablemates like Frisius to keep the Fox on his toes.

To others, that tendency to slow down looked like he was sulking, unwilling to give his best effort. Such an impression drove William Woodward to call his trainer, who was still in New York, and ask Fitzsimmons to bring another horse to Pimlico to work out with the Fox.[35] On May 7, he turned in his last one, a good six furlongs and then a slower gallop out to a mile total.[36] Woodward's involvement with his colt's preparation for the Preakness Stakes coincided with the visiting Lord Derby's sojourn to New York and Kentucky, where he was entertained by racing's elite, including Woodward and Joseph Widener and others.

While the Fox was the overwhelming favorite for the Preakness, his price almost as short as that of Man o' War a decade before, he was not the only horse in the race: ten others were slated to join him. Some were familiar foes like Crack Brigade and Gold Brook, who the Fox beat in the Wood Memorial; others were new to him, like Armageddon and Full Dress, both sons of Man o' War, and Woodcraft, who was representing Audley Farm at Pimlico while his stablemate Gallant Knight would see the Fox at Churchill Downs—if Woodward decided to send him.[37] The horse that seemed to concern William Woodward the most was the sprinter Tetrarchal, slated to start from post position three while Gallant Fox was on the rail in post position one.[38] From that position, Tetrarchal could win the start, seize the lead quickly, and cut off a slow-starting Gallant Fox going into that first turn. Of all of the horses in the Preakness, several of whom would also be in Louisville for the Kentucky Derby, that sprinter seemed the most problematic for the Fox.

"Sunny Jim" Fitzsimmons arrived in Baltimore on Thursday, May 8, to saddle the Belair horse for the big race the next day. Along with the famed trainer, William Woodward was on hand for Friday's big test, joining Ral Parr, owner of the 1920 Kentucky Derby winner Paul Jones, and others in Vice President Charles Curtis's box. Also present at Pimlico was a special guest of the Maryland Jockey Club, eighty-year-old George Barbee, the jockey who had ridden Survivor to victory in the first Preakness Stakes in 1873.[39] In all, nearly forty thousand people jammed into Pimlico Race Course for the day's racing. A beautiful May day greeted the crowd, and a band on the brick lawn played a variety of tunes, including "Maryland, My Maryland." The state's signature song played as Governor Albert Ritchie climbed the steps to the judges' stand to watch the race and then present the Woodlawn Vase to the winning owner.[40] With the sun getting lower in the sky, starter Jim Milton presided over the parade of horses milling behind something new for the 1930 Preakness Stakes: a starting gate.

The Bahr starting gate, another version of the technological innovation that was still gaining traction at the country's racetracks, resembled the starting gates modern fans know with its metal frame and individual padded stalls for horses. However, the gate's stalls did not have barriers on the front or the back to keep horses in; instead, the familiar cabled barrier was strung across the front of the gate, lifting at the starter's push of the button. As the barrier went up, the gate's bell would ring, signaling the start of the race.[41] Pimlico had started using the Bahr gate in 1929, and others would adopt different versions of the starting gate in the early 1930s.[42] What the gate did not do was prevent horses from acting up as they waited for the start, and the 1930 Preakness had its bad actor in Armageddon. This son of Man o' War held up the start long enough that Milton sent him to stand at the end of the gate, rather than in a stall, for the start.[43] Gallant Fox, too, fell out of line a couple of times, but Milton finally got the whole field to stand still long enough to send them away. Sure enough, Tetrarchal jetted to the lead, crossing to the rail and cutting off the horses behind him, including Gallant Fox. Crack Brigade moved into second with Sweet Sentiment and Gold Brook behind him. Gallant Fox found himself boxed in on the first turn, sitting far back in eighth position. Sande realized, though, that staying in that position would mean trouble later. Taking Gallant Fox to the outside was the only way to go.[44]

On the backstretch, Sande took his horse out from the rail, going around horses rather than waiting for an opening. Even though he had lost ground moving out toward the middle of the track, that path on the straightaway gave him space to accelerate.[45] Gallant Fox picked up his pace, moving from eighth at the half-mile call to third at six furlongs, with three and a half furlongs to go. That meant Sande needed Gallant Fox to make another move after a breather on the far turn. A tiring Tetrarchal started to fade, surrendering to Crack Brigade, who assumed the lead with only a furlong and a half to go.[46] Gallant Fox accelerated again, running even with Crack Brigade for a few yards before Sande tapped him with the whip twice. The jockey told Woodward later that the Fox had not wanted to pass Crack Brigade, given his fondness for running in company and all, so he had to use the whip to remind the colt to pass his competitor. Gallant Fox pulled away to win by a length, a brilliant performance that Sande summed up with "He is a great horse, Mr. Woodward."[47]

In the winner's circle, Governor Ritchie gave a grinning William Woodward the prized Woodlawn vase, presented annually to the winner of the Preakness Stakes. Earl Sande had his photo made with George Barbee and showered praise on the colt that brought him what would be his only Preakness Stakes. Team Gallant Fox was jubilant after a hard-fought victory, but the evening was not done until the question had been asked: Would Gallant Fox start in the Kentucky Derby and would Earl Sande be riding him?

Sunny Jim passed the day receiving congratulations from friends and keeping a watchful eye on his horse as he cooled out from the tough trip. With Gallant Fox back in his stall, Woodward returned to the barn to find Fitzsimmons already arranging to send his Preakness winner on to Louisville for the Kentucky Derby. The master of Belair insisted on shipping the Fox with his workmate Rattler, a pony, a dog, six men, and Fitzsimmons's friend and longtime farrier Bill Dallimore on Sunday afternoon.

Before leaving Pimlico, William Woodward visited Earl Sande in the track's jockey quarters to ask if he would ride Gallant Fox again. Sande had originally agreed to only two races, and those two had come and gone. Woodward offered Sande $10,000 to ride Gallant Fox in 1930, but the famed jockey, who had been on some of the era's best horses, including Man o' War, Zev, and Sir Barton, wanted different terms, agreeing to a 10% share of the colt's winnings.[48]

"We're going to win a lot of races," Sande said, predicting the ride that the Fox was about to take the three of them on over the course of this extraordinary season.

7

Roses Are Red

By early 1930, nearly six million Americans were standing in bread-lines as the Great Depression accelerated into record unemployment and endless debates about how best to mitigate the economic emergency. Desperate for any respite, people turned to the diversions that promised a few hours' reprieve from the troubles that surrounded them. They flocked to sports, filling baseball stadiums to watch players like Babe Ruth and Lou Gehrig, and to the racetrack, seeking an idol to cheer on through the spring and summer.[1] With the Kentucky Derby right around the corner, thousands gathered in Louisville to celebrate another year of a grand tradition, one that attracted the attention of another racing fan, this one from the very country that inspired the contest at the center of the city's attention.

The name "Derby" for a horse race has its origins in England, the progenitor of many things now American, with the name more happenstance than purposeful, as the legend goes. The 12th Earl of Derby and Sir Charles Bunbury witnessed the running of the first Oaks for three-year-old fillies in 1779, and both commented that a similar race was necessary for three-year-old colts. This new race should be named after one of those gentlemen, but which one? A coin flip later, it is the Derby, not the Bunbury, that fans look forward to each year.[2] In 1930, when it was Gallant Fox's turn, how appropriate that Edward George Villiers Stanley, 17th Earl of Derby, a descendant of the race's namesake, was present to witness William Woodward's first Kentucky Derby win.

Lord Derby had traveled to the United States specifically to see the Kentucky Derby, another sign that the Run for the Roses had ascended to the status of America's greatest race in the world's estimation. For William Woodward, Lord Derby's attendance must have been quite the personal coup: nearly three decades earlier, Woodward had spent much of his time in England attending the races and rubbing elbows with the country's racing elite, including Lord Derby and the late King Edward VII.[3] Even better, the horse that Woodward himself had bred was the focus of attention at this year's Derby; his distinctive Belair white with red polka dots stood out alongside the famed silks of Colonel E. R. Bradley, Audley Farm, and others.

As Louisville geared up to welcome the namesake of its greatest race, the Pennsylvania railroad carried the Preakness victor onward from his Baltimore triumph to a date with Churchill Downs's starter. Fitzsimmons originally had engaged a stall space in a car with Crack Brigade and Ned O., also Derby bound, but Woodward insisted on shipping his horse in his own car—and agreed to pay for part of the car that the other two were in.[4] Gallant Fox would travel in style and certainly looked every bit the part of the favorite when he arrived at Churchill Downs on Monday, May 12, sleek and fit and ready to run.[5]

The field for the fifty-sixth Kentucky Derby still numbered sixteen, despite the focus on Gallant Fox and his victories in the Wood Memorial and then the Preakness. He started out the favorite, but then sentiment swung toward the colt Tannery, especially as the weather started to trend toward a possible wet track. Tannery had won his two most recent starts at the Kentucky Association racetrack in Lexington after winning five of his eight starts at two and was showing good form in the mornings, a contrast with Gallant Fox's tendency to loaf through his workouts.[6] The big strapping chestnut did not have Earl Sande on his back, though, and certainly the two-time Derby winning jockey gave Gallant Fox an edge that other horses did not have.

That did not stop the speculation that precedes any race of this magnitude. With sixteen horses on the list, a potential dark horse could have been out there, waiting to upset the balance of the race. Could it be Gallant Knight, Audley Farm's consistent colt, or Crack Brigade, who gave Gallant Fox a run for his money in the Preakness?[7] Time would show that the Fox was the best of them all, but as the hours ticked down to the Run for the Roses, bettors gave Tannery and even Colonel Bradley's entry of Breezing Through and Buckeye Poet a chance. Gallant Fox remained at the top of the list of probables for the Kentucky Derby.

Then the weather started to turn toward rain, and reports surfaced that Gallant Fox might scratch if the track turned muddy on Derby Day. "I have never even worked the colt in muddy going, let alone race him," Fitzsimmons told W. C. Vreeland.[8] The decision would be up to Woodward, who had already declared his colt for the Belmont Stakes. "And if he says 'scratch,' it's all right with me. I'd rather save him for a dry track and take the chance of winning the Belmont."[9] On Wednesday, May 14, Gallant Fox appeared for his lone workout during that intervening week between the Preakness and the Derby. Under Earl Sande, he worked a mile and a quarter on the sticky surface, completing the ten furlongs in 2:19.[10] Opinions on Gallant Fox's taste for the mud were divided. Some claimed the workout showed that he had no problem with the wet going and others pointed toward the slow time as evidence that Gallant Fox disliked his first experience with mud. The man on his back, the one who would know best, was pleased with the colt's effort three days before the big race.[11] "My doubts about Gallant Fox's ability over a heavy or muddy course are gone," the jockey told reporters. "I have no worry about the outcome Saturday."[12] Sande was not worried, and William Woodward was not either: his memoir about Gallant Fox's career does not mention any wavering about starting his colt. When asked about the Fox's chances to win the Derby, the master of Belair said, "No horse can beat Gallant Fox in the Derby unless he is just about as good as Man o' War."[13] On Thursday, the Fox turned in another workout, besting Wrattler over three furlongs in a stiff 35½ seconds. Both Sande and assistant trainer George Tappen reported their pleasure at Gallant Fox's show when "Sunny Jim" Fitzsimmons arrived from New York.[14] The Fox was ready.

On Friday, the post-position draw gave Gallant Fox a break that might be sorely needed on a muddy track: he would start from post seven, the middle of the field. From there, Earl Sande could pick his running lane, away from the traffic jams of horses vying for position from the inside.[15] This time, Churchill Downs was using the Waite starting gate, which differed from the Bahr gate used at Pimlico. The Waite starting gate consisted of a series of low stalls, ten feet long and three feet wide, with padding on both sides.[16] Each stall had a soft barrier across the front to keep the horse in and a small rubber door across the back to prevent any injury should a horse kick backwards.[17] Unlike the Bahr gate at Pimlico, the Waite gate featured no overhead structure; the stalls were completely open from the horse's shoulder level up. After the horses were off, the gate was folded up with a crank and then was carried off by assistant starters.[18] After years of standing at the starting line, waiting for each horse in the field to stand still in the assigned post position, and then making sure the horses all got away at the same time, the process, hopefully, was now condensed into a simple load, line up, and push button release. A new way to go.

Another addition to that year's Kentucky Derby was a new viewing stand, built specifically for their honored guest. Colonel Matt Winn ordered the construction of a glass-enclosed square viewing stand located about a hundred feet from the finish line. There, their royal visitor would watch the day's racing and then present the gold trophy to the winning owner while the winning horse would be led into the adjoining enclosure for the presentation of the blanket of roses and the traditional winner's circle photographs.[19] The viewing stand also had a platform with enough space for the National Broadcasting Company (NBC) to set up an area where Lord Derby could address their listening audience during the day's festivities. In addition to the anticipated address from Lord Derby, Clem McCarthy, famed radio sportscaster, and Graham McNamee were on hand to call the race for NBC and their affiliates across the country.[20]

The Derby Day forecast called for a cool, cloudy day with the possibility of some showers. As workers dressed Churchill Downs up for the next day's festivities, the racing surface was "in excellent condition, a trifle cuppy, and it was not anticipated that a shower or two would affect racing conditions."[21] If questions still remained about Gallant Fox's ability to run on an off track, they likely would not be answered in the Kentucky Derby. Any rainy weather was expected to hold off long enough for the dirt oval to remain ideal for the next day's spectacle. With more than fifty thousand spectators expected, a fast track would make for an ideal day of racing.[22]

Lord Derby himself was apparently the worse for wear on this whirlwind trip to the former colonies. He had arrived nearly two weeks earlier and had spent much of that fortnight being ushered from place to place: a visit to Belmont Park with his host, Joseph Widener; a dinner in his honor put on by the Jockey Club at William Woodward's New York home; a visit with President Hoover in Washington, DC; a trip to Lexington to Widener's Elmendorf Farm, where Lord Derby's stallion Sickle was standing for the 1930 breeding season; and then acceptance of other honors while in Louisville, including the keys to the city.[23] Feeling under the weather, the Englishman had canceled several engagements to rest up for his appearance at Churchill Downs.[24] Lord Derby, though, was looking forward to attending the race that bore his family name, ready to celebrate the American version of one of England's treasured classics.

Another Earl, this one named Sande, was ready to roll, too. With Sande on board, Gallant Fox seemed invincible, despite the Kentucky leanings toward Tannery. With two Derbies behind him, Sande was going for another mark: his third win, one that would tie him with the legendary Isaac Murphy. After battling through injury and then the ignominy of losing his money to the caprices of racing luck, Sande deserved the plaudits following him around that year. The crowd would cheer on Derby Day, all right, but perhaps more for the fair-haired man piloting the favorite than for the horse him-self. He was on the comeback trail, after all, back in the saddle once again, his "aw, shucks" attitude easy to like and easy to root for. By extension, then, they were cheering for Gallant Fox, and the horse, with his sleek coat and his tendency to pose for the cameras, was easy to love.

The days were down to hours. The preparations were almost done. Louisville's hotels were full, and the city seethed with an influx of humanity via rail and road and even the air, ready for roses. From aristocrat to average Joe, they waited for the show with the same seed of anticipation blooming with the advent of the new day. It was Saturday, May 17, 1930, Derby Day.

Time to run.

Airplanes buzzed over the expanse of Churchill Downs, landing at nearby Bowman Field and offloading passengers eager to see the Twin Spires and enjoy the day's racing. Special rail cars came and went throughout the day, spilling out more and more revelers to tax the capacity of Louisville's historic racetrack.[25] On the backside, Colonel Matt Winn had authorized $10,000 to build a new set of bleachers that could hold up to five thousand backstretch workers so that they could also watch the day's racing.[26] Celebrities and the sport's elite mixed among the box seats and clubhouse. Al Jolson got shots for his next movie in between the day's races while Arthur Hancock, the man behind Ellerslie and Claiborne Farm and its inti-mate connections with William Woodward, expressed his support for Gallant Fox.[27] Despite the chilly air and the gray skies, the day was a celebration of the best of the Bluegrass as upwards of seventy thousand people filed into Churchill Downs for the big race.

Radio networks set up for their broadcasts, observing the day's events for those who were not able to join the fray in person. NBC anticipated that they would reach at least seventy stations over the course of their national broadcast, with Clem McCarthy set to call the race for the audience at home. Lord Derby arrived at about

1 p.m., accompanied by a coterie of breeders and owners and his host, Joseph Widener.[28] They attended a luncheon given by the Downs's president, Samuel Culbertson, with a long guest list that included Arthur Hancock and William Woodward. Woodward gives no details about the day's events save for the running of the race itself in his memoir about Gallant Fox.[29]

Meanwhile, "Sunny Jim" Fitzsimmons sent his colt on a walk around the track with a stable hand, with the goal of acclimatizing the Fox to the festive crowd and the changing surface. After one lap around the oval, the stable hand guided Gallant Fox to the runway leading to the paddock, but the colt would not move. He stood there for ten minutes, unmoving, as if taking in the masses gathered to see the country's biggest race. The stable hand knew not to push the Fox, so he waited for the colt to finish his surveillance and then rode him patiently back to the paddock.[30] The Fox of Belair was ready.

After the field for the third race was sent away at 3:28 p.m., a light rain sent the crowd scrambling for cover and continued through the fourth race. The Derby was the fifth race on the card, scheduled for 5 p.m. The drizzle continued, just enough to dampen even the hardiest of millinery but not enough to take the track from good to muddy. Gallant Fox would not have to worry about the mud this time. The crowd began to shift back toward the rail despite the rain: they wanted to find a spot to watch the show. [31]

Just before the fourth race, Lord Derby joined the festivities. The crowd around his viewing pavilion had been waiting to see when the distinguished guest would appear and, finally, he did, with a derby hat—which he called a billycock—topping off his double-breasted gray suit. Umbrella in hand, the aristocrat emerged to the broadcast of a military band playing the British national anthem over the loudspeakers, eager to watch the coming feature race, the one he had traveled four thousand miles to see.[32] The 17th Earl of Derby stood in the misty rain, watching the fifteen horses slowly make their way through the tunnel to the track, on their way to the post for the race named for his ancestor.[33] Led by a red-coated outrider on a dappled pony, they paraded down the Churchill Downs's straightaway, the rain dripping off of everything in sight.[34] Lord Derby took in the sight of the best that the East and the West had to offer as the field walked by, cheers erupting at the sight of Gallant Fox and Tannery.[35]

Single file, the field made their way to the Waite gate while the crowd strained for a glimpse at the horses, their numbers barely contained by the rails on both sides.[36] The horses milled around behind the contraption, new for 1930, each one taking its position within a padded stall. Thirteen colts, gelding Ned O., and the filly Alcibiades lined up, Longus on the rail and Buckeye Poet on the outside. Clem McCarthy took his spot overlooking the track, clad in a dark overcoat, holding binoculars while another man held the radio microphone for him. William Woodward watched Gallant Fox from the directors' box, his eyes focused on the maroon blinkers in the seventh post. The whole of Churchill Downs stopped, and, for a moment, the world was quiet, reduced to the breathless anticipation of the unleashing.

The pop of the gate and the field was off, Alcibiades the fastest away. Behind her were Buckeye Poet, Tannery, and then Gallant Fox. Sande held the Fox there for the first quarter, staying off the deepest part at the rail, waiting for the chance to move forward to take the lead.[37] Generally, Gallant Fox preferred to run just behind the leaders, but, at the half mile, Sande moved his horse to the front to his owner's surprise. Really, the move made sense: "The horse was going well and he did not want to check him, but also—and more important—he found that his contender was in trouble at that particular point and he felt that if he went on, others would follow him and the contender would not get out of his trouble."[38] The identity of that contender was unclear, but Tannery was still in close quarters with Gallant Fox, just behind Alcibiades, and Gallant Knight was moving through the pack, passing the filly and Tannery to find the right place to make a run at the front-running Gallant Fox as they approached the mile mark. Sande had the Fox two lengths ahead of the field, running as he pleased in the lane he wanted.[39] This was almost too easy.

Every horse race, no matter how long or short it might be, has phases. Some are marked in bare yards while others are in furlongs. Most involve at least one turn, usually the marker for the beginning of the end, where front-runners might fade as the closers begin to accelerate, a frantic push for position as the race fast approaches its end. That frenetic swing into the final turn of the Kentucky Derby whips the crowd into a frenzy as that last phase of the race begins, the denouement imminent. Gallant Fox swept into the stretch in total control, with the closers behind him trying to find the key to beating him.[40] Would it be going to the inside or around the front runner? Would whatever final kick a horse had be enough to catch Sande before he could boot 'em home?

At the top of the stretch, Lord Derby put down his binoculars and said, "Fine stuff. I'm glad," as Gallant Fox swept into that straightaway with a sure lead. The roar of the crowd ascended higher and higher as Gallant Knight mounted his bid to catch the Fox, but no one was catching the Belair colt this day. Sure enough, Sande had allowed Gallant Knight to get just close enough to keep his mount on his toes, but today Gallant Fox was an undeniable force.[41] As he swept under the wire first, he duplicated Sir Barton's double, only the second horse in history to take home both the Preakness Stakes and the Kentucky Derby. Sande had also made history this day, winning his third Derby, only the second jockey to do so.[42]

For William Woodward, it was his first Derby victory, and, while the victory might have been easy for Gallant Fox, it was not easy for Woodward to get down from the directors' box to the winner's circle set up next to Lord Derby's pavilion. Not only did he find his knees weaker than he had anticipated, but he went down the wrong stairs and had to climb over a couple of railings to get to the right spot, much to the amusement of the unknown persons helping him down to accept the trophy.[43] When he finally found himself down at ground level, Woodward met Gallant Fox and Sande; he shook the champion jockey's hand and then led his prized colt into the winner's circle, where the blanket of roses was draped across Gallant Fox's shoulders as the shutters of a myriad of cameras clicked around them. The Fox did not turn a hair at the attention of the enthusiastic crowd or the garland of roses, remaining docile in the whirlwind of activity around him.[44] The winning owner climbed the pavilion's steps and joined the Earl of Derby on the platform, as the NBC microphones recorded Lord Derby's remarks and the presentation of the gold cup to the winning owner.[45] In the hubbub of aristocrats and exultant connections no one seemed to notice the absence of the man responsible for preparing Gallant Fox in the first place: "Sunny Jim" Fitzsimmons.

After saddling Gallant Fox for the race, Fitzsimmons had ventured to the infield rather than remain part of the crowd in the grandstand. He watched the race from there and, after Gallant Fox won, he was among the rush of people that crowded onto the track. Concerned for his horse, Fitzsimmons attempted to cross to get to the winner's circle and check up on his charge. A mounted policeman stopped him from crossing, clearly not recognizing the famed trainer.[46] Sunny Jim finally made his way to the presentation stand, where Earl Sande, the blanket of roses now draped over his shivering shoulders, stood with Lord Derby, William Woodward, and the radio men dodging wires and raindrops as they carried the proceedings to their national audience. "He's a good horse," the respected trainer said. "He did just what I expected."[47]

With the ceremonies done, the celebrants dispersed and Gallant Fox headed back to the barn with his owner and trainer trailing behind him.[48] Effusive, George Tappen shared details about the horse and his routine as reporters hung around the Fitzsimmons barn, taking in the atmosphere of supreme satisfaction, while a crowd tried to peer in and get a glimpse at the newly minted Derby winner.[49] Earl Sande answered questions in the jockeys' room and then slipped into a waiting car, bound for the train station and home in Jamaica, New York.[50] With the Preakness and the Derby behind them, Team Gallant Fox focused on their next target: the Belmont Stakes. Looming large there was a potential confrontation with a familiar foe: Whichone. Harry Payne Whitney's two-year-old champion was fresh off his layoff and ready to run. Could he derail Gallant Fox's pursuit of racing immortality? It was time to find out.

8

In Pursuit of a Crown

Whichone's knees had been a question mark for months. After winning five of his seven starts at age two, Harry Payne Whitney's prized son of Chicle had been sidelined with rumored knee issues for nearly eight months when he appeared at Belmont Park in mid-May and jogged a mile around the big sandy oval.[1] His recuperation at Whitney's Brookdale Farm in New Jersey had prepared this champion colt for his first test of the year, the Withers Stakes. After that, Whichone likely would meet Gallant Fox again in the Belmont Stakes. The two had already met once in the Futurity at Belmont Park the previous September, where the Fox, hampered by a troubled trip, finished three lengths behind Whichone. Who would come out on top in a second meeting?

Before that question could find an answer, Whichone had to get through his first two starts in preparation for that 1½-mile Belmont Stakes. First, trainer Tom Healey sent his charge to the one-mile Ballot Handicap, where he carried 126 pounds against two other horses and easily won the race. Observers agreed that the Whitney colt, who pulled at the reins throughout the race, seemed full of vim and vigor.[2] Three days later, Whichone started in the one-mile Withers Stakes, this time against five others. Starting on the rail, jockey Sonny Workman tried to get Whichone away first, hoping to avoid being boxed in. However, Black Majesty beat him to it, his stablemate Maya running just behind him to the outside of Whichone. Settling in behind the front-runners, Workman had to bide his time until Black Majesty ran himself out. Workman kept his mount on

Whichone, with jockey Raymond "Sonny" Workman, at Belmont Park, May 31, 1930. Keeneland Library Cook Collection.

the rail and sent him on when Black Majesty began to fade. Though Whichone won by four lengths, his performance was less than impressive: "Better watch out for Gallant Fox in the Belmont," W. C. Vreeland heard from the crowd on Withers day.[3]

Jockey Sonny Workman galloped Whichone out another quarter of a mile after the one-mile Withers was over, giving him a test of ten furlongs in anticipation of the twelve they would run the following week. Sportswriter John Lewy commented that while the stakes might have marked the three-year-old champion in years past, "the 1930 renewal was regarded as nothing more than qualifying effort for Whichone, in preparation for the battle to come at the end of this week."[4] Given his two-year-old season and now these two wins in his 1930 efforts, Whichone gained slight favoritism over Gallant Fox going into the Belmont Stakes. Despite all that Gallant Fox had done to that point, winning the Wood Memorial, the Preakness, and the Derby, Whichone remained the horse to beat in the minds of Eastern horsemen.[5] The Belmont Stakes was shaping up to be the race of the year, a battle between two heavyweights.

Walter Vosburgh bore this out with his announced weights for the Brooklyn Handicap, set for a week after the Belmont: he had Whichone at 114 pounds while Gallant Fox was at 112 pounds. When the Whitney colt turned in a twelve-furlong workout in 2:32, a time that matched multiple winning Belmont efforts, even sportswriter John Lewy thought Whichone was the choice over Gallant Fox, despite having picked the Woodward colt to win the three races he had already in 1930.[6] Given that Whichone had defeated Gallant Fox in the Futurity at Belmont Park the year before, the idea that Whichone was the better of the two, especially knowing how great he had been in 1929, lent an air of excitement to the race. Gallant Fox had won his first three races of 1930, including two of the great stakes races run in the United States, but he had not yet met Whichone, and that was enough to raise doubts about the abilities of Woodward's colt. Whichone had been the best horse of 1929 and Gallant Fox was shaping up to be the same in 1930, making the Belmont Stakes a clash of champions, a titanic event. Indeed, Frank Getty went so far as to bring in the biggest horse of them all when talking about the anticipated confrontation: "Not since Man o' War's day has there been promise of such a race as these two Thoroughbreds and their two capable riders should put on from the flick of the barrier at Belmont."[7]

After a day's rest in his stall at Churchill Downs, Gallant Fox started on his Belmont Stakes journey on Monday, May 19, traveling back to Fitzsimmons's base at Aqueduct in the company of assistant trainer George Tappen.[8] The Derby winner remained there and logged his first post-Derby workout on May 24 under Earl Sande. He went five furlongs in 1:05, his trainer pleased with the colt's fitness.[9] All the Fox needed to do was maintain his form; he had already run three times, with each of his starts carefully curated for this point in the racing season. Woodward had identified the Belmont

Stakes as a goal for the Fox, and all Fitzsimmons needed to do was to keep the colt on edge. Gallant Fox remained in such good form that the trainer contemplated starting him in the Withers, but Woodward declined the opportunity. That stakes was only a mile, and the Fox was tuning up for a race that was even longer than the Derby. Instead, Gallant Fox worked three more times in the lead-up to the June 7 Belmont, including a 1⅛-mile turn around Belmont Park in 1:49⅘, within a second of the world record.[10] Whichone's 1½-mile turn in 2:32 garnered more attention than the Fox's near record. All eyes appeared to be on the Whitney blue and brown, the two-year-old champion, Whichone. Could he play spoiler to the Fox's try at the Triple Crown?

Something else almost spoiled the Fox's try: a car accident. On Thursday evening, less than forty-eight hours before the race, Earl Sande was a passenger in jockey Eddie Barnes's car when they were involved in a chain reaction accident at the intersection of 121st Avenue and Sutphin Boulevard in Jamaica, New York. A blown tire sent a car careening into Barnes's car and one other. The force of the accident overturned Barnes's car, and the two men were fortunate that they were not pinned beneath their automobile. Three others were also injured, but, other than cuts and bruises, Sande was relatively unhurt.[11] Though he was released from the hospital after only a few hours, his ability to ride Gallant Fox in the Belmont was uncertain. Would Sande's injuries, especially the cuts on his hands, be enough to keep him out of the saddle on Saturday?

William Woodward visited with Sande for a time on Friday afternoon to ascertain his condition before the next day's race. Despite speculation that Gallant Fox would be at a disadvantage without Sande in the saddle, the master of Belair was confident that his colt had the necessary talent and preparation to win the prestigious race regardless of who was riding him.[12] For his part, Earl Sande had survived worse than that car accident, including that spill at Saratoga in 1924, when Spurt threw him after being impeded by another horse.[13] Despite injuries that should have grounded him permanently, Sande was back in the saddle the next year.[14] In 1930, having survived that spill and the loss of his wife and much of his fortune, the famed jockey was not about to let some cuts and bruises keep him from this race. He assured Woodward that he was ready to ride.[15] The team was ready for its next big test.

The stage was set: Whichone versus Gallant Fox, and a couple of others. Big Sandy was ready for the battle. Earl Sande would play his part, come hell or high water. When William Woodward fretted about the competition, Fitzsimmons assured his boss that "*we* have the horse" for the coming race.[16] With the Kentucky Derby and the Preakness Stakes behind him, Gallant Fox stood on the precipice of another trial, another chance to prove his greatness. History was his to make.

William Woodward started June 7, Belmont Stakes day, standing on the lush greens of his Long Island home in his robe and slippers, staring out at the vista before him. "I was able, also, to watch the weather which was very threatening and didn't look good," the master of Belair reported.[17] The rain started to come down about 1 p.m., soaking the crowd, estimated at more than forty thousand, who had descended upon Belmont Park for the day's show. With them came a sense of "intense excitement over the coming of a great event" despite the showers that continued to dampen everything in sight. The traffic jam outside of Belmont Park, drivers desperate to get into the historic racetrack so they could see the show, indicated that feeling of wanting to be a part of something great.

At 3:32 p.m., a field of eight two-year-olds, including Harry Payne Whitney's Equipoise, met the barrier for the National Stallion Stakes, the rain still falling. The future Hall of Famer won his race on what the *Daily Racing Form* called a fast track, but within the hour, Gallant Fox and the winner's stablemate Whichone would do battle on a surface that had taken on enough moisture to be downgraded to "good" instead.[18] The weather might have drenched the waiting crowd, but it was not going to diminish the anticipation of the battle to come.

After the Fox's stablemate Flying Gal scratched, the field was down to four, including Swinfield and Questionnaire. Both were decent horses on their own, but they lacked the reputation and the record that the other two had. William Woodward had expressed concern about Questionnaire's ability after his win in a 1⅛-mile race earlier in the week, but Sunny Jim remained unconcerned: they had *the* horse. Even knowing that Whichone was an experienced mudder, the team behind the Fox was confident,[19] especially knowing that a bruised and bandaged Earl Sande would be in the saddle. The betting public, though, still made Whichone the favorite, with the Fox second choice.

The horses were saddled under cover in the paddock, as the rain dripped on the galleries of spectators assembled to watch the preparations.[20] Fitzsimmons kept his instructions to Sande simple: do not let the horse get mud in his face. Breaking from the first post made it possible that Gallant Fox would get behind horses that would break and then move in toward the rail. The Fox had not had mud in his face before and Fitzsimmons worried that the sensation would cause an already curious horse to pause and wonder at what was happening.[21] Finally, a gentleman in a raincoat came out, raised a bugle to his lips, and blew the call to the track.[22] Sonny Workman was boosted into Whichone's saddle and Earl Sande onto Gallant Fox. Rain continued to trickle down, slowly soaking the silks both jockeys wore. Underneath his cap, Sande's bandaged face appeared composed as they trickled through the tunnel onto the main track, Whichone in the lead.[23] The paddock had swelled with admirers as the horses prepared for the race; out on the Belmont apron, the rail was lined with thousands more, standing deep in the mud and heedless of the downpour.[24] To the tune of applause from the overflowing crowd, the four competitors walked down to the barrier and lined up behind the elastic strip strung across the track for a standing start.[25]

Gallant Fox stood on the rail, with Questionnaire next to him, Whichone in the third post, and then Swinfield on the outside. Per his custom, Gallant Fox broke through the barrier, cantering for twenty yards and turning to look at the other horses before Sande took him in hand and brought him back to the line.[26] The jockey patted and cooed to his mount, knowing that the Fox was eager to get going.[27] They stood together at the line, starter George Cassidy's eyes trained on the four, waiting for the right moment to spring the barrier. He pressed the button and released them; the tense crowd shouted "They're off!" as the four found their stride.[28]

Swinfield showed in front first, a neck ahead of Gallant Fox, with Questionnaire and Whichone behind them. Within a few strides, Sande had Gallant Fox on the lead, moving him to the rail as the horses rounded the first turn. The rain misted over the course, making the field look like a blur as they straightened out into the backstretch, Gallant Fox at least a length in front at each call. Sande gave his horse a breather and then would push him a bit anytime he felt the press of another horse in his vicinity.[29] As the field entered that last sweeping turn, Sonny Workman urged Whichone to make his move, their sights set on the red-hooded horse in front. This was the confrontation the crowd had waited for, what everyone was expecting: for Whichone to challenge Gallant Fox, for the two champions to duke it out for the Belmont Stakes.

But that battle was not to be. As the four turned into the stretch, any ground that Whichone had gained on his opponent was met by effortless grace and speed, Gallant Fox a stark contrast to the laboring Whichone behind him.[30] Questionnaire and Swinfield were mere props in the show now: the eyes of the crowd were fixed on the white with red dots streaking to victory. Gallant Fox crossed the finish line triumphant, three lengths in front, winning the race in a stakes record time of 2:31⅗ despite the rain-heavy track.[31] On the heels of a hard-fought victory in the Preakness Stakes, where he showed his gameness, and a tour de force in the Kentucky Derby, where he showed a versatility indicative of the sport's most elite, here, on a rainy day, he was the sun, shining bright on the crowd there to see his triumph. Gallant Fox had won the sixty-second Belmont Stakes and, with that, the second Triple Crown in American racing history.

William Woodward and Earl Sande accept the Belmont Stakes trophy from Joseph Widener after Gallant Fox's victory. Keeneland Library Cook Collection.

The outrider caught up to Earl Sande and Gallant Fox, the jockey "jiggling up and down in the saddle, a wide smile splitting all of his freckles" as they jogged back past the judges' stand for their turn in the winner's circle.[32] William Woodward, clad in his raincoat, took his champion's bridle and led him into the winner's circle, pleased that Gallant Fox had fulfilled the ambitions that he had for his son of Marguerite since the colt's debut.[33] The Fox was still full of run after his long test: every time he moved his head, he would lift his owner off the ground, the power and strength of the second Triple Crown champion evident as the master of Belair had his hands full simply holding on to his bridle.[34] In the winner's enclosure, they faced a barrage of microphones and cameras, eager to capture this moment for all posterity.

Joseph Widener presented Woodward with the silver plate that served as a permanent memento of a Belmont victory. Mrs. August Belmont II was there to award the August Belmont trophy to the master of Belair, along with the option to take the historic trophy home for the next year.[35] Earl Sande stood with Widener and Woodward, his left eye obscured by the bandages protecting those infamous cuts, his face ebullient with the moment's significance. When asked about Gallant Fox, Sande said, "He is a great colt." When asked to compare the Fox to Man o' War, who Sande rode in the Miller Stakes in 1920, the famed jockey demurred: "Gallant Fox is a great colt. You know Man o' War was a superhorse."[36] Like many veteran turfmen, Sande was not going to make that pronouncement, though others were willing to compare the two, including Joseph Widener, who called the Fox "unquestionably the best colt since Man o' War."[37] The best part? The Fox was not done yet.

All along, William Woodward had his sights on the Belmont Stakes; the other races that the Fox had won in the interim were bonuses on top of that. In pursuit of them all, Woodward managed to do something that had been done only once before: win the Triple Crown. Sir Barton had established that standard a bare decade earlier and now the Fox had copied that feat. However, the term "Triple Crown" had limited usage in the context of Gallant Fox's triumph. Since Sir Barton's win in 1919, the phrase "Triple Crown" had been attached to the Kentucky Derby, the Preakness Stakes, and the Belmont Stakes by several turf writers, though in limited usage. In the immediate post-race coverage of the Belmont Stakes, the same appears to have been the case. Even William Woodward himself mentioned it only in passing in his memoir of Gallant Fox's career: "It's called winning the triple crown, the Preakness, the Derby, and the Belmont. It was also the fulfilling of the ambition that we had had for the colt from his earliest racing days."[38] These three races would mark the careers of both Sir Barton and Gallant Fox, serving as blueprints for the champions to come after them, including one named Omaha.

With the Belmont Stakes behind him, Woodward was content to let his champion rest until the late summer meet at Saratoga. Some news reports touted the American Derby at Washington Park near Chicago for the Triple Crown winner's next start. Fitzsimmons wanted to race Gallant Fox more rather than wait for Saratoga: "I want this horse to do what no horse has ever done before. I want you to let me race him; although I may get him beaten, I am sure we can do what others have never done."[39] Woodward agreed to take it start by start, building on what his colt had already done in 1930. The next day, Gallant Fox stood in his stall, munching his oats and looking fit after his historic win. While W. C. Vreeland stood talking to assistant trainer George Tappen, Gallant Fox stopped eating to stick his head out of his stall, twitching his ears as if to say, "Are you talking about me?"[40]

Of course, they were. He was the ever curious and famously fast Fox of Belair, Triple Crown champion.

9

The Fox Rolls On

A horse who wins twenty of twenty-one starts in his career is destined to be a topic of discussion long after his racing days are over. The odds of retiring with only one loss are stacked against all horses, claimer or champion, but, for that one horse, that singular loss is an eternal blemish, surely a mistake. How could Man o' War *lose?* The idea was anathema, inconsistent with all that he was on a racetrack. To this day, Man o' War stands as the embodiment of immortality, so great that to compare other horses to him is borderline blasphemy. How could one ever hold another horse up next to near perfection and state that one is like the other with a straight face? Horsemen bristled.

Yet there they were; those very comparisons between Man o' War and Gallant Fox popped up in the pages of newspapers following the latter's victory in the Belmont Stakes. Joseph Widener, owner of Belmont Park and witness to the Fox's victory, had said as much in a cable to Lord Derby after the race.[1] Unlike Man o' War, the Fox had been hit or miss at two, but, at three, he had done all that they had asked of him; he ran in the slop or the sun, bulldozed his way through obstacles, and pulled out victories while he flew home with proverbial ease over the best of his crop, almost yawning at their challenges. Such performances invited the comparisons, but still the horsemen that had borne witness to the flights of Man o' War in 1919 and 1920 resisted that appraisal. Arthur Hancock, the man who had helped make Gallant Fox possible, called the colt the "best since Man o' War."[2] While the debate went on in the inches of newspaper columns, Fitzsimmons looked toward what was next for his horse.

92

The trainer had told his boss that he wanted to race Gallant Fox, the sooner the better given the colt's form. Woodward had wanted to wait until Saratoga for the Fox's next start.[3] With the Belmont behind them and about six weeks until Saratoga's meet, another race or two seemed to be logical. The American Derby in Chicago? The Latonia Derby in Kentucky? Where would the newly minted Triple Crown champion go? As it turned out, he would stay put and run in the Dwyer Stakes at Belmont Park. This 1½-mile test had once ended the winning streak of Sir Barton, the first Triple Crown winner. Would it spell the end of Gallant Fox's as well?

The question was, what horses had he *not* beaten at that point? So far in 1930, he had faced at least two dozen other three-year-olds, from two-year-old champion Whichone to Kentucky Oaks winner Alcibiades, and had defeated them all. It did not matter who he faced, really, because now a new reality sank in: Gallant Fox was going to carry weight. Racing uses the weight-for-age scale, a system that determines how much weight a horse will carry in a race based on their age, sex, the race's distance, and the time of the year.[4] The scale advised that three-year-olds should carry about 126 pounds maximum, so that was the weight the Fox would have in the Dwyer. Handicappers would then assign horses their weights based on their record. Since most of the other horses had records that were not as consistent as Gallant Fox's, they would carry less weight, potentially as much as twenty pounds less. The list also included a name that suddenly made the Dwyer more than a celebratory romp for the Fox: Whichone.

If Whichone started, he was slated to carry four fewer pounds than Gallant Fox, 122 pounds to 126. That might not sound like much of a difference; but consider that both colts carried the same weight in the Belmont Stakes and Whichone then was coming off a shorter rest between races than Gallant Fox. This time, Whichone would have the advantage of both less weight and a longer layoff than he had prior to their meeting at Belmont Park. He also would have a new jockey, Linus "Pony" McAtee, rather than Sonny Workman, who had piloted the Whitney colt in the Belmont. Tom Healey, the Whitney stable's trainer, wanted to try a new rider, hypothesizing that Whichone had not run well for Workman in that race.[5] McAtee had won the Kentucky Derby twice and the Preakness once and was as experienced a jockey as Sande, though perhaps not as well-known. He also had ridden Whichone in the Hopeful the previous year. If Whichone started, McAtee's experience could make a difference.

The countdown to the Dwyer was on. Advertisements for racing at Aqueduct on June 28 touted a "mighty struggle for supremacy" in the offing that Saturday. In expectation of a record crowd for the Dwyer, track officials moved the Winfield Steeplechase Handicap from the day's second race to the first. Once that race was complete, they could then open the infield to spectators for the meeting between the Fox and Whichone, the fourth race on the card.[6] Memories of the 1920 Dwyer, where Man o' War faced his greatest test from John P. Grier down the Aqueduct stretch, only heightened the anticipation. Once again, it was a horse owned by Harry Payne Whitney challenging the dominant horse of the year. Once again, fans hoped for an epic confrontation, hoping that Whichone could pressure Gallant Fox as John P. Grier had pushed Man o' War in 1920. Alas, that test was not to be.

On Friday, twenty-four hours before that mighty struggle, Healey found himself on the receiving end of another round of bad luck. After a banner year in 1929, when the Whitney horses seemed unbeatable, Whichone again would miss racing time, this time with a blind quarter crack in one hoof, a vertical crack in the widest part of the hoof between the foot and the heel. The two-year-old champion of 1929 would not be seen under colors again until Saratoga's late summer meet.[7] In the meantime, the field for the Dwyer was now bereft of a serious challenger for Gallant Fox. Instead, he faced four others, including stablemate Flaming, and was giving each of them fifteen to twenty pounds, but that did not matter. He was still the overwhelming favorite.

Fitzsimmons had the Fox more than prepared for the twelve furlongs. Two days before the race, Gallant Fox worked out with a relay of stablemates, going 1⅜ miles in 2:18⅖; this was faster than the trainer might have intended, but the colt was full of run, unable to resist the challenge of racing those horses sent out with him.[8] Whitey Abel, Fitzsimmons's exercise rider, did his best to handle the Fox's bountiful energy, while Earl Sande supervised from the sidelines, nursing a sore ankle. Sande had been unseated when Petee-Wrack kicked his mount, Distraction, before the Brooklyn Handicap nearly two weeks earlier.[9] Normally, the legendary jockey would have worked Gallant Fox himself, but Sunny Jim wanted Sande as healthy as possible for the Dwyer. His familiarity with the Fox and his ways made him too valuable to risk any further injury.

Gallant Fox would need the right pilot for this race. The Fox was not going to turn it on just for the fun of it, even if a big crowd showed up to watch the show.[10] He needed a challenge, and the scant list of other starters did not promise that. What he found instead was trouble at the barrier. With the filly Bannerette on the rail in the first post position and the lightly raced Xenofol in the third post, Gallant Fox was sandwiched between two bad actors. Chaos reigned for a few minutes. Xenofol pushed the Fox into the rail at one point and the assistant starters moved Bannerette to the outside of the field, before starter George Cassidy could get them all in line.[11] The field got away in good order, but not without Woodward lamenting that he wished the starting gate were in use to cut down on the pre-race antics.[12]

Jockey Laverne Fator put Limbus on the lead within the first quarter, with Sande content to move Gallant Fox within a couple of lengths behind him. The famed jockey let out a notch on the back-stretch, moving the Fox even with Limbus until they reached the mile mark.[13] Limbus ran out of steam, his stride shortening as Sande picked up the pace on Gallant Fox. Behind him, Xenofol began to move as the Fox started his customary loafing without company. Sande shook him up with a couple of taps of the whip and the Triple Crown winner refocused on his task, moving to the rail and running with ease into the stretch. As the field turned for home, the Fox had a two-length lead, but Xenofol was coming on fast in the end, getting as close as Gallant Fox's tail, when Sande shook up his mount one more time.[14] The margin between the two increased to a length and a half in that last sixteenth. Gallant Fox took home the Dwyer for his fifth straight stakes victory and increased his career winnings to $210,220, putting him at seventh on the list of all-time money winners of the turf.[15] That number inspired a new pursuit for the Fox: could he win enough money to pass Zev's mark of $313,639?

If he were going to pass Zev, Gallant Fox would need to do it in 1930. With Woodward's goals for his spring campaign already behind him, races at Arlington Park in Chicago and Saratoga were all on his dance card, but, once the year was done, so was the Fox. His owner admitted to the same concern that stopped Samuel Riddle from racing Man o' War beyond his three-year-old season: weight. Woodward knew that the fifteen-to-twenty-pound difference in weights in the Dwyer was simply the beginning. At four, handicappers likely would not hesitate to assign weights that would have the Fox carrying upwards of forty pounds more than his competition.[16] No, the master of Belair wanted to race his champion's sons and daughters, "securing for myself really greater benefits through his offspring than the winning of this or that race."[17] Once his three-year-old campaign was complete, the Fox would move on to the next phase: making more Foxes for his breeder and owner to race. First, though, he had a few more races to win.

With the Triple Crown and the Dwyer behind him, the Fox was doing so well that Woodward and Fitzsimmons considered his next move as they counted down to Saratoga. Despite the long trip and the heat of summer, they sent Gallant Fox westward to Chicago for a turn in the Arlington Classic.

The Monday following the Dwyer, Gallant Fox and company rolled into Chicago and straight into the dog days of summer. In his private car, the horse came with two others, Flaming and Bobbles, a pony, a dog, and six men; these included assistant trainer George Tappen, Gallant Fox's groom Bart Sweeney, an exercise rider, two watchmen, and Bill Dallimore.[18] The goal was to run in both the Arlington Classic on July 12 and then the Arlington Cup on July 19, the latter against older horses.[19] At stake were two high-value purses, $70,000 for the Classic and $25,000 for the Cup, money that would push the Fox closer to Zev's mark. First, though, he had to get through a field of five others, including Gallant Knight and Alcibiades.

Gallant Knight had finished second in the Kentucky Derby, Audley Farm's best finisher in that classic race. Since that race, he had won the Fairmount and Latonia Derbies and finished second in the American Derby at Washington Park.[20] With each victory, at ten furlongs or better, Gallant Knight had developed into a colt that could have bid for the best three-year-old of the year in any other year, but, in 1930, his accomplishments simply made him the Fox's biggest rival in the list of probables for the Arlington Classic. Alcibiades had led the Derby for the first half mile, fading to tenth in the end. Then she won the nine-furlong Kentucky and Arlington Oaks but finished well behind the boys in the American Derby. Ned O. was back after winning a seven-furlong sprint just two days before the Classic, his first win since his third-place finish in the Kentucky Derby. But these were all horses that Gallant Fox had faced before and had beaten with little trouble. What could stop the Fox from flying home?

Since the Belair contingent's arrival in the Chicago area from New York the previous week, the weather had presented a bit of an issue. Temperatures hovered in the eighties, more intense than what Gallant Fox had encountered previously. With more intense heat, horses need to drink more to stay hydrated, but the champion did not like the taste of Chicago-area water and Fitzsimmons had not shipped any with the horse and his entourage. Fortunately, the neighboring E. R. Bradley stable had some that the Fox would drink.[21] Between the water and the heat, Gallant Fox did not prepare well for the race, but he turned in a nice workout the day before, five furlongs in 1:00⅘. He was ready to roll and fans were ready to watch him, with a crowd of at least fifty thousand expected.[22]

The week had been sunny, baking the track to a hard fastness, but Saturday had a chance of rain so Dallimore shod the Fox with mud caulks just in case. As the race got closer, the weather held off so the caulks were filed off as Fitzsimmons saddled Gallant Fox for the Classic.[23] The race had allowance conditions. The only filly, Alcibiades, carried 116 pounds, ten pounds less than the Triple Crown champion; Gallant Knight was assigned 123 pounds, despite his own stakes victories; and the other three colts all carried 121 pounds. Even with the weight differences, Gallant Fox seemed practically unbeatable. Fitzsimmons remarked that his horse "can't lose" and Sande assured the press that the Fox could set a new record in this ten-furlong test if pressed.[24] The $70,000 purse had a $10,000 bonus if the winner had also won the Kentucky Derby, American Derby, the Preakness Stakes, or Belmont Stakes.[25] Alongside the rich purse, the day featured a star-studded crowd of attendees, including Vice President Curtis, who had been in attendance when Gallant Fox won the Preakness at Pimlico; William Wrigley Jr., owner of the Chicago Cubs and the namesake of the club's legendary field; and William and Elsie Woodward, both in attendance from New York.

Arlington Park used the Bahr starting gate, a familiar sight from the Preakness Stakes. Gallant Fox was in the third post, with Ned O. on the rail and Alcibiades in the second post. Gallant Knight was farther out, in post position five.[26] At the break, Maya sprinted to the lead, running two lengths in front of Gallant Fox and Gallant Knight. When Maya drifted out from the rail, Sande sent his mount through that opening, passing him and taking a short lead. Gallant Knight, still running toward the middle, hung just back, waiting for the one-mile mark to make his move. As Gallant Knight picked up momentum, Mrs. Woodward tugged at her husband's sleeve, concerned about the potential for the Audley horse to pass Gallant Fox. Mr. Woodward remained unconcerned, certain that Fitzsimmons had his horse fit as a fiddle and that Sande knew exactly how much horse he had under him.[27] The two horses appeared to duel through the last few furlongs, Gallant Knight pressing and whittling the margin down to a neck, but "Gallant Fox had too much speed, too much courage, and too much Sande on his back to allow that upset to happen."[28] The jockey tapped Gallant Fox with the whip and the Triple Crown champion finished with ears pricked like he was enjoying himself immensely.[29] Though the margin of victory was close, a neck, at no point was Gallant Fox in danger of losing the race. Sande was conscious of each inch between the Fox and Gallant Knight as they approached the wire. They blew past in 2:03⅘, just a fifth of a second off the track record for a mile and a quarter.[30] The record crowd with its celebrity attendees and fans overflowing Arlington's grandstand had come to see a show, and what a great show it was.

As Earl Sande trotted Gallant Fox back to the winner's circle, the Triple Crown champion's ears pricked at the reception from the nearly sixty thousand who had witnessed that battle, whose cheers "all but lifted the roof off the huge stand."[31] As William Woodward wound his way down from his box to the winner's circle, he found his progress stymied by the mass of fans, much as he had at Churchill Downs after the Derby. He joined James Fitzsimmons and Earl Sande to receive accolades and a gold cup from Governor Emmerson.[32] In addition, he received a check for $64,750 for the win in the Classic, bringing Gallant Fox's career total to $274,980, just $38,659 short of Zev.[33] His next race, the Arlington Cup, could go a long way toward making up that gap.

The Arlington Cup was another ten-furlong stake at Arlington Park, this time against older horses. Gallant Fox was to carry 114 pounds, based on the weight-for-age scales at this point in the year and at that distance.[34] This would have been a decided advantage against older horses like Blue Larkspur, the best horse of 1929, who would be carrying 126 pounds. George Tappen sent the Fox out for a workout a couple of days after his Arlington Classic victory, but the colt seemed reluctant to train, sulking rather than responding to his rider. His attitude was better the next day, but Tappen called his boss to let him know that the Fox probably should not run in the Arlington Cup. Fitzsimmons agreed, advising Woodward that staying for another week in that heat might affect the rest of Gallant Fox's campaign, including starts in the Saratoga Cup and the Jockey Club Gold Cup.[35] Since his victory in the Wood Memorial in late April, he had run at six different tracks and traveled from New York to Maryland to Kentucky and now to Illinois, long trips and tough races that clearly had Gallant Fox ready for a break. With the scratch from the Arlington Cup, Fitzsimmons sent his Triple Crown winner straight to Saratoga for some down time before preparation for the important races to come.[36]

In ten weeks, Gallant Fox had become a sensation, the best horse since Man o' War and a veritable super horse. But not all of his biggest challenges were behind him. Another loomed in the distance: a rematch with Whichone.

10

A Dandy Show

Many go back to the old maxim: "Anything can happen in the mud."
—Bryan Field

The quirks of racing luck are well-known to anyone who has anything to do with the sport of horse racing. On any given day, a myriad of tiny details can challenge even the most favored of favorites: a jockey operating on a surplus of a hangover and a deficit of sleep; a substitute starter throwing off the rhythms of the day; an ill-timed start igniting a cavalcade of trouble. Such was the 1919 Sanford Memorial Stakes for jockey Johnny Loftus and his mount in that race, the immortal Man o' War.

There is a reason why Saratoga is known as the Graveyard of Champions. Man o' War was about to have some company in infamy.

The win at Arlington in mid-July came in the stifling heat of summer after weeks of racing in the cooler late-spring temperatures. Even with the advantages of traveling in style, Gallant Fox was still a horse and Fitzsimmons knew that the colt's reluctance to train after the Arlington Classic signaled that it was time for a much-needed breather. The trip to upstate New York was a chance to let down and recover until the Travers in mid-August. And then the fans found the barn.[1]

Nearly a year after Black Monday, the descent into the Great Depression left millions out of work; breadlines formed to feed hungry families seeking relief of any sort while still others took to the roads in search of something, anything to sustain them. The Fox's exploits on the racetrack were a welcome distraction from the bad news that dominated the headlines. A series of photographs chronicled Gallant Fox's daily routine in newspapers across the country in early August, but fans around Saratoga wanted to see the sights for themselves. They arrived in droves to visit Fitzsimmons's barn and watch the goings-on around the second Triple Crown winner. Woodward himself commented on the crowds lining up to see his colt, remarking, "It was thought that on one Sunday there were a thousand people there to see him at different times during the day."[2] This plethora of visitors prompted Fitzsimmons to bring in guards for the prized colt. One sat by his stall during the daytime and two at night. A fence five feet high by eight feet wide was erected around the Fox's stall to limit outside access: he could be seen but not touched. Fitzsimmons's barn was open to visitors, but none could get near Gallant Fox.[3]

About the same time rumors swirled that the Fox would spend his four-year-old season abroad, racing in England with the ultimate goal of the Ascot Gold Cup.[4] The master of Belair usually would send a consignment of yearlings to England to race under trainer Cecil Boyd-Rochfort, so the Fox was to join the other Woodward horses at Freemason Lodge, sailing for jolly old England after the Jockey Club Gold Cup.[5] He had conquered many of America's biggest races already, so racing in England seemed like a natural next step for the second Triple Crown, right?

Except that none of it was true. Woodward had considered it for a moment, but realized that Gallant Fox was much too valuable to ship overseas for any kind of racing, even a race as iconic as the Ascot Gold Cup.[6] Sunny Jim had never heard anything about it from his boss, and, of all people, he was sure he "would be the first to know."[7] Gallant Fox might not be going to England for another year's racing, but another Belair horse would follow up his Triple Crown with a trip to Boyd-Rochfort's yard. Woodward's tries for an Ascot Gold Cup of his own were still to come.

"Sunny Jim" Fitzsimmons with Gallant Fox in 1930. National Museum of Racing and Hall of Fame Collection.

Regardless of where Gallant Fox would spend 1931, he still had races ahead in 1930, four more to go in fact. The Travers Stakes was set for August 16, and waiting for him at the barrier would be Whichone—and the specter of Upset.

A blind quarter crack in late June had kept Whichone from meeting Gallant Fox in the Dwyer, which the Fox won easily. A month later, the Whitney juvenile champion was at Saratoga with trainer Tom Healey and stablemates like Equipoise, another Whitney-bred horse destined to shine. Even with his future champion turning in nice performances in the two-year-old stakes, Harry Payne Whitney was focused on one goal for his stable's season at Saratoga: he wanted Whichone to beat Gallant Fox and he was willing to push Whichone to the limit to get there.[8]

Because of that forced layoff, Whichone could not simply wait for the Travers. Healey needed to get the colt back in the swing of things, so he entered Whichone in the one-mile Saranac Handicap for three-year-olds on August 6. There, the Whitney colt was top weight of 123 pounds, giving five to thirty-one pounds to others in the field, including Maya, Sun Falcon, and Caruso. He won easily, running the mile in 1:37; the next day's headlines declared him to be "as good as he ever was."[9] Even W. C. Vreeland seemed impressed with Whichone's performance, claiming that the colt "served notice yesterday on Gallant Fox, the champion of 1930, that he was ready to topple the present-day titleholder off his throne."[10] With ten days to go before the Travers, Whichone seemed primed to meet Gallant Fox at the barrier and challenge him one more time.

Three days later, Healey sent Whichone out for the Whitney Stakes against older horses, but his presence in the race caused all but two starters to drop out. He won the ten-furlong race in 2:04 and seemed to have speed in reserve as he crossed the finish line.[11] With only six days left before the Travers, Whichone fit in one more start before that special Saturday, the Miller Stakes at a mile and three-sixteenths. On Tuesday, he faced only two other three-year-olds, Spinach and Gone Away, and won with no problems. He had logged three races in less than two weeks and had one more, a big one, just four days hence. Meanwhile, Gallant Fox had not faced the barrier since July 12, four weeks and four days before the Travers. If fitness was a question, the Fox readily answered it.

When the master of Belair arrived in Saratoga to check in on his champion, one of Fitzsimmons's exercise riders reported that "the horse had never been better, that he was stronger and more powerful than he had ever been."[12] His workouts were showing that same turn of foot that was characteristic of Gallant Fox: only giving enough until challenged. A workout the week before the Travers had Earl Sande up rather than one of the stable's other exercise riders. Under Sande and wearing full tack, 131 pounds in all, Gallant Fox worked a mile and a quarter, the Travers distance, in 2:04⅖.[13] Whichone had won the Whitney Stakes in 2:04 carrying 117 pounds in that weight-for-age event. Other than a touch of colic the weekend before the Travers, a frightening moment that passed quickly, Gallant Fox seemed spoiling for a fight.[14]

Two days before the big race, the two contenders were out for a morning stretch of their legs, getting short and quick workouts before returning to their respective barns. The eyes of the racing world were on them; the other horses that might be part of the Travers were almost afterthoughts. Whichone and Gallant Fox returned to stalls that were under guard; racetrack security was assigned to keep watch over whoever ventured close to their barns. The meet's opening days had been marred by the "sponging" of at least two horses, incidents where saboteurs had inserted small sponges into the horses' nostrils to impede their performance.[15] Tensions were high and "anyone approaching either stable must give a good account of himself or leave the vicinity."[16]

The headlines all pointed toward the same thing: a battle between two turf titans. Gallant Fox versus Whichone. Whitney versus Woodward. Whichone had beaten Gallant Fox in the Futurity nearly a year earlier; Gallant Fox had beaten Whichone in the Belmont Stakes two months earlier. The Belmont, though, was not conclusive evidence of one's superiority over the other. Whichone had been done wrong by Sonny Workman's ride that day, "outgeneraled by the wily Sande," but the Travers would be the chance to right the wrong, to answer the questions once and for all.[17]

The question no one was asking was, what about the other horses in the race?

William R. Travers was the first president of the Saratoga Racing Association and the namesake of the track's first race, the Travers Stakes, won by Kentucky on August 2, 1864. Travers was a man of great wit despite a lifelong stutter, a social butterfly with his memberships in twenty-seven private clubs—a testament to his preference for the sunniness of sociability. The track and his namesake race owed much of its success to the congenial atmosphere that Travers and his compatriots crafted when they created the Saratoga Racing Association. William Collins Whitney, father of Harry Payne, and friends continued that ambience when they rescued Saratoga in 1901.[18] Despite the drab weather that greeted them on Saturday, August 16, a crowd of an estimated forty thousand spilled into the grandstand for the day's show, Governor Franklin D. Roosevelt and his wife Eleanor among the throng.[19] Traffic in Saratoga Springs was so bad that racegoers abandoned cars two miles away and walked to the famed track.[20] Clem McCarthy was there to broadcast the proceedings for a national radio audience while famed heavyweight boxer Gene Tunney watched from the grandstand. In front of them was a surface laden with at least a day's worth of rain, soaked by steady showers.

To dry the track out after the heavy rain Friday evening, superintendent Thomas J. Clare set out wooden "dogs," beams about forty feet long that prevented any action within forty or fifty feet of the rail. When horses worked Saturday morning, they ran over the center of the track instead, cutting up that section of the dirt surface. This made those areas deeper and more cut up and left the inner areas untouched.[21] In essence, the best part to run on even with the continued intermittent rain was closer to the rail rather than out toward the middle of the Saratoga oval.

If one picked up a *Daily Racing Form* that day, one would find the past performance for the day's six races, including the Travers Stakes, the day's feature. Right before that race was the Waterboy

Handicap, a one-mile handicap for three-year-olds and up with a purse of $1,200 added.[22] Listed were seven horses, with Bobashela as the highest weighted entrant at 118 pounds. Also in the list of entrants was Sun Falcon at 111 pounds and Jim Dandy at 103 pounds. These two names also appear in the list of starters for the Travers, along with Caruso and Gallant Fox and Whichone, of course. W. R. Coe already had scratched Caruso, who had beaten Gallant Fox in the United States Hotel Stakes the year before and who had finished seventh behind the winning Whichone in the Saranac.

With Caruso out and the two superstars set to battle for the win, the third- and fourth-place purses—$2,000 and $500, respectively—were technically open to any horse who could stay upright long enough to cross the finish line with a jockey on its back.[23] So, instead of the Waterboy Handicap, Sun Falcon and Jim Dandy were switched to the Travers, destined to become bit players in the drama unfolding on the soaked surface. The race might have been down to three had it been any other race. As Tom Healey prepared Whichone for the Travers, he had the colt shod in bar plates, horseshoes that had a bar across the usually open portion at the back of the foot. The trainer, who knew that his horse would be hampered by the mucky track, was reluctant to start him and communicated his concerns to Harry Payne Whitney. The owner felt that he had no choice but to send Whichone to post given the excitement around the race and the large crowd that had turned out to see his colt face Gallant Fox again.[24] Whitney was content to take his chances, despite Healey's concerns. The duel would go on as advertised.

In the paddock, showers continued to drip on the crowd gathered around the four horses that appeared for saddling. Fans pressed against the roped barrier between them and the saddling area, straining for a sight of the equine combatants. Jim Dandy's trainer, John McKee, joked with Woodward and Fitzsimmons about running for third-place money, which was almost three times what Jim Dandy would have collected if he won the Waterboy Handicap. Gallant Fox came out with a light sheet to protect him from the rain, which was shed when he was saddled under the trees.[25] After Whichone was saddled under the cover of the paddock shed, Raymond "Sonny" Workman, in the legendary Eton blue and brown of the Whitney stable, boosted himself onto his back. Earl Sande came out in the red polka dots on white of Belair, folding his five-foot, six-inch frame into the tiny saddle on Gallant Fox's back. Nearby, Jim Dandy and Sun Falcon, both carrying less than the 126 pounds assigned to the two champions, had their saddles and jockeys Frank Baker and Frank Coltilleti in place.[26] The four horses followed the red-coated outrider from the paddock onto the wet oval, a surface that, as William Woodward observed, "was muddy and on the heavy side. Perhaps it was greasier than it was sticky."[27] As the four paraded to the barrier for the ten-furlong Travers, Gallant Fox observed the packed grandstand, his innate curiosity at his surroundings reminding him that it was time for the show. He had an audience to please.[28]

Behind him, wearing number two, was Whichone, and then Jim Dandy and Sun Falcon as three and four. When they lined up at the barrier, though, their order was reversed: Sun Falcon on the rail, then Jim Dandy, then Whichone, and lastly Gallant Fox on the outside.[29] In the Belmont, Gallant Fox had drawn the rail with Whichone to his outside in the third post position. For the Travers, Whichone was to his inside. As in the Belmont, Sande's instructions were simply "not to have mud thrown in his face and that was all."[30] Determined to prove his colt's superiority to the Fox, Harry Payne Whitney had given jockey Sonny Workman specific orders: "Stay with the Fox, match his strides in every department, and then race him into submission."[31] With Whichone to his outside, Sande could be forced to stay with the Whitney colt or take Gallant Fox behind him and try to get to his inside. On a fast track, that might have been an easier task. On a heavy surface like this one, such maneuvers might not be so simple, especially if a horse has a harder time handling the footing on that part of the track. To leave a running lane that has the ideal surface for a horse's feet to grip and then move to less certain ground might be too much to ask of even the best horse in the country. Split-second decisions like that can make or break a race. This time, Sande's only option was to hustle Gallant Fox to the front and hope that he could get enough ground between his mount and Whichone to have a say in his running lane.

Racetracks in New York were still using a standing start, rather than the gates that the Fox had seen in his other races. George Cassidy dropped his flag right when Gallant Fox was moving sideways so it took a beat for him to find his feet and go forward. Workman put Whichone on the lead, whip flying, and Sande went after him. The Whitney colt was about fifteen feet off the rail, running toward the center of the track, with Gallant Fox right on him. Jim Dandy was three lengths behind them, with Sun Falcon last of all. Sande took Gallant Fox into the first turn on a diagonal, pulling even with Whichone. As they straightened into the backstretch, the two rivals were still running head to head, Sande unable to shake Workman and his mount. He gave Gallant Fox some rein and the Fox pulled away to a half-length lead, but Workman again took to the whip and Whichone responded.[32] As they went into the final turn, something curious happened.

Because of the turns, the shortest route on any conventional track is to stay as close to the inside as possible. If a horse runs on the outer paths, they inevitably run farther than horses who run closer to the rail. To force a horse to run on the outside and to do it in close company is asking the horse to expend more energy, both in running farther and with other horses. Some horses dislike running in company and will react adversely; others, like Gallant Fox, *need* another horse to keep them engaged or else they will linger or even pull themselves up. As Whichone and Gallant Fox entered the final turn of the Travers, Workman seemed to gradually push the Fox farther and farther out. Again, Earl Sande could not take Gallant Fox back and then go around Whichone without losing a tremendous amount of momentum and ground. As a result, he was carried wide, waiting for a chance to escape Whichone's pursuit, the two far enough off the rail that it was open for anyone who wanted to take it. Jockey Frank Baker on Jim Dandy saw the two leaders drift wide and ducked his mount in toward the rail as they rounded the far turn into the stretch. Entering the Saratoga straight, Sande hesitated on Gallant Fox, losing about a half-length and expending more energy to pull even with Whichone once again. With a quarter of a mile to go, the Fox and Whichone were pushing each other to the limit, their struggle the focus of the assembled fans—but another sight drew their eyes away from the tussling rivals.[33] It was Jim Dandy, his ears flicking back and forth, relishing that inside path and taking the lead from the two titans.

The previous year, owner Chaffee Earl had a horse, Naishapur, run second to winner Clyde Van Dusen in the Kentucky Derby. While in Louisville for the Derby, his trainer John McKee purchased Jim Dandy, a promising two-year-old by Jim Gaffney, winner of the 1907 Hopeful Stakes and sire of 1923 Preakness Stakes winner Vigil.[34] Jim Gaffney had been a good mudder and Jim Dandy seemed to be of the same ilk, winning a race in the slop the day after McKee purchased him. Years later, jockey Frank Baker recalled his ride on Jim Dandy, remembering that the colt had "eggshell feet, the walls being very thin, so that when the track was hard, it hurt him to run. He was at his best running in the mud."[35] Later that summer, Jim Dandy showed that propensity for racing well on a wet track. He bested a field of ten others to win the Grand Union Hotel Stakes over a muddy surface at Saratoga. "I doubt if he's won another race since," said columnist Damon Runyon of Jim Dandy and he was right; the colt was winless in ten starts in 1930, his best showing a third-place finish.[36] But not this day, not this race.

In the race's final furlongs, as Jim Dandy rode the rail and put more and more distance between himself and the rest of the field, Whichone had finally had enough. With an eighth of a mile to go, Gallant Fox had his neck in front of the Whitney colt, but Jim Dandy was far too gone and the Fox far too spent to have a shot at catching the surprising presence racing toward the wire.[37] Whichone stopped so badly that he was in danger of finishing behind Sun

Falcon, who was bringing up the rear having played no role in the race other than to collect his $500 for fourth place.[38] To the supreme shock of the thousands present, a horse that William Woodward had called "a bad horse on a dry track and on a wet track he is not a superior horse" had won the Travers Stakes at odds of 100–1.[39]

The cheering stopped as Jim Dandy approached the finish line, silence greeting this surprising victor when he returned for his moment in the winner's circle.[40] Jim Dandy had done the improbable: he had beaten two horses from the two most prolific stables in the country by eight lengths. As William Woodward observed, "The boys on the two horses fought the duel up a back alley and did not watch to see what was going on along Broadway."[41] The two jockeys had tried to play each other, and, in doing that, were themselves played by the longest of long shots. Additionally, neither Workman nor Sande had a mount on earlier on the card, nor had either walked the racetrack prior to the Travers, so they had no idea that the rail had the firmer footing than the outer areas, the section of the dirt oval that Whichone and Gallant Fox had raced over while Jim Dandy and Frank Baker sailed through on that inside path.[42]

Sonny Workman jumped off of Whichone soon after they had crossed the finish line and walked the colt over to the judges' stand. In the process of dueling with Gallant Fox, he had bowed a tendon and would never race again.[43] Despite the injury, Whichone had finished the Travers in third, three lengths in front of Sun Falcon. The other half of the battle, Earl Sande, was chagrined at the losing turn in the Travers and lamented the defeat: "I am sorry, more than you can imagine, for it hurts to lose on such a great horse," he told the waiting reporters after the race.

For his part, the Fox came out of the race in good condition, and both Woodward and Fitzsimmons were relieved that the sloppy conditions did not take their toll on their colt. "That horse Gallant Fox does not like the mud," Sande had observed after the Travers. Both trainer and owner took that to heart.[44] "He will never start in that kind of going as long as I have charge of him," Fitzsimmons told

W. C. Vreeland.[45] The Fox's dislike for the mud had made itself plain at a historically inopportune moment. Man o' War was no longer the only champion who had a notorious defeat at the Spa.

Jim Dandy had one more start at Saratoga in the American Legion Handicap and then Chaffee Earl was thinking about sending him to Belmont Park for another meeting with Gallant Fox in the Lawrence Realization. Either way, though, most thought little of Jim Dandy's chances unless the surface was muddy, even after his win in the Travers. He would not win again in 1930, but his Travers victory was to follow him everywhere he went, long after his days on the racetrack were done.

Even if others were not convinced of the son of Jim Gaffney's quality, contractor Sam Rosoff surely thought rather highly of Jim Dandy. He had laid $1,000 on the colt at 100–1 and walked away with $100,000, a jim-dandy of a wager.[46] Chaffee Earl came away with the $27,050 purse and the honor of owning a Travers winner. Jim Dandy exited his unexpected performance with the glory of adding his name to the august list of victors in the Midsummer Derby: Man o' War, Roamer, Hindoo, Kentucky. He also had another claim to fame: he was on par with Upset, the only horse to ever beat Man o' War to the wire.

And who owned Upset? Harry Payne Whitney.

William Woodward was philosophical about the whole deal in the end: "It was a great disappointment to lose the Travers, of course, but the hard satisfaction was that we had killed our adversary in spite of the fiasco."[47] Whichone would not race on, but the Fox had business left to handle. With no more rivals to challenge him, all that was left for the Fox was to win a few more races to cement his legacy and establish his place in the pantheon of greatness. How did he stack up to the likes of Man o' War and Exterminator, Salvator and Colin? With only a few starts remaining, it was time to find out.

11

Record Breaker

You only dream the thing that happened here this afternoon.
—Damon Runyon, August 17, 1930

After the lone defeat of Man o' War's career and now Gallant Fox's spectacular rout, Saratoga must have seemed like it had a bit of a Bermuda Triangle quality to it. The Fox came out of his defeat by the mud and Jim Dandy just fine, though news reports did start surfacing to suggest that the champion had been tampered with at Arlington and that those rumored meddlings had contributed to his unexpected defeat.[1] In reality, that was unlikely since Gallant Fox had been in Saratoga for several weeks; he had been shipped there right after he was scratched from the Arlington Cup. The Fox had come out of the Travers much better than Whichone and looked forward to the Saratoga Cup on August 30.

The 1¾-mile Saratoga Cup was celebrating its jubilee, fifty years as one of the Spa's premier races. The list of past winners read like the roster of some Hall of Fame of horse racing: Kentucky, Beldame, Roamer, Exterminator, and Reigh Count. William Woodward valued distance races and sending his champion in the Cup was a given. However, this was the first time he was stepping out of his division and facing older horses. Would he regain his form and find himself victorious again or would another surprising defeat happen on Saratoga's final day of racing?

The fourteen furlongs of the Saratoga Cup would be the second longest race that Gallant Fox would run in his short career. The Derby and the Travers were ten furlongs, the Belmont twelve. At two, though, Gallant Fox had been less consistent, likely because his form worked best at distances longer than the typical six- and seven-furlong races carded for juveniles. The longer distances of these later races suited him much more, but William Woodward had a short time to enjoy this. Additionally, as a three-year-old, the Fox enjoyed a weight advantage in races against older horses that he would not get at age four, under the weight-for-age scale. In the Saratoga Cup, with his status as a three-year-old, he would carry 116 pounds. Much like Man o' War, if he raced another year, he would carry more weight than his competition, an unfavorable outcome in William Woodward's eyes. Though his days on the racetrack were numbered, the Fox still had three more races to go, all long-distance tests, the kind that the Belair colt preferred.

The field for the Cup included three three-year-olds, a four-year-old filly, and two older horses, including the Fox's stablemate Frisius. Frisius had won the Merchants and Citizens Handicap at 1¾₆ miles the week before, so he possessed the chops to run in a race like the Cup. Truly, though, this son of Star Hawk was there for one reason: to be pacemaker for his more illustrious stablemate.[2] The field also included Gone Away, who had finished second behind Whichone in the Miller; Ben Machree, winner of the 2¼-mile Latonia Cup; and Folking, the winner of the Waterboy Handicap, the race that had come just before the Travers two weeks earlier, the race that both Jim Dandy and Sun Falcon had passed up in favor of the Midsummer Derby.[3] The field was a fair one, but without names like Petee-Wrack and Sun Beau and a number of other older horses, the Saratoga Cup lacked the punch of a big-name challenger.

Unlike Travers day, the last day of Saratoga's 1930 meet was a dry one, with a fast track greeting the six horses for the Saratoga Cup. The previous race, the Hopeful Stakes, had featured an upset, in which Epithet beat the previously undefeated Jamestown. Would the Saratoga Cup feature another upset? Two weeks had elapsed since Jim Dandy had surprised everyone by taking advantage of the gap left by the dueling Gallant Fox and Whichone. Could another upset be in the offing in this prestigious race?

Frisius took the lead as soon as the six broke from the barrier, with jockey Alfred "Whitey" Abel donning the red cap while Sande had the white cap with the Belair silks.[4] Gone Away ran with Frisius while Gallant Fox sat a couple of lengths behind them, Sande keeping his mount under a tight hold while waiting for the right moment to move.[5] That came ten furlongs on, when Sande let down on the Fox and allowed his colt to move into second place. As they rounded the final turn into the stretch, Woodward savored the sight of his great colt pouring on the speed: "It really was a thrilling sight for an owner to see his colors on both horses, in red blinkers head and head, destined to run first and second."[6] Gallant Fox, powered by his stablemate, drew away to win by a length and a half.

As he jogged back to the judges' stand and then into the winner's circle, Gallant Fox received a twelve-minute round of applause from the crowd of twenty-five thousand. He always looked toward them in the post parade, as if to take in the sight of the people that had flocked to see him as he walked to the starting line. The spectators present appreciated the fourteen furlongs he ran in 2:56, just one second under the stakes record set by Reigh Count two years earlier.[7] They delighted in the ease of his victory on that day, symbolic of his seven of eight victories in 1930. That closing day crowd especially loved bearing witness to the Fox of Belair taking home $9,275 for his win in that prestigious race, which catapulted him to second on the all-time winnings list, just $26,000 behind Zev.[8]

The Fox came out of the Saratoga Cup with the relish of a horse that loves running long; the colt was "so full of zip, so full of animal spirits that he dragged the man who held him by the head several feet."[9] Yet, when the race was done and it was time to rest, the Fox showed he was full of energy only on the track. His owner found him standing untied and halterless in his stall later while two stable

Gallant Fox and Earl Sande at Saratoga Race Course, August 30, 1930. Keeneland Library Cook Collection.

hands sat in the straw and unwound tape from the champion's ankles.[10] Through all of the travel and hard racing, Gallant Fox had maintained that curious and friendly disposition that had given Fitzsimmons fits the year before.

As the long campaign began to wind down, Gallant Fox and the rest of the Belair horses moved back south to their home base at Aqueduct and the autumn racing there. With just two more races left in his illustrious career, Gallant Fox had another famous long-distance test ahead of him, the Lawrence Realization, and some stiff competition in the form of a horse named Questionnaire.

At a mile and five-eighths, the race was just an eighth of a mile shorter than the Saratoga Cup and boasted the same sort of gravitas. Like so many of the Fox's other races, the list of winners ran deep into the well of equine greatness: Fair Play, Reigh Count, Zev, and

Man o' War were just a few of the legends who had taken this prize. William Woodward wanted to add Gallant Fox's name to that roster of immortals, but he would need to get through another short field of challengers to get there.

Like the Triple Crown classics and the Travers, the Lawrence Realization was for three-year-olds only and, to no one's surprise, only three others answered the call. Besides the Fox, Spinach, Yarn, and Questionnaire were all set to meet the starter for the race on Saturday, September 6. All three had met Gallant Fox in 1930 and all three had seen the back of him each time. Spinach had last seen the Fox in April at Jamaica for the Wood Memorial, finishing last, but had won his last three races. Yarn had been part of that short field for the Saratoga Cup, finishing fourth nearly eight lengths behind Gone Away. Questionnaire appeared to be the race's biggest threat. Sure, he had finished third behind the Fox and Whichone in the Belmont Stakes, but he had won seven races in a row since then, including the Empire City Derby, the Yonkers Handicap, and the Hourless Handicap. His win in the Hourless came just four days before the Realization, a six-length victory over nine furlongs. Raymond "Sonny" Workman, the same jockey that had pushed Whichone into a suicidal duel with Sande and the Fox in the Travers, rode Questionnaire in the Hourless and knew that his mount was ready to give the Belair colt a run for his money.[11] Could Questionnaire prove to be the Fox's foil? He stood out as the most likely challenger for the Triple Crown winner.

Noticeably absent were horses like Gallant Knight, Crack Brigade, and Whichone, horses that had made their run at the Fox of Belair in previous races.[12] Crack Brigade had forced Sande to take Gallant Fox around horses to get clear in the Preakness but had been absent since a training mishap sent him to the sidelines. Gallant Knight had finished second to the Fox in the Kentucky Derby and then had pressed him in the Arlington Classic, but injury prevented a chance to face the Fox again in the Realization.[13] Whichone had beaten Gallant Fox in the Futurity in 1929, lost to him in the Belmont Stakes, and then ended his career trying to beat him in the

Travers. Meanwhile, Gallant Fox had won at Jamaica, Pimlico, Churchill Downs, Belmont, Arlington, and Saratoga in the space of less than six months, demonstrating a sturdiness that seemed to elude his competitors.

A section of the paddock was roped off, accessible only to the connections of the starters, away from the press of a public eager to catch a glimpse of Gallant Fox and his challengers. The day was humid, and sweat rolled off the Fox and Questionnaire as they were saddled and Sande and Workman were boosted onto their backs.[14] The stage was set, the battle joined. Today was the day that Gallant Fox could break Zev's record, but he needed to beat this short field of competitors first.

The four walked to the barrier, as the crowd of thirty-five thousand craned and jostled for a spot to see the spectacle before them. The horses milled around the starting line, taking up their positions for the skirmish. Carrying 119 pounds, Spinach stood at the rail; next to him was Gallant Fox with 126. Then it was Questionnaire with 123 pounds and the still-maiden Yarn on the outside, laden with only 116 pounds. In the Travers, Workman and Whichone had been inside of Sande and Gallant Fox, a position that had allowed Workman to push the Fox into a running lane he did not want to be in. This time, Workman was on his outside, giving Sande more options for positioning Gallant Fox through the race. He would not allow Workman to get the better of him as he had in the Travers. Earl Sande would not be fooled again.

As usual, Gallant Fox instigated a false start, breaking through the barrier and running a sixteenth of a mile down the track before Sande was able to pull him up. The colt looked at the crowd for a beat, taking in the scene before him, before he trotted back to the line with the field. With all four in line, George Cassidy sprang the barrier and Workman went to the whip on Questionnaire. He sprinted out three lengths ahead of Gallant Fox and took a position on the rail. Gallant Fox ran behind him with Yarn and Spinach running together to his rear. The first half mile went by in 0:48⅗, Questionnaire picking up the pace in an effort to lengthen his lead as

Sande readied Gallant Fox for their move. Into that final sweeping turn, the Fox turned on the speed and closed the gap with Questionnaire with increasing urgency. As the two dueled, Questionnaire on the rail and Gallant Fox on the outside, Workman made a familiar move: he guided his horse out from the rail, carrying the Fox wide with him, leaving space for a Jim Dandyesque surprise to pass them both. Neither Yarn, who was third, nor Spinach, trailing in fourth, were the horses to pull off something like that.[15]

Instead, Questionnaire and Gallant Fox were locked in battle as they straightened into the stretch, Workman freely using the whip on his tiring colt. Running head to head with Questionnaire, the Fox of Belair seemed to hang, neither fading nor flying ahead, until Sande tapped him with the whip three times. That seemed to bring the Fox back to the task at hand. Sande put his whip away and hand rode Gallant Fox to the wire, knowing that his horse had that last bit of speed necessary to keep fighting while a tired Questionnaire started to give way. At the wire, the Fox on the outside and Questionnaire on the rail, only a head separated the two. [16]

William Woodward waited for the results to go up on the tote board. Finally, the Fox's number shone bright over the others, along with another: 2:41⅕. Gallant Fox's time for the Lawrence Realization was just two-fifths of a second off Man o' War's record from a decade earlier.[17] It was the closest finish of his career, a scant head over another good three-year-old, another example of the Fox's propensity to give just enough to win. Fitzsimmons knew why his colt had allowed such a short margin of victory. "Something like seventy yards from home and Gallant Fox gets his nose out in front," the trainer remembered. "Now he's only a couple of jumps from the wire and anything can happen. But Pop! The ears went straight up, as if he was saying, 'That takes care of that.'"[18] With the Lawrence Realization done and Questionnaire beaten, the Fox was seemingly out of competition. He was also a record breaker—again.

With that victory in the Lawrence Realization, Gallant Fox brought home a purse of $29,610, bringing his career total to

Gallant Fox (outside) gets a head in front of Questionnaire (on the rail) in the 1930 Lawrence Realization. National Museum of Racing and Hall of Fame Collection.

$317,865; this passed Zev's mark of $313,639 and usurped his throne atop the list of highest money winners of all time.[19] Thirty-five thousand racegoers greeted the new king with voracious applause, as Sande paraded the second Triple Crown winner before the grandstand so that the colt could receive the congratulations due such an achievement.[20] William Woodward met the two on the track and, as he led the Fox to the winner's circle, the colt nearly knocked his breeder and owner off his feet. "I went down to lead in the horse and found him still full of run and very strong," Woodward observed of his champion, "but each time he started to carry me forward I would speak to him and he would immediately come back in hand."[21] Even after that long duel with Questionnaire, even after months of training and travel and racing, the Fox thrived on his job as a racehorse and stayed curious about the people and places around him.

After the race, Workman claimed a foul against Sande, which angered the winning jockey. Although the claim was disallowed and Gallant Fox remained the winner, Workman's ride on Whichone in the Travers Stakes plus the claim of foul put Sande over the edge. After the race was declared official, the two "had a set-to in the jockey room, resorting to fists, which was an unknown thing from Sande's point of view," according to William Woodward.[22] Even the usually easy-going Earl Sande had a limit, and Workman's antics in both the Travers and the Realization had clearly gotten under the famed jockey's skin.

The next day, W. C. Vreeland paid the Fox a visit at Fitzsimmons's Aqueduct barn. He found the champion in fine fettle, cleaning his feed box and acting playful, full of vim and vigor after his hard race only twenty-four hours earlier. Gallant Fox seemed ready for his next challenge: racing against older horses like Sun Beau. After nine races, all against other three-year-olds, a horse like Sun Beau, the year's leading older horse, was a new kind of opponent, a five-year-old horse with more experience and more seasoning. In July, Woodward and Fitzsimmons had bypassed the Arlington Cup against older horses in favor of giving their colt time off after his strenuous spring campaign. He had beaten every horse with whom he had shared a barrier or a starting gate in 1930—save for one, Jim Dandy. Like Man o' War, he was saving the challenge of facing older horses for his last hurrah. At two miles, the Jockey Club Gold Cup at Belmont Park was another long-distance race that should suit the Fox just fine.

In 1930, the Jockey Club Gold Cup still was a relatively young race, but, in the decade since it had first been run as the Jockey Club Stakes at Belmont Park, the list of its illustrious victors, including the likes of Man o' War and Reigh Count, had made it an obvious target for a horse like Gallant Fox. William Woodward was a vice-chairman of the Jockey Club, so he was expected to run his champion in that race.

Would this be the Fox's last race? Reports had him running at Hawthorne in the Hawthorne Gold Cup and at Latonia in the Latonia Championship Stakes after this trip to Belmont. But Gallant Fox had been in training continuously since March and now it was mid-September. Could he maintain this form into mid-October? He had run in nine stakes races since late April, over more than twelve miles. Was this it? Was this the end?

If it were to be the last, it likely would be an easy one. The field for the race shaped up to be only three horses: Frisius, the stablemate that had set up the Saratoga Cup for Gallant Fox; Yarn, who spent the whole of the Lawrence Realization behind the Fox; and the Triple Crown champion. Sun Beau passed on the chance to meet the Belair contingent because this was two miles at weight-for-age conditions. It was one thing to give Gallant Fox weight at a distance like a mile and a quarter, but to give him eleven pounds at two miles was something that Sun Beau and his owner Willis Sharpe Kilmer were unwilling to do.[23] With Blue Larkspur on the sidelines with an injury, Gallant Fox was virtually devoid of competition.

He literally had little left to prove.

Under the signature ash trees of Belmont Park, Gallant Fox was saddled along with Frisius. Yarn was the lone other horse joining them in the paddock. Frisius was to carry 125 pounds and the two three-year-olds were to carry 114, the Fox's lowest weight of the season. Earl Sande found that number a challenge he did not need to meet since all they needed to beat was a stablemate and a horse he had already beaten.[24] He was boosted into the saddle at four and a half pounds overweight. Really, though, the weight did not matter. The winning did.

A crowd of five thousand showed up on a Wednesday, the final day of Belmont's fall meet, to see the feature, Gallant Fox's last Gotham hurrah. They crowded into the paddock to watch the horses prepare for the race and then ran to the lawns to wager on the entry and the plodder, betting the Fox and Frisius down to 1 to 25 and Yarn to 20 to 1. It was not quite Man o' War's 1 to 100 odds from his 1920

Jockey Club Stakes, but it was surely a sign of the times: Gallant Fox was virtually unbeatable.[25] That showed throughout the race.

From the break, the three ran together head to head, but, after a quarter of a mile, Frisius from his spot on the rail took a short lead, with Gallant Fox trailing and then Yarn last of all. They stayed that way until ten furlongs in, when Sande let the Fox catch up to Frisius, a reminder that this was still a race after all. Yarn was only three lengths behind, waiting for the stretch to mount a serious bid at Gallant Fox. As Yarn started his move, Frisius seemed to quit; an ankle injury forced him to hobble home, but he already had served his purpose in this race. Gallant Fox was in stride by this point, with more than enough to hold off his challengers with ease. He won by two lengths and finished the two miles about three seconds off of Exterminator's record, but he did not need to extend himself to taste victory. The victory was enough.

William Woodward met Joseph Widener in the winner's circle to collect his trophy for winning the Jockey Club Gold Cup. In his speech, Belmont Park's president referred to the Gold Cup as "perhaps his [Gallant Fox's] last race." Woodward chimed in with "I hope not."[26] Whether he bowed out at Hawthorne or at Latonia, Gallant Fox was not supposed to be done yet. His latest victory added $10,300 to his record winnings, to bring the total to $328,615, still short of Ksar's world record of $335,000 (1,562,025 francs).[27] One more race might definitively establish the Fox as the leading money winner in the world, not just in North America.

Alas, that was not to be. As Fitzsimmons prepared his charge for the Hawthorne Gold Cup, he found that the Fox had developed a cough. His ailment was not accompanied by a fever, just some congestion, but Gallant Fox would need several days to recover. By the time he would be able to resume training, it would have been too late to prepare properly for either race. So, with that, Gallant Fox was done. On October 7, the news of his retirement hit the papers, with the details of his exit followed by a recounting of his time on the track. He was the greatest since Man o' War, but the big red horse, "great as he was, never in his career won at a mile as a two-year-old or never won as a three-year-old at a mile and three-quarters or two miles as Gallant Fox has done."[28] In 1930, Gallant Fox had won nine of ten races, losing only to Jim Dandy in the Travers, at distances from a mile and seventy yards to two miles. He was impervious to weight, carrying as much as 130 pounds in his workouts and regularly winning as the highest weight in the field.[29] Fitzsimmons felt that the Fox should have won all of his races, but his propensity to slow down when alone on the lead coupled with those early slow starts kept Gallant Fox from ending his two-year-old season with more victories.[30] Earl Sande, who had ridden both Man o' War and Gallant Fox, compared the two a few months after the Fox had retired: "Man o' War gave his speed willingly. He loved to race. Gallant Fox loved to race—when he felt in the mood. He needed companionship to spur him on."[31]

In the end, as a racehorse, Gallant Fox was tireless, effortless, and peerless. Physically, he was a "grand raking horse," as Neil Newman described him, a bay colt with black points and a blazed face with an extra bit of white showing around his left eye, a walleye that was said to intimidate his foes. He stood sixteen hands, one inch at his withers and weighed eleven hundred pounds; with "a well-laid shoulder he has unusual heart room and a middle piece indicating his rugged constitution."[32] He loved distance, craved competition, and won for fun. Most of all, though, his personality was one of "striking individuality," as Newman put it: "Nothing escapes his notice and as soon as he sees anything he wants to examine it—the examination completed he pays no more attention to it."[33] Before most of his races, he would look up into the crowd, as though he needed to take in his audience before he performed. His weaknesses might have been an off track and a lone lead, but he could carry any weight, run almost any distance, and beat almost any horse that joined him on a racetrack. He was not generous with his speed or stamina as some great horses were, but "so long as he had competition, he would run like the wind," Fitzsimmons said of his Belair champion. "But as soon as he whipped everybody and got the lead, he would slow to a walk. He was a fire eater when he had the competition though."[34] The Fox competed in blinkers in every one of his seventeen starts, the cups progressively cut away with each start. Too superstitious to stop using the blinkers, Fitzsimmons trimmed the leather cups on the red hood so that the Fox would see his competition and light that fire that would propel him to the lead.

Sir Barton had pioneered the Triple Crown in 1919, but those races needed a horse like Gallant Fox to come along and sweep them again, to make a show of his trips around these classics and establish these races—the Kentucky Derby, the Preakness Stakes, and the Belmont Stakes—as the prime showcases for three-year-olds, a yardstick for the greats for years to come. The Belair colt had broken records over and over, his career already historic. He would make history again in just a few short years.

His racing career over, Gallant Fox remained at Aqueduct with his trainer and the people who had cared for him for two seasons until it was time for his trip to Claiborne. Three weeks later, he boarded a train bound for Paris, Kentucky, traveling with veterinarian Dr. Edward A. Caslick, groom Bart Sweeney, and assistant trainer George Tappen. William Woodward went too, riding in an observation car while his champion rode loose in a box stall in another car. At every stop, people gathered to see Gallant Fox, bringing their children to pet him. The city of Paris was eager to receive their new celebrity resident and even offered to greet his arrival with a band, but that offer was declined for the horse's safety. The Fox arrived in Paris without incident and was put on a small van and driven to his new home in the stallion barn at Claiborne Farm.[35]

The next day, Gallant Fox was turned out in his paddock at Claiborne, his first true freedom of space in months. At first, he stood still, like he was contemplating the situation, taking in his new surroundings, and then he wheeled and ran around his paddock at breakneck speed. At one point, he ran at the fence, and then, as he turned to avoid it, he slipped and fell, cutting his hock. The Fox immediately got back up and allowed himself to be caught so he could be treated. The next time he was turned out, he behaved much better, settling into his retired life with aplomb.[36] The Fox of Belair was ready for what was next.

Algernon Daingerfield, assistant secretary of the Jockey Club, addressed Gallant Fox's secondary status to Ksar; he appraised the value of the cups and trophies the colt had won in his two seasons of racing, and then added their material value, which amounted to $13,200, to his career winnings. With that valuation, Gallant Fox became the world's leading money winner, passing Ksar's $335,340 by $6,025.[37] His mark would not stand for long, with Sun Beau surpassing his record the following year, but that total was another illustration of the dominance that Gallant Fox unleashed on the racetrack in 1930.

Like his sire Sir Gallahad III, Gallant Fox's stud book was full; breeders were eager to pair their mares with the champion, a horse who ran far and fast and remained sound through all of it. William Woodward sent his own mares to his beloved colt, including Flambino, another homebred that showed a propensity for racing at long distances herself, a descendant of that original group of mares he had imported from France a decade earlier.[38] From Gallant Fox and Flambino came another history maker, a colt that Woodward would name Omaha.

12

Boys and Girls

Since the retirement of Man o' War no horse has captured
the imagination of the American public as has Gallant Fox.
—Neil Newman, *Famous Horses of the American Turf*

With that, the master of Belair said goodbye to the Fox's racing days
and greeted the prospect of the next generation of his great champion. Gallant Fox stood at Claiborne Farm, his birthplace, whose
bucolic setting was perfect for breeding the hopes of many a dreamer
who relished the idea of winner's circles great and small. Alongside
him were his sire Sir Gallahad III; Durbar II, Epsom Derby winner;
and Diavolo, Saratoga Cup and Jockey Club Gold Cup winner. In
Paris, Kentucky, he was part of the sport's future and also its past,
the historic grounds awash in potential as he took his place next to
his sire at the head of Hancock's stud, standing for a stud fee of
$3,000 in his first season.

Thanks to the success of the Fox, Sir Gallahad III topped the
sire's list for 1930, despite having the fewest winners among the leading sires of the year. He had fourteen winners to Wrack's forty-nine,
but the $403,430 in purses Sir Gallahad III's foals earned, $308,275
from Gallant Fox, led the second-place sire Pennant by more than
$150,000.[1] Since his first breeding season in 1926, 1930 was the first
year that the imported stallion had topped the list and it would not
be the last. The question was, would the Fox duplicate his sire's success at stud?

The other half of the Gallant Fox equation, Marguerite, started 1931 as the leading broodmare of the year thanks to her son's accomplishments.[2] Her sire, Celt, was also the leading broodmare sire of the year. The late stallion's daughters produced fifty-three winners from thirty-seven mares. Marguerite's colt far outpaced the other Celt horses, winning the bulk of the $452,850 in purse money credited to the stallion.[3] Gallant Fox's success led Woodward to again send his prized mare to be covered by Sir Gallahad III, hoping for lightning to strike twice. That nick, the nebulous miasma of genetic contributions from sire and dam, had already yielded the Fox. Why not try again? Her last foal from the imported stallion had died just days after he had been foaled. Since Gallant Fox's debut in 1929, the mare had not had another foal come to the races.[4] Yet his success as well as that of Petee-Wrack made her one of the era's greatest broodmares despite her bad luck with losing foals in consecutive years. Woodward would continue sending her to Sir Gallahad III for the rest of her breeding career, undeterred by the misfortune.[5]

Gallant Fox was not the only one making the transition from track to stud. Whichone's Travers had ended with his resounding defeat by both Jim Dandy and the Fox and a career-ending injury. The former two-year-old champion had been retired since that day at Saratoga and had been relocated to the Whitney Farm in Lexington. With the death of owner Harry Payne Whitney in October 1930, Whichone became part of his son Cornelius Vanderbilt Whitney's breeding operation, standing alongside his sire Chicle; Upset, the conqueror of Man o' War; and his stablemate and fellow juvenile hopeful Boojum.[6]

Speaking of Jim Dandy, the benefactor of the Whichone–Gallant Fox battle continued to race on, long past the Fox and Whichone and even beyond the stars of Gallant Fox's earliest crops. The son of Jim Gaffney returned to the races five weeks after his Travers win and finished last in the Potomac Handicap.[7] After finishing next to last in the Hawthorne Gold Cup, he finished third in the

Gallant Fox at Claiborne Farm. Keeneland Library Sutcliffe Collection.

Cambridge Handicap at Laurel and then toward the back of the field in the mud in the Prince George Autumn Handicap at Bowie.[8] The conqueror of the Fox continued racing through 1939, amassing a final tally of 141 starts with seven wins; the 1930 Travers was the last of his stakes victories. His trainer, John McKee, bought Jim Dandy from Chaffee Earl and then turned him out when the gelding finally retired at the age of twelve. McKee could see that the veteran, despite his long career, thrived when put to work, so he gave the gelding to Major L. G. Otto, who trained Jim Dandy to become a hunter and jumper. He lived out his life at Otto's riding academy in California, his place in racing's history immortalized in a stakes race run annually at Saratoga.[9] The Jim Dandy is a graded stakes race that, rather appropriately, serves as a prep race for the

Travers Stakes.[10] A fitting tribute for a horse who continued Saratoga's tradition of being the graveyard of champions.

Earl Sande had been lured out of retirement by Woodward's offer for Gallant Fox, and, now that the Fox was retired, the legendary jockey knew that his days in the saddle were numbered. The eternal struggle to regulate his weight was wearing on the thirty-two-year-old veteran, who had started to look elsewhere for employment. Sande retired a second time, and took his talents to show business. He took voice lessons from former Broadway performer Estelle Wentworth, landed a few movie roles, and performed at the Stork Club in New York.[11] More than four years after his first wife Marion Casey died, Sande married Marion Kummer, widow of jockey Clarence Kummer. He continued his riding career until August 1932, when he signed a contract to train horses for Colonel Howland Maxwell Howard, a lawyer and owner of a paper manufacturing company.[12] Among the horses that Sande trained for Howard was Stagehand, who won the Santa Anita Derby and the Santa Anita Handicap, beating Seabiscuit by a nose in track record time in 1938.[13] When Howard died in late 1944, the loss of his biggest employer left Sande struggling. In 1953, the fifty-five-year-old Sande was still toiling as a trainer. He attempted one last comeback as a jockey in an effort to attract new owners, and won one race from ten mounts before he hung up his tack for good.[14] The proud and stubborn Sande would not take any jobs offered to him by racing officials, insisting that "he would do it with horses or not at all." Ailing after his permanent retirement from riding, Sande eventually moved to Oregon to be with his father.[15] There, he died in a nursing home at age sixty-nine, far away from the racetracks and winner's circles that had made him a Hall of Famer. Nearly forty years after his glorious season with Gallant Fox, Sande's story ended on a tragic note; sportswriter Jimmy Breslin said his life "ranks with one of the saddest in sports."[16]

As Sande continued to struggle with his weight and his riding career, William Woodward continued his ascendancy through the sport he loved. After holding roles as member and then steward of the Jockey Club, he was elected chairman of the sport's governing body in November 1930, replacing the retiring Frank K. Sturgis.[17] In addition to his duties with the Jockey Club, the master of Belair had between twenty-five and thirty horses in training with "Sunny Jim" Fitzsimmons, another twenty-five mares at Claiborne Farm, and then fifteen yearlings sold at auction, most of whom were fillies. In England, Captain Cecil Boyd-Rochfort had eight to ten Belair horses in training, and Woodward maintained a few broodmares in Ireland.[18] Belair Stud's first two imports, Fair Game and The Scout, won in England, and Woodward's good two-year-old Sir Andrew won the Scarborough Stakes in 1930. Sir Andrew was Woodward's Derby candidate for 1931, but he finished eighteenth, later winning the Prince of Wales's Stakes at Royal Ascot.[19] The American Belair contingent was not as successful in 1931 as they had been the year before, but they did manage to win twenty-eight races that year, including the Pierrepont Handicap with Ormesby, the King Edward Gold Cup and Toronto Cup Handicaps with Frisius, and the Autumn Handicap with Flaming.[20] With the Fox at stud, Fitzsimmons admitted that the Belair contingent was "a fine lot of Thoroughbreds, but there's no Gallant Fox among the group."[21]

Certainly, Woodward could have kept the Fox in training for his four-year-old season and amassed more wins and more money. But the master of Belair was a breeder, not just an owner; he was deeply invested in improving the breed as well as developing more good racehorses. William Woodward's fondness for his champion prompted him to craft a privately printed memoir of the horse's life and racing career to preserve his memories of Gallant Fox's accomplishments. He was eager to see the Triple Crown winner's impact as a sire, and the stud fee of $3,000 reflected the esteem in which both he and Arthur Hancock held the colt.[22] In early February 1932, the first of Gallant Fox's foals arrived at Claiborne Farm. A new day had dawned, a new opportunity for the master of Belair to find the next champion to realize his ambitions.

As the first generation of the Fox's progeny greeted the world in relative comfort, away from the concerns of the wider world, they were coming of age in a sport that was evolving by necessity as a global financial disaster made horse racing less of a diversion and more of an economic engine.

Horse racing has been a part of American life since colonial times, since that first racetrack was established on Salisbury Plain on Long Island around 1665.[23] The sport survived a revolution, entrenched itself into the history of the nascent republic, and then grew as the country expanded from sea to shining sea. The Civil War interrupted racing in the former Confederate states; this shifted the heart of the sport northward to states like New York and Maryland. Kentucky, which had been neutral in the Civil War, became the hub of breeding in the United States.[24] By the end of the nineteenth century, not only had racing expanded far and wide, from coast to coast, tracks "popping up like dandelions across the country," but so had gambling, with competing interests, including those running the racetracks, trying to milk all they could out of the people and horses.[25] Bookmakers were the predominant conduit, although parimutuel wagering, in which gamblers pay into a pool and then the money is distributed to the winners according to the odds, had already been used in some jurisdictions. Bookmakers were essentially small wagering markets, setting odds and paying out with the goal of trying to keep a balance among bets; this made them a target for reformers, who felt that bookmakers took advantage of their customers.[26] While there may have been some corruption and a few bad actors, as is the case with all human endeavors, bookmakers were the choice of most tracks, even with the fairer and more equitable parimutuel option available. Regardless of its source, reformers felt that gambling was a vice that was a scourge on American society, much like alcohol, and thus needed to be eliminated. A wave of bills from California to New York effectively shuttered large swaths of racing in the United States.

The combination of reform measures and the oversaturation of the sport led to a radical contraction, from a high of 314 racetracks in twenty-six states in 1897 to just twenty-five in nine states in 1908.[27] Laws like Hart–Agnew in New York left horse racing on the brink of extinction just two decades removed from its height. When racing finally did resume in New York in 1913, only Aqueduct, Belmont Park, and Empire City remained, whereas tracks in Kentucky and Maryland continued to flourish and even grow.[28] The glorious Gotham tracks like Sheepshead Bay, venues that had been the scene of so many triumphs for people like "Sunny Jim" Fitzsimmons, were closed for good as racing in New York limped along through the latter half of the 1910s and into the 1920s. The economic gains of the 1920s helped the purse for the Belmont Stakes jump from $14,200 in 1919 to $77,540 in 1930. By the end of the decade, the number of race-tracks in the United States had grown to thirty-four in 1929.[29] The sport had been growing since the end of World War I, as Americans sought diversion from the tragedies that war and the Spanish flu pandemic had brought on the country. Over the next decade, that growth would turn a trip to the races into more than just a day's recreation.

October 29, 1929, was a Tuesday. Gallant Fox had run the final start of his two-year-old season a month earlier. Empire City was in the final week of its meet while Laurel was running its fall season in Maryland. Whichone's and Boojum's wins accounted for more than half of Harry Payne Whitney's $344,480 in winnings that year.[30] Bask and Questionnaire both had wins at Empire City for James Butler, as the white and cherry colors came home first at the race-track that he owned.[31] Twenty miles away, the New York Stock Exchange was seeing far more losers than winners as the sell-off that had begun in mid-September intensified.

By late 1929, though steel production was down and automobile sales were lagging, easy credit had allowed too many Americans to incur debt so they could buy into the stock market, which then seemed to be on a permanent upward trend. The idea was that con-sumers would buy the stocks on credit and then use the profits from selling them to pay off the debt. However, as stock prices fell, the profits disappeared; when creditors came to collect, consumers did not have the funds to pay back what they owed.[32] This all came to a head on October 28 and 29, days now known as Black Monday and Tuesday, when the stock exchange lost 23 percent of its value, devastating thousands of investors. Despite the best efforts of financiers like the Rockefeller family and William C. Durant, cofounder of both General Motors and Chevrolet, the damage had been done.[33] People could not pay their debts, leading to foreclosures and bankruptcies. Consumer spending fell, which in turn forced employers to slow down production and lay off workers. Those who remained employed saw their wages cut, leaving them with less income to buy goods and property. This cascade of financial cause and effect grew into the economic emergency known as the Great Depression.

As most governments at the local and state level depended primarily on property taxes for their income, bankruptcies and foreclosures led to decreases in income needed to run necessary services, especially the limited social safety net available for those hit hardest by the economic downturn.[34] Fuel taxes were another source of revenue, but they did not provide enough to make up for the deficit in property tax collections. This left state and local officials looking for new sources of revenue. With Prohibition still the law of the land, the legalization of alcohol was seen as a potential generator of both taxes and jobs, one way to stimulate the economy.[35] Another way was gambling.

In 1929, twelve states had tracks. Canada, Mexico, and Cuba each had at least one, from Oriental Park in Havana to Agua Caliente in Tijuana, just over the Mexican border.[36] While New York still used bookmakers for their wagering, Kentucky and, later, Illinois adopted pari-mutuel wagering, which had been sold as more egalitarian than bookmaking.[37] Both methods of gambling had takeout that went to the tracks, which, in turn, provided funds for the purses offered for each race. Additionally, admission and any sort of nomination, entry, and starter fees also made up the monies awarded for all races.[38] Purses awarded reflected the money coming in and going out. In 1929, sanctioned American racetracks, those that ran meets under the auspices of the Jockey Club, ran 1,599 racing days with 11,133 races contested, an average of about seven races per day. Those tracks distributed $13,417,827 in total purse money, an average of about $1,205 in purse money per race. This total, more than three times what had been awarded just a decade earlier, showed that the sport had benefited from the boom economy of the 1920s.

In 1930, as the effects of the Great Depression set in across the country, racetracks added fifty-four race days and 344 races, with $13,674,160 in purses awarded. New York led the way, with just over $2.5 million in purses awarded over 181 racing days; Maryland and Kentucky lagged behind, which accounts for the difference in purse monies earned by Gallant Fox and Omaha in their careers.[39] The devastation of the economic crisis took another year to set in, with only $10,082,757 awarded in 1932 and then $8,516,325 in 1933. From 1930 to 1933, as purse monies fell, so did attendance and bloodstock values. Fewer people were coming to the races save for the sport's biggest days, like the Kentucky Derby. Bloodstock values plummeted, with the average price going from $2,538.63 in 1929 to $1,966.15 in 1930.[40] Prices continued to fall through 1933, as did the price of admission. In order to fill their grandstands, tracks cut ticket prices, in some cases down to a dollar from a high of three to five dollars.[41] Though 1933 had more racing days and more races contested, the sharp drop in purse money from 1930 to 1933 was due to the state of the American economy, which was in the direst of straits when Franklin Delano Roosevelt, the governor of New York, who had witnessed the triumph of Jim Dandy over Gallant Fox and Whichone in the 1930 Travers Stakes, was elected president.[42] Along with the new administration's solutions for alleviating the crisis, state and local governments adopted another remedy: expansion of pari-mutuel wagering.

In 1933, California, New Hampshire, New Mexico, North Carolina, Ohio, Oregon, Texas, Washington, and West Virginia all approved pari-mutuel betting, giving their governments another avenue for generating income.[43] Because bookmakers were harder to regulate, racetracks preferred the more transparent pari-mutuel system. By taxing the wagering revenue each racetrack took in, state governments created much-needed funds to continue operating as well as to provide relief to the millions of Americans who were out of work and displaced by the Great Depression. Racetracks offered people a chance to get away from the troubles in their lives, a diversion where they could spend a few dollars for a day of fun with the possibility of making a little money in the process. Before the end of the decade, twenty-one states would approve pari-mutuel betting, which allowed the industry to grow by 70 percent before 1939.[44]

With the expansion of wagering came the construction of more tracks. Santa Anita Park in Arcadia, California, opened in late 1934, followed by Del Mar Thoroughbred Club near San Diego in 1937.[45] Rockingham Park in New Hampshire had briefly hosted Thoroughbred racing in the early years of the twentieth century but, since gambling was illegal at the time, it was shut down after three days. After a stint as an auto racing venue, Rockingham returned in 1933, with Narragansett Park in Rhode Island following the next year.[46] By 1935, purses were back up to $12,794,418; this was distributed over 15,830 races run over 2,133 days at nearly sixty racetracks across North America.[47] By the middle of the decade, thousands of people would attend the races daily, with upwards of fifty million attending annually.[48]

For William Woodward, whose own fortunes had not been affected by this major financial crisis, the proliferation of racing was not necessarily an ideal development. As chairman of the Jockey Club, he took his position as the chief steward of the sport seriously. With an eye on the sport's future while also mindful of its past, the master of Belair remarked in a speech in 1935, "Do not misunderstand me: I believe in changes if they mean advance and improvement, after careful study."[49] As an owner and breeder who had been a keen observer of the sport, from his earliest years through his time in England and his years building up to the success of Gallant Fox,

Woodward wanted to maintain racing as he knew it. He saw the commercialization of racing, as pari-mutuel wagering expanded and the number of tracks multiplied, and feared that it would dilute the sport to the level of a mass-produced product rather than an endeavor that was backed up by generations of experience:

> It is well to improve the rules of racing when one can, but when one says the rules are old-fashioned, I say, "Thank God they are." Not only have they been built up on experience and tradition, but it has been the experience and tradition of many nations and of many sportsmen and of many men who have devoted their lives to this, and it is such experience that is embodied in the rules.[50]

The Great Depression had sent state and local governments scrambling for solutions as President Roosevelt and his New Deal sought to provide federal responses to the dire financial situation of the United States; the slow-rolling global disaster would last at least a decade and have worldwide implications. For the sport of horse racing, though, the 1930s and the Great Depression became a transitional moment: starting gates and pari-mutuel wagering, among other innovations, would challenge the men that had overseen the sport for the first decades of the twentieth century. Woodward's ambitions as an owner and breeder were not only to win the classic races he valued but also to better the sport and the animal at its heart. To him, integrating innovations and making changes in how racing worked should not be undertaken with haste, but with careful consideration and over time: "The thought underlying this rather unpleasant, complicated picture is for those interested to consider carefully just what the public *does* want and not to imagine too hastily what such things may be, or place in that category some profitable, glamorous things which it does not want."[51]

As Woodward lamented the commercialization of the sport and expressed his hope that no more states would join the fray, he hit upon the heart of issues that are relevant still today. The questions about maintaining the quality of the sport and the welfare of the horse while also balancing the needs of the business side of racing are not unique to our moment. The sport in all its facets has been pondering the same issues for decades. The master of Belair kept his focus on the sport; he was cognizant of the business side but also of the downsides of overexpansion.

The average gestation for a horse is eleven months or 330 days, and so it is nearly a year before breeders meet the foals that might fulfill their hopes and dreams.[52] Since all Thoroughbreds have an official birthday of January 1 regardless of their actual foaling date, the North American breeding season starts in February and runs into early July, as breeders send their mares to their selected stallions in the hopes that the pairing will produce something special. With a full book in 1931, Gallant Fox's first season augured much hope that the next superstar would result, another grand champion to carry the white with red polka dots on the sport's biggest stages.

When the Fox's first foal, a colt out of Merry Princess, arrived on February 6, the *Blood-Horse* ran a photo of this "upstanding youngster" who looked "very much the same cut as his sire at the same age."[53] The first of the many, the next generation, he was just the tip of the iceberg, the next best hope for his breeder and owner, who was seeking good horses to do great things. The future was rich with promise for the get of Gallant Fox. From this first crop would come seventeen foals, with one standing head and shoulders above the rest, both literally and figuratively. From the first crop of this Triple Crown winner came something special: Omaha.

13

Second Generation

When those five Ajax mares arrived in America, they came with the foals they had produced as they waited out the conflict that kept them from joining the Belair broodmare band. La Flambee came with La Rablee, her filly by English stallion Rabelais, and a yearling filly by 1914 Epsom Derby winner Dunbar II. That yearling William Woodward named Flambette, and leased her to his friend P. A. Clark. After an injury forced her retirement, the daughter of La Flambee produced thirteen foals, including her first, Flambino, by Wrack.

For Woodward, Flambino would win the Gazelle Stakes; and, much like Ruthless, the first winner of the Belmont Stakes, she stepped out of her division and took on the boys in that long-distance classic. She finished third, just 2½ lengths behind the winner, Chance Shot, in a better showing than Woodward's earlier starters in the Belmont. Five years later, Woodward paired this daughter of Flambette with Gallant Fox and produced a horse who would improve on his dam's third-place finish, a colt who would wear a crown of his own.

Retiring as the world's richest horse, Gallant Fox had left the days of competition behind for the quiet country life of covering mares and running through Claiborne's lush and ample paddocks. After going nine for ten at age three, Gallant Fox, after two seasons on the race-track, had his name in the same company as Man o' War and Colin, at least in turf writer W. C. Vreeland's estimation.[1] Earl Sande, too, called the Fox "the greatest long distance colt I threw a leg over."[2] At

Flambino finishes third behind Chance Shot and Bois de Rose in the 1927 Belmont Stakes. Keeneland Library Cook Collection.

stud, his book was full; the Belair star covered his share of good mares, including Flambino. On March 24, 1932, she foaled a lanky chestnut colt with a wide blaze and one white sock and with flecks of gray in his golden tail, a colt that Woodward would name Omaha.[3]

The story of how this son of Gallant Fox got his name has two versions: either Woodward named the son of his champion after one of the country's best-known meat processing cities, Omaha, Nebraska, as a reference to the foal's beefiness or, as Woodward himself put it, "my Thoroughbred stock comes from the Ormonde line. I was looking around for a good name starting with 'O' and Omaha came to me first."[4] Like his sire, he was foaled at Claiborne and then brought to Belair Stud as a weanling, where he awaited his owner's decision about what was next.[5] Each year, trainer and owner would look over the Belair yearlings and Woodward would single out one horse with a pronouncement, "This is the Derby winner." The desire to win the Epsom Derby, an honor that eluded him still, remained strong for this sportsman even after he had won the Kentucky Derby and then the Triple Crown with Gallant Fox. In 1933, he looked at Omaha, standing there in his Belair paddock, and told Fitzsimmons, "This is the Derby winner."[6] Did Fitzsimmons merely smile, familiar with the eternal hopes and infinite ambitions of the owners he worked for? Or did he spy Omaha, lanky and awkward, and see the potential inherent in the colt's long frame? In either case, when the son of the Fox arrived in New York, Fitzsimmons might have reconsidered his good opinion.

Omaha was a nervous horse. Years later, "Sunny Jim" Fitzsimmons would call this son of Gallant Fox the most excitable horse he ever had; his nervousness would cause problems on the racetrack.[7] He was big too—sixteen hands, two and a half inches at the withers—and long, often requiring the enlargement of two standard stalls into one.[8] His torso was long, "a homebred of a stayer's admirer, and with a stayer's build."[9] He was built to run all day—and he would. At two, however, the baby races of five and six furlongs were not quite suited to the long legs of this particular chestnut colt. At three, though, those longer distance races would suit Omaha much better. At four, he would follow that up with a European adventure.

First, though, Fitzsimmons had to get him ready for the tests to come.

The problem with a long body and long legs is that it takes some ground to settle into stride. That makes those shorter two-year-old races less ideal for those horses that need some distance to find their stride. The problem with Omaha was that his high-strung nature caused him to dislike running in company, so much so that he would turn his attention to fighting a horse that brushed him rather than focus on the task at hand.[10] To keep him out of trouble, his jockey often would need to bring him to the outside of horses to have a clear running path. That alone meant covering more ground than most of

Omaha with jockey Jimmy Stout at Aqueduct, June 23, 1934. Keeneland Library Morgan Collection.

his competition. So, for Omaha to succeed, he needed to have space to run and ground to get up to speed. That made those early races tough.

He opened his career on June 18, 1934, at Aqueduct in a five-furlong maiden special weight race, where all of the starters carried the same amount of weight. With a purse of $1,200, the race was not quite a Triple Crown classic, but it was a good place to start at least. Jockey Jimmy Stout had the assignment aboard the son of Gallant Fox, breaking from post position thirteen, with only one other horse to his outside. With a field of fourteen, the race was a large group of mostly green juveniles; the most experienced horse had six starts and the majority of the field were making their first or second start.[11] This was the kind of race that was for experience. If Omaha were to win, all the better.

Sir Lamorak broke fast from near the rail, grabbing the lead from the get-go. Omaha broke fourth and Stout settled him in fifth by the first quarter of a mile. Sir Lamorak held the lead for the whole of the five furlongs, but his lead was never more than a half-length. In the stretch, Stout set Omaha down for a final drive, and he might have even passed Sir Lamorak had the son of Gallant Fox stayed straight as they drove for the wire. Instead, he finished second by a neck, the race's form chart commenting that "Omaha moved up fast on the outside but bore in and his rider could not do him justice."[12] Green in his first start, he showed potential with that burst of speed, and his performance promised more from the big colt.

For his second start, again at Fitzsimmons's home base of Aqueduct, Omaha faced a smaller field, only four others, again at five furlongs. Jimmy Stout was back on the big horse, breaking from the third post, the middle of the field.[13] He went into the gate as the heavy favorite for this first race of the day, only five days after his first race.[14] At the start, only Allen Z. beat Omaha, but it was Tea Talk who grabbed the lead by the first quarter of a mile, with Moisson just behind him. Stout held Omaha back in fourth, biding his time and then moving Omaha as they entered the stretch. By then, Allen Z. had moved to the front, but Omaha gobbled up ground to challenge him.[15] In the last eighth, the green son of Gallant Fox bore in again, bothering Allen Z. a bit, before swerving outward again. Stout's hands must have been full with the big horse zigging toward the wire and eking out a slim victory by a head. Allen Z.'s jockey Sam Renick lodged a claim of foul against Stout, alleging that Omaha impeded his colt. The judges disallowed the claim and the result stood.[16] Omaha had broken his maiden, covering the five-eighths of a mile in 0:58⅘, the fastest time for that distance during the whole Aqueduct meeting.[17]

W. C. Vreeland had seen his share of great Thoroughbreds in his lifetime. In his years with the *Brooklyn Daily Eagle,* he had access to the backside of each racetrack and relationships with each barn that dotted Gotham. He visited Sunny Jim and his coterie of horses on

Omaha, with jockey Jimmy Stout aboard, wins an allowance race at Aqueduct, June 23, 1934. Keeneland Library Morgan Collection.

the backside of Aqueduct. Only four years removed from Gallant Fox, the veteran trainer was not one to linger on past successes; instead, he was always looking forward to the next race, the next horse. Fitzsimmons brought out Omaha for Vreeland, and the turf writer's practiced eye assessed the young horse with his sire in mind: "He has the length and bone of Gallant Fox, but not the substance of his sire. His barrel—body—is light as compared with his frame."[18] Still growing, Omaha had not filled out that frame, had not yet reached that solidity that made his sire such a success.

But it was coming, and, when he was finally fully grown, watch out.

For any two-year-old, especially a juvenile of import, Saratoga was a place to see and be seen. In order to be in the conversation for the next year's big prizes or to gain any sort of notoriety, a horse needed to be at the Spa competing in its roster of historic stakes races for the youngest Thoroughbreds allowed on a racetrack. This was where a horse could learn the lessons that needed to be learned. Fitzsimmons brought his contingent of horses from the Belair and the Phipps stables to upstate New York for another year's late summer racing. Even though he was not the only two-year-old sired by Gallant Fox in the Fitzsimmons barn, Omaha's recent success had made him one to watch, alongside stablemate Vicaress, a daughter of Flying Ebony. This was his chance to find the winner's circle again and show what he could do. It was Omaha's time to shine.

His first try at Saratoga came in the United States Hotel Stakes, the same six-furlong race that his sire Gallant Fox had run in five years earlier.[19] The Fox had come in second behind Caruso in his try. Would Omaha do his sire one better? He would face horses that would become familiar to him over the next year: Balladier, a son of Black Toney, who was making his second start and still seeking his first win; Psychic Bid, a colt by Chance Play, winner of the Jockey Club Gold Cup and the Saratoga Cup; and Today, whose sire was familiar to the Belair barn.[20] Today was owned by Cornelius Vanderbilt Whitney, or C. V., who had inherited his father Harry Payne Whitney's stable just months after Jim Dandy beat Gallant Fox and Whichone in the Travers Stakes.[21] Today was from Whichone's first crop of foals, just as Omaha was part of Gallant Fox's. The Fox and his erstwhile rival would meet once again on the Saratoga oval, this time their progeny standing in as their surrogates.

The United States Hotel Stakes came with allowance conditions so, of the twelve starters, only Try Sympathy, the most experienced horse in the field, carried the full 124 pounds while Omaha's Belair stablemate Pitter Pat had 122 pounds. Omaha was assigned only 117 pounds, despite having the same record as the filly, who had beaten Try Sympathy in their previous meeting in the Flash Stakes the week before.[22] As Bert Collyer saw the United States Hotel Stakes, "It should be a corker."[23]

The field stood ten across at the starting line, and George Cassidy waited until the undulating line of horses was sufficiently in place before he tripped the barrier. Pitter Pat had been scratched, leaving only Omaha to face the starter for Belair. With jockey Tommy Malley on board, Omaha had drawn the second post position toward the rail with Today to his left on the rail and the favorite, Try Sympathy, in post position seven.[24] At the start, Balladier zoomed to the lead, with Polar Flight just behind him. Today and Omaha both got off to slow starts, the Gallant Fox colt lingering at the back of the pack. Sonny Workman moved Today up behind the two leaders by the half-mile mark while Malley and Omaha hung back. Polar Flight gave way to Today in the last furlong of the six-furlong dash as jockey Don Meade on Balladier tapped his colt twice and pulled away from the Whitney colt.[25] Balladier won by three lengths, with Today second and then Polar Flight third.[26] Omaha had "closed with a rush," but had not been a factor in this race, ultimately finishing fourth. The United States Hotel Stakes was not a win, but it was a learning experience for this son of Gallant Fox, another step toward becoming the racehorse that his pedigree promised.

Next up was the Saratoga Special and another go at Today, one week after the United States Hotel Stakes. Also in the six-furlong Special was Boxthorn, whose sire, Blue Larkspur, had won the same race in 1928 and had been one of the older horses most people had expected to challenge Gallant Fox. An injury had prevented Blue Larkspur from ever meeting Gallant Fox, but here were Omaha and Boxthorn to duke it out on the racetrack in their stead. In a field of only seven, Omaha broke from the inside, again starting slow.[27] Instead, the Greentree Stable's Plat Eye took the lead at the start, Psychic Bid behind him until the stretch. At the top of the stretch, Plat Eye stumbled, opening an opportunity for Boxthorn to rush up from the outside and take the lead. As Psychic Bid tired, Today moved up too, the three leaders with scant space between them. Boxthorn hit the wire in front by a length, with only a head separating Plat Eye and Today in second and third. Omaha followed the same path that he had in the United States Hotel Stakes, gaining after his slow start to finish at the heels of Today, again moving up with a rush.[28] For both the Flash and the Special, Omaha had drawn a post toward the inside and for both he had slow starts, finishing with a head of steam but ultimately unsuccessful. After posting one win already, what did this son of Gallant Fox need to find the winner's circle again?

Saratoga's long list of stakes races included the Sanford Stakes, which boasted legends like Regret, Billy Kelly, and others on its list of victors, but perhaps the race is most famous for one that did not win: Man o' War.[29] While 1934 did not feature its own super horse, the Sanford nevertheless was another opportunity for Omaha to show off his potential. Joining him in the field of nine were familiar foes Psychic Bid, Boxthorn, and Today, all returning for another chance at a Saratoga stake.[30]

Again, Omaha drew a post position close to the rail, starting from the third stall. To his left was Boxthorn on the rail and to his immediate right was Psychic Bid, both of whom gunned to the lead at the break, with Psychic Bid holding a one-length advantage. Omaha was seventh, then sixth four furlongs in. By the top of the stretch, jockey Lee Humphries gave Omaha the green light, moving up to fourth place and building momentum to challenge Today and Boxthorn in second and third. Psychic Bid had extended his lead to three lengths, and, while Omaha would not catch him, the son of Gallant Fox was able to pass Today to finish second, his best showing since his win nearly eight weeks earlier.[31] These six-furlong races, coupled with Omaha's preference to come from behind rather than run on the lead, showed that he simply lacked the distance to maximize the talent he had.

Damon Runyon saw this. In his long experience writing about racing and hanging around racetracks, he had seen his share of good horses, ones with the potential to win the contests that America valued, with the Kentucky Derby at the top of that list. He went out on a limb, though, in late August 1934 when he made his pick for the 1935 renewal of America's best-known race, which was still about nine months away. "It is the custom of this writer to nominate a winner of the Kentucky Derby along in the winter," he wrote on August 21, boldly making his choice early:

> This year, he will take time by the forelock and name his horse now.
>
> The horse is Omaha, a son of the Derby winner of some years back, Gallant Fox. Omaha is owned by Mr. William Woodward, master of the Belair Stud and chairman of the august Jockey Club. . . . But Omaha is the horse, bar accident. He hasn't been much in sprints, but when they stretch the races out you will commence hearing of him. He is always running like a scared wolf in the late stages of his races. He will eventually run past all the two-year-olds that have been showing their heels to him up here. Remember the name—Omaha. The name of a great city, and a great colt.[32]

The son of Gallant Fox had won only one race to this point, had finished second in two races, and fourth in the other two. Omaha was five starts into his career and yet here was Damon Runyon singing his praises months before a blanket of roses was in the offing. The scribe's predication was bold, but Omaha had plenty of time to show everyone else what Runyon had already judged for himself: that he was a champion.

A decade into his Hall of Fame career, Charles Kurtsinger had already logged his own personal Triple Crown, winning the Kentucky Derby and Belmont Stakes on Twenty Grand in 1931 and then a Preakness Stakes on Head Play in 1933.[33] By 1934, Kurtsinger was among the country's most successful jockeys, a natural choice to ride Omaha as he sought another victory, this time in the Hopeful Stakes on closing day at Saratoga.

The Hopeful had taken a hit to its purse, as the Great Depression took its toll on racing as it had on the country. To keep people coming, racetracks had to reduce or even eliminate admission fees, which affected the amount of money available for purses. Nevertheless, the Hopeful maintained its traditional prestige, and the 1934 edition included all of the leading two-year-olds seen under colors at the Spa.[34] Omaha would be there alongside stablemates Pitter Pat and Sir Beverley. Colonel E. R. Bradley had Balladier and Boxthorn while Brookmeade Stable brought their own contingent of challengers, including Psychic Bid. Saratoga Special winner Plat Eye was back for another go at a big stakes race, to add to his five wins in seven starts so far in 1934. The field of sixteen was a star-studded affair that offered a chance to establish some supremacy over the rest of the division ahead of the Futurity at Belmont Park two weeks later.

At six and a half furlongs, the Hopeful offered Omaha something he had lacked in his last few starts: more ground to cover. Would the extra 110 yards afford the son of Gallant Fox enough space to overcome his slow starts and bring home the victory? Couple the extra space with the race's allowance conditions, and Omaha's 117 pounds to Plat Eye's 126 pounds seemed a distinct advantage, especially to learned observers like W. C. Vreeland.[35] With Kurtsinger aboard and something of a weight advantage plus extra distance for his late move, Omaha seemed ripe for a second victory.

Alas, even the extra half furlong was not enough for this Belair hopeful. Starting from post nine, the middle of the pack, Omaha stayed true to form and broke slowly, tenth at the start but rallying to hang in seventh or eighth for most of the race. Boxthorn sprinted to the front by a head over St. Bernard and held on to that lead until the stretch. Meanwhile, Psychic Bid and Plat Eye lingered just behind those two, but, as the field turned into the Saratoga stretch, Mack Garner hustled Psychic Bid to the lead as Boxthorn called it quits. Plat Eye gave it up about the same time, allowing Rosemont and Esposa, both among the longer shots in the field, to pass him in those waning yards. Kurtsinger put down Omaha for a drive to make up enough ground to finish just a head behind Esposa in fourth place.[36] Even that extra distance did not help Omaha in the

Hopeful. How was he going to overcome these slow starts? What did he need to do to find the winner's circle again?

Perhaps, like his sire, he needed to find the right jockey. Lee Humphries was back on Omaha for the Champagne Stakes five days later at Belmont Park. The action might have shifted from one part of New York to another, but the competition was still the same: the Champagne featured familiar faces like Balladier, Plat Eye, and Boxthorn.[37] This time, though, rather than running around the oval, the six-and-a-half-furlong Champagne was on the Widener course, the familiar straightaway that cut through Belmont's infield. At the start, it was 150 feet wide, more than enough space to accommodate the large fields for races like the Futurity; at the finish, it was one hundred feet wide, still wider than most American racetracks. The only problem? The width of the straightaway made it more difficult for jockeys to judge their place within the field.[38] This wee issue reared its head in the Champagne.

Omaha started from the far outside of the twelve-horse field with Balladier toward the rail and then Plat Eye and Boxthorn between them. Running straight allowed Omaha to stay in his lane and build up speed without having to adjust for a turn. Black Gift joined Omaha on the outside when he acted up in the gate, and then starter George Cassidy moved him to stand alone to the side of the gate.[39] At the start, Wayne Wright sent Balladier away from the gate fastest, but joining him early was Omaha. In his previous races, this long-bodied son of Gallant Fox had not shown much in the way of early speed, but, in the Champagne, he was toward the middle running on a straight path in second, two lengths behind Balladier. They stayed that way until the last furlong: Wright kept Balladier in a drive, but Humphries misjudged the distance between Omaha and the leader and believed that they had succeeded in passing Balladier. Instead of driving Omaha harder to make up the scant gap between him and the leader, Humphries stopped riding his colt and lost the Champagne by only a nose.[40] Humphries said later that he thought they were almost a full length ahead, not two scant inches behind.

In another stride, he would have caught Balladier, who set a track record for the six and a half furlongs in his win over Omaha.

The Futurity was shaping up to be quite the affair with fifteen of the country's leading two-year-olds scheduled to meet the starter for the $100,000 purse. Balladier, Boxthorn, Psychic Bid, and Plat Eye were all back for a share of the massive purse. Rosemont and Esposa wanted another crack at the division's leaders as did the still-maiden Sir Beverley, Omaha's stablemate. New to the list was Chance Sun, whose sire, Chance Shot, had won the 1927 Belmont Stakes and had sired the 1934 Belmont Stakes winner, Peace Chance.[41] Chance Sun was owned by Joseph Widener, owner of Belmont Park, so winning the Futurity would definitely be a feather in the cap of his breeder and owner.[42] Omaha's showing in the Champagne, though, made him a popular choice for the Futurity. The frustration at his Saratoga form was giving way to hopes that the Futurity on the Widener course offered him another shot at a victory.[43] With another clean start on this straight path, surely Omaha could bring home the prized Futurity to Belair Stud.

William Woodward had nominated this son of Gallant Fox for the Futurity in utero, betting that Flambino's unborn foal would make it to Belmont Park on September 15, 1934. He did, only to find the Widener course muddy, a first for Omaha. With his stablemate Sir Beverley scratched and Charley Kurtsinger back for another ride, he was to start from post thirteen, with Plat Eye to his left and only Chance Sun to his outside. Rosemont went to the lead from the break, only a head in front of Balladier and Chance Sun two furlongs into the six and a half. Omaha did not get the same quick start he had in the Champagne, laying fifth throughout the race. By the final eighth of a mile, Chance Sun had shaken off a fading Rosemont and surging Plat Eye and Balladier to pull ahead of the pack by two lengths. Omaha splashed past Rosemont as that colt lost ground to finish fourth.[44]

For his part, Chance Sun took home the winner's share of the Futurity's $100,000 purse and a place on the historic roster of winners to add to his previous stake victory in the Grand Union Hotel Stakes at Saratoga, also in the mud. With that, Widener's colt logged his third win in twelve starts, with five seconds in addition. Satisfied with this two-year-old season, the president of the Westchester Racing Association sent his promising son of Chance Shot to his Elmendorf Farm in Kentucky to rest until 1935.[45] Omaha, on the other hand, had one more date with the starter before he was done for the year.

At a mile, the Junior Championship Stakes at Aqueduct was one of the longest stakes races for two-year-olds. After racing at shorter distances, a mile seemed a more ideal fit for the slow starter and fast closer that Omaha had proven to be. It also happened to be the last race that Gallant Fox raced in and won in 1929, auguring well for his record-breaking 1930 season.[46] A win in this race would do the same for Omaha; it would capitalize on the promise of his fast finishes at shorter races and give everyone a preview of what observers like Runyon had already predicted. The "next-time horse" was ready to run.[47]

The field was small, only six horses. Most were well raced, logging as many as seventeen starts for the year, and most carried lighter weights, 111 to 116 pounds, but only Sailor Beware, the winner of the Babylon Handicap, had the gravitas of Omaha's previous competition. Cheshire and Sailor Beware were one-two on the rail with Omaha in the middle and then Sound Advice and Abner on the outside, while Brookmeade's Special Agent scratched.[48] With Charley Kurtsinger aboard again, Omaha took his spot in the gate and stood ready for this one-mile test. He was the 4–5 favorite over the entry of Cheshire and Sailor Beware.

Sound Advice got out to a one-length lead at the start, with Abner and Sailor Beware running behind him. Omaha took up his usual position toward the back of the pack, until three furlongs in when he passed Cheshire to sit just behind Sailor Beware as Abner moved ahead of Sound Advice. Sailor Beware sat in third still, but, as they entered that final turn, Sonny Workman gave his mount the go-ahead to move. Sailor Beware "leaped into an open lead" with Kurtsinger taking Omaha wide to find a running lane for his late move.[49]

Into the stretch they swept with Sailor Beware ahead by a length and a half, Omaha on his heels. They dashed down the stretch in what W. C. Vreeland called "a ding-dong battle," with Omaha closing fast, but not fast enough to catch Sailor Beware. In the end, the margin of victory was a head, with Sailor Beware barely outlasting Omaha's sprint for the finish. "A cut of the whip on the part of Kurtsinger would have changed the outcome," Vreeland observed.[50] Again, Omaha had moved just a bit too late to use that closing kick to its fullest. With another hundred yards, he might have passed Sailor Beware. Regardless, it was another loss, another promising performance rife with concerns about what it meant for Omaha in 1935.

Supporters of the Belair colt held fast to their observations about his potential. John Lewy put Omaha's season in perspective: "Omaha has had the tough luck to be beaten by a snoot by Balladier in world record time for six and one-half furlongs and a head by Sailor Beware in one of the fastest miles ever run by two-year-olds."[51] Both Balladier and Sailor Beware had to run faster than expected in order to beat Omaha's closing rush. Though Gallant Fox had a better record than his son at two, the Fox was spectacular at three, thanks to a rider change. Had Earl Sande not taken up the charge of piloting Gallant Fox in 1930, would the Fox of Belair have been as brilliant? Perhaps, as W. C. Vreeland pointed out, Omaha needed a new jockey, "a strong, skillful rider like Earl Sande."[52] If Fitzsimmons and Woodward could find the right rider, then perhaps Omaha would be "likely to measure up to dear old dad."[53] Who could that rider be?

After the Junior Championship, Omaha spent some time in Maryland, resting in anticipation of his three-year-old campaign. In late December, he was shipped back to Aqueduct for the legendary trainer to prepare him for the new year's challenges. Ahead of him were longer races, bigger purses, and tougher competition. As Beau Belmont observed, the son of Gallant Fox was nominated for the very same stakes races that his sire had conquered in 1930: the Kentucky Derby, the Preakness Stakes, and the Belmont Stakes. "It would be quite the feat," noted Belmont, "if he could win all three, for the writer, without the records at hand, can recall no horse has gained the American triple crown and then sent forth one of his sons to repeat the feat." Omaha had his supporters, including Damon Runyon, those who thought he was capable of the same greatness that had marked his sire. As he grew out of the juvenile awkwardness into a maturing three-year-old, the son of Gallant Fox was ready to capitalize on the promise inherent in his pedigree and his changing physique.

14

Following the Fox

William Woodward had experienced many fortuitous moments in his life to this point. As the calendar rolled over from 1934 to 1935, he already boasted two Belmont Stakes winners in addition to his Triple Crown with Gallant Fox. His English stable had a classic winner of its own: Brown Betty, who won the One Thousand Guineas, the filly version of the Two Thousand Guineas; it also had success with Alcazar, who had won several stakes, including the Ebor Handicap and the Doncaster Cup.[1] Woodward was chairman of the Jockey Club and a breeder of champions. His original investment of only a few thousand dollars for those Ajax mares from France had yielded the good filly Flambette, winner of the Coaching Club American Oaks in 1921 and dam of Flambino, who came in third in both the Coaching Club American Oaks versus fillies and the Belmont Stakes versus colts. In turn, Flambino's pairing with Gallant Fox brought Woodward something else: a chance at an unprecedented achievement that likely would never be duplicated, a second Triple Crown, thanks to a colt named Omaha.

Omaha's slow development as a yearling led to Woodward's decision to keep him stateside rather than sending him to England. Fitzsimmons pointed this golden chestnut son of Gallant Fox toward the American classics. The master of Belair still sought an Epsom Derby winner, but he had something else he valued in 1935: another horse deep in stamina, built for the distance racing that his owner cherished. Now three years old, Omaha had grown into a horse with "heroic lines, standing over 16½ hands tall . . . at the same time being of great length and his room behind the saddle exceptional."[2] The brevity of the juvenile races in 1934 had not suited Omaha's running style, with his long and sweeping stride, but Damon Runyon had prognosticated more for the lanky chestnut, marking him as his choice to win the Kentucky Derby 256 days before the actual event. This Belair star, awash in obvious potential not yet realized, was about to ascend to his sire's throne.

By this point in the 1930s, Belair Stud had risen to a dominance that would be rivaled only by Calumet Farm in the next decade. Calumet, though, was in its early stages of development as a Thoroughbred powerhouse; Warren Wright was still transforming his father's Standardbred farm into what would become a premier breeding and racing operation. To this end, Wright had purchased the Preakness-winning mare Nellie Morse in foal to American Flag, a son of Man o' War, for $6,100.[3] The foal she carried also happened to be a filly, who Wright would name Nellie Flag.

As a juvenile, Nellie Flag shone. She won the Selima, the Matron, and the Kentucky Jockey Club Stakes in 1934, marking her as the best two-year-old filly of the year. This bay filly carried the blood of both Man o' War and Abercorn, the best Australian horse of the nineteenth century, which made her an ideal candidate for classic distance races like the Kentucky Derby. Her best performances at two had come at a mile so it was no surprise that she was listed among the favorites for the 1935 Kentucky Derby.

Omaha's performances at age two earned him a spot on that favorites list with the filly, but, with his lone victory at two alongside his in-the-money close calls, he was behind Nellie Flag, Chance Sun, and Roman Soldier.[4] Along with his status as a Derby contender, the son of Gallant Fox gained another potential advantage: a regular rider. Over his two-year-old season Omaha had four different jockeys, including Jimmy Burke, who would later win a Derby and a Belmont on Johnstown for Belair, and Charles Kurtsinger, the jockey who would pilot War Admiral to a Triple Crown of his own just two years later. Fitzsimmons had signed Montana native Willie Saunders to a contract, tapping the young jockey to ride Omaha in 1935.

Born in Bozeman, Montana, and later raised in Calgary, Alberta, Saunders had started exercising horses on Canadian racetracks. He returned to Bozeman to live with his uncle and ride half-mile races on Montana's "kerosene circuit," the area's smallest meets. Later, he went to work for trainer L. T. Whitehill in California and rode at Tanforan in San Francisco in 1932.[5] Two years later, he came east to ride for Fitzsimmons and the Wheatley and Belair Stud stables. Saunders was unmarried and twenty years old, about the same age Earl Sande had been when he debuted in 1918; he also had a mouth that got him in trouble with Mrs. Henry Carnegie Phipps and almost cost him his position with Wheatley. Instead, Fitzsimmons put him on the Belair horses, which is how he came to ride Omaha in 1935. Saunders worked the big colt in the mornings and discovered something surprising: Omaha liked to bite. Always high-strung and nervous, Omaha disliked it when horses got close to him. He would try to take a chunk out of any horse that made contact with him. As a result, whenever Saunders rode Omaha, he knew to take him around horses to avoid any possible bumping that might result in the colt getting distracted rather than surging past.[6] Saunders knew that to keep Omaha on track, he would need to be the right rider for the tests to come.

His first race of 1935 came in the South Shore Purse, an allowance race at Jamaica; at a mile and seventy yards, the race gave Omaha a chance to hit the ground running just under two weeks before the Kentucky Derby. Omaha hung back at the start, and Saunders bided his time until the far turn. He took the big Belair colt around his competitors and drove through the stretch to win by two lengths.[7] After having won only one race in nine starts at age two, Omaha was one for one at age three, a great way to start the new season. With this win, he was primed for the Wood Memorial; he joined eleven others in the starting gate for that prep race.

Like his previous start, the Wood Memorial would ask Omaha to run a mile and seventy yards; allowances brought the colt's weight

Jockey Willie Saunders. Keeneland Library Cook Collection.

down to 114 pounds, despite his earlier victory. Even though he was the first out of the gate, Omaha dropped back to last in the field of twelve. He lumbered through the early part of the race while Psychic Bid took the lead, with C. V. Whitney's Today and Greentree's Plat Eye right behind him. Coming out of the final turn, Today passed both Psychic Bid and Plat Eye to take a two-length lead while Omaha came on "like a whirlwind," his stride "long and sweeping."[8] The son of Gallant Fox finished just a nose out of second after picking his way through the field of twelve; he finished third only because he ran out of track. The Wood Memorial was three-sixteenths of a mile shorter than the Kentucky Derby; if Omaha could make up ground that quickly in a race that short, he was sure to come home victorious at 1¼ miles in the Derby. His Wood Memorial made him the co-favorite with Chance Sun on the list of Derby probables, at odds of 5–1.[9] On the same day, Nellie Flag won the Cherokee Park Purse at Churchill Downs, beating a field of colts, including Chance Sun, by six lengths. The win sealed her place on that same list as Omaha, her 8–1 odds putting her up there with Today and Roman Soldier.[10] Her performance already had observers comparing her to the great Regret, the only filly to win the Kentucky Derby.

As Derby Day approached, the field numbered twenty-two horses, a wide-open extravaganza of Thoroughbred excellence, but one notable name was not among them. Chance Sun was out of the running after X-rays showed that the colt had a bony growth in his left front foot, an injury responsible for his poor finishes in his last two races before the Derby.[11] Among the remaining horses were six geldings and one filly; Nellie Flag was running in the tradition of both her dam, Nellie Morse, who had won the 1924 Preakness, and 1915 Kentucky Derby winner Regret, fillies who had beat the boys soundly in their time. Could this filly, "hailed as the greatest member of her sex to run in the Blue Grass Special in the twenty years since racing history was made by the daughter of Broomstick [Regret]," master the large field and come home in front? As rain sheeted down over Louisville, the odds swung from Omaha, who had become the odds-on choice after Chance Sun had scratched, to Nellie Flag, who had won the Cherokee Park Purse in the mud the weekend before. As Calumet Farm seemed set to win its first Kentucky Derby, jockey Eddie Arcaro looked forward to the same on the first Derby mount of his young career.[12]

As the sun dawned with a chill on Churchill Downs, the crowd looked forward to a thrilling race to warm them all up.

In a double-wide stall in the Fitzsimmons barn stood the Belair hopeful and son of Gallant Fox, his golden chestnut coat shining beneath the wide white streak that ran down his strong face. His last workout in anticipation of this day had been on Wednesday, May 1, when he completed the ten furlongs in 2:10 over the Churchill Downs dirt. Mere days after running the Wood Memorial at Jamaica, Omaha had breezed 1⅛ miles in 1:55⅘, leisurely cantering with stablemate Gallant Prince. His fast-closing finish in the Wood Memorial promised that the Kentucky Derby, at 1¼ miles, should be no problem for the son of the 1930 Derby winner. With the Wood Memorial winner looking weary, Omaha looked all the more attractive as a Derby pick.[13] He was part of a sextet of horses given the best chance to win it all, including Nellie Flag, Today, Plat Eye, Commonwealth, and Boxthorn. Indeed, the six were so close that writer Henry McLemore was predicting a six-way dead heat. Eventually, though, on the day of the Run for the Roses, McLemore landed on Omaha as his choice, saying that "he is going to look as big as the place he was named for and sweet as peaches and cream when he comes roaring down the stretch today."[14]

Albert Johnson, former jockey with two Derbies to his name, landed on Omaha for his 1935 Kentucky Derby pick, with the caveat that one would need to watch Nellie Flag if it rained on race day.[15] Given the size of the field, though, it was a wide-open race when it came to selecting a winner. Sportswriter Ralph McGill, who judged the field to be "a poor lot of colts and one filly," selected Omaha to win over Boxthorn, Nellie Flag, and Commonwealth.[16] With the

Omaha with jockey Wayne Wright. National Museum of Racing and Hall of Fame Collection.

filly and Today, son of Whichone, one of Gallant Fox's rivals, as the odds-on favorites, turf writer Damon Runyon reminded his readers that Omaha was still his pick, noting that the come-from-behind colt "will be running when most of the others are folded up like opera hats."[17] Even famed writer Grantland Rice pronounced himself an advocate of Omaha; he said that the colt "might not be another Gallant Fox, but he isn't so far away," possessing "all that you can ask for in a 3-year-old."[18] The bettors started swinging the momentum away from Today after trainer Jack Healey reported that the colt had a slightly bruised hoof and put their money on Nellie Flag, making the filly the tepid favorite. When the day's card began with rain cascading down on the one-mile oval at Churchill Downs, a chill settled on the gathering crowd and on the betting, with Nellie Flag sitting at 4–1, and Omaha just behind her as second choice.[19]

Nellie Flag with trainer B. B. Williams and jockey Eddie Arcaro, 1934. Keeneland Library General Collection.

A crowd of fifty thousand braved the drizzle and chill of the day; temperatures dropped into the forties as the rain soaked the hardy fans out to see another historic contest despite the continued effects of the Great Depression on the country. At 4:05 p.m., the Old Kentucky Handicap, a six-and-a-half-furlong dash for three-year-olds and up, went off with a field of six. Vitamin B won by a head over Hank McTavish after a stretch drive in which the winner caught the place horse in the race's waning strides. With the fifth race done, the day's sixth race, the Kentucky Derby, loomed an hour in the future, and the throng of young and old, male and female, well-heeled or threadbare, awaited the bugle's call.[20] When the strains of "My Old Kentucky Home" resounded through the Downs, the crowd of umbrellas, the lone barrier against the miserable drizzle, surged forward as the horses trickled out onto the fast-deteriorating track.

The twenty-two had been whittled down to eighteen: one filly, six geldings, and eleven colts. The colorful silks of some of America's most famous owners—Whitney, Woodward, Calumet, Bradley—stood out in the gray of the day. America's best breeding stock were part of the milieu; Gallant Fox, Nellie Morse, Bostonian, and Blue Larkspur, champions of the American classics themselves, were counted among the sires and dams of the contenders.[21] Future Hall of Famers graced the list of trainers and jockeys, names like Fitzsimmons and Jones, Woolf and Arcaro that would become iconic in the history of the sport. The eighteen paraded out to the Bahr starting gate as the chilled fans strained to see something, *anything,* of the spectacle before them.[22] The field loaded into the gate, Nellie Morse in post nine, with Omaha next to her in post ten. She needed to beat the crush to get into stride; he needed to find running room and build up his speed. With that many horses, a clean trip would be essential to success. For a horse like Omaha, who did not relish running in company, finding a clear lane for the ten furlongs was key and Willie Saunders knew it.

At the break, Nellie Flag darted to the lead, but, in the rush to find running room, she was squeezed back to eighth, as Plat Eye and others formed the front-running pack on the first turn into the backstretch. Omaha got away twelfth, content to hang out on the outside while the field jostled for position in front of him. Saunders was careful to keep the long-striding colt from getting boxed in while he patiently waited for the right moment to call on Omaha's gathering momentum. With a half mile to go, Saunders gave the big chestnut colt a nudge.

On the outside, Omaha's long stride took him past horses, ticking off competitors one by one. He reached Plat Eye and Boxthorn as they surrendered the lead coming out of the turn and then repelled the onslaught of Roman Soldier, who also had gotten clear of the field as he made his move for the lead. Behind Omaha, the field stretched out, Roman Soldier, Whiskolo, and Nellie Flag accelerating into their own stretch drives. No one was to catch Omaha this day, though, as Saunders simply needed to cluck at the colt and Omaha responded, his lead a length and a half at the wire.[23] Despite the slow track and the constant drizzle that soaked into the surface, the son of Gallant Fox bettered his sire's Derby time by more than two seconds and the two became the third sire–son duo to win the Kentucky Derby.[24] William Woodward had his second Kentucky Derby winner and he made the familiar trip down to the winner's circle at Churchill Downs, greeting the assembled crowd of dignitaries with gruff lamentations on the weather.[25]

When asked to compare his newest champion to his sire, Woodward said that the Fox's accomplishments had given him "[his] greatest race track thrills."[26] For Saunders, however, the thrill of his victory became even bigger when Woodward threw his arms around the jockey, and "warned him to 'go on and get out of this weather for we've got to win a lot more races this year.'"[27] Still stunned by his victory on his first mount in the country's biggest race, the Montana native called the race "the greatest thrill of my life" and Omaha "the greatest horse I ever rode."[28] While Omaha might not have been the top of the heap for his owner, his jockey sure was fond of the tall and leggy chestnut colt, a newly minted Derby winner.

As the day wound down, William Woodward declared his son of Gallant Fox for the Preakness Stakes one week later. After his performance at Churchill Downs, there was no question about a trip to Pimlico and the home state of Belair Stud for a horse who had won the Derby as he pleased, coming home in a rain-soaked romp.[29] Woodward had affection for the American classics. Gallant Fox had won the second Triple Crown in 1930 and then Faireno had won the Belmont Stakes in 1932, so sending Omaha to Baltimore was the logical next step. The question was, could Omaha duplicate his sire's success there?

The newest Derby winner boarded a train the next day, his ticket stamped for Baltimore, Maryland. Joining him on the train were

eight others, including Sun Fairplay, Plat Eye, Today, and Commonwealth.[30] Sun Fairplay's friend, a stern-faced Great Dane, joined him
for the journey while Omaha had the company of Gallant Prince,
another son of Gallant Fox.[31] Nellie Flag followed the next day, her
fourth-place performance in the Derby owed to the misbehavior of
horses like Plat Eye rather than some shortcoming on the filly's
part.[32] Owner Warren Wright was confident that his filly would
duplicate the feat of her dam, Nellie Morse, and take the Preakness
for herself.[33] Omaha, though, was the name on everyone's lips,
installed as the race's favorite in the scant week between his Derby
triumph and his Pimlico test. The chance to watch the horse that
some called the "Belair Bullet" take another race that his sire also
had won promised to attract a record crowd to Old Hilltop.

Meanwhile, new faces Firethorn, Mantagna, and Brannon
joined the four others returning from the Kentucky Derby to challenge Omaha. Firethorn won an allowance race on May 6, with a
come-from-behind style that resembled that of the Derby winner.
Looking sharp in this tune-up made Firethorn a potential threat to
Omaha.[34] Mantagna joined the fray on the strength of his second-
place finish in the Florida Derby in March at Hialeah. Brannon,
who also ran in the Florida Derby, came in as another long shot, but
both Mantagna and Brannon were question marks, their quality in
doubt next to the likes of Nellie Flag and Omaha.[35] Firethorn,
though, loomed as a potential dark horse to threaten Omaha's ability to close in a race like the Preakness.

The preponderance of the Preakness coverage focused on
Omaha. He exited the Kentucky Derby in good shape and was
shipped to Pimlico more than prepared for the test ahead. From
pedigree to previous performances, the Belair colt was a standout
who counted turf writers like Bruce Copeland among his admirers:
"There is nothing in the shape of a three-year-old in training that
can match strides with this son of Gallant Fox at distances of more
than a mile."[36] Copeland was so high on Omaha that he predicted
the colt would win the "triple crown" before the colt had even

entered the gate for the Preakness.[37] With ideal spring weather predicted for May 11, the Preakness was shaping up to be another crowning moment for the Belair Bullet.

The Preakness field half the size of the Derby had Nellie Flag's connections looking for a cleaner trip for the filly that had classic winners in her pedigree. Commonwealth had also had a troubled trip in Louisville and also counted a Preakness winner in his pedigree; his sire, Bostonian, had taken the race in 1927. Boxthorn's sire was Blue Larkspur, the 1929 Belmont Stakes winner. So, despite finishing sixteenth in the Derby, he also had distance in his pedigree, which made him another horse that could threaten Omaha. The weather forecast predicted a much warmer day than the chill of Derby Day with no chance of rain, making a fast Pimlico track likely.[38] With better weather and track conditions on their side, if any of those horses got a clean trip, they could thwart Omaha's chokehold on the race—but not if the big horse had anything to say about it. He was primed for a sensational performance.

The Preakness Stakes, named for the horse who won the first Dinner Party Stakes at Pimlico in 1870, was even older than the Kentucky Derby. First run in 1873, the Preakness stayed in Maryland until 1888; it moved temporarily to New York (Morris Park and then Gravesend) from 1890 to 1908, and was revived at its original home in 1909. The Woodlawn Vase, America's most valuable sports trophy, was the prize for the winning owner, alongside a purse of $25,000.[39] William Woodward was no stranger to the race's history. His Belair Stud was located only forty miles from Old Hilltop and Woodward's favorite son Gallant Fox had won the Preakness in 1930. Once again, as the Woodward silks, white with bright red dots, graced the favorite for the Preakness Stakes, the Jockey Club's president had the opportunity to take home an American classic.

The day indeed turned out to be ideal weather for the forty-five thousand that filled Pimlico Race Course, the largest crowd to ever see a race at the track. For the first time since the match race between

Parole, Ten Broeck, and Tom Ochiltree in 1877, both the Senate and the House of Representatives adjourned early so that the members could go to the races.[40] The crowd wagered nearly $900,000 on the card of eight races; this was down from the all-time high but was far healthier than the year before, given the economic realities of that moment.[41] At the center of it all was the spectacle that was the Preakness Stakes. The race was the thing and Maryland was there for it.

The late afternoon sun shone brightly on the eight horses as they trickled from the Pimlico paddock to the main track. The record crowd roared in anticipation of the much-ballyhooed test before them, standing as the band first played "The Star-Spangled Banner" and then "Maryland, My Maryland." Eagerly clutching their betting slips, the crowd overflowed the stands and spread into the infield. All held their breath as the horses entered the starting gate.[42]

In a race that was a sixteenth of a mile shorter than the Kentucky Derby, how would the long-striding Omaha, who needed ground to get into gear, handle the change in distance? Jockey Willie Saunders answered that question immediately. Omaha drew the sixth position, a post that ensured he would be to the outside of horses like Nellie Flag and Firethorn. At the start, Brannon jetted out to the lead, with Boxthorn and Psychic Bid following. Nellie Flag sat behind them, tucked in behind the leaders on the first turn, with Omaha following in sixth. Coming out of the first turn, Saunders moved Omaha into fourth, much closer to the front runners than he had been in the Derby. As they entered the second turn, the jockey loosened his grip on the favorite, signaling it was time to make his move. On the outside of the front-runners, Omaha's long stride ate up ground like he was starving for it, taking the lead and then stretching his advantage to six lengths as the field thundered into the stretch.[43] Behind him, Brannon and Boxthorn gave way to Psychic Bid and Firethorn, who chased Omaha to no avail. Nellie Flag faded, unable to find the form she had shown before the Derby. Omaha stormed home in 1:58⅖, a fifth of a second slower than the Preakness record and two-fifths slower than the track record. He had won both the Kentucky Derby and the Preakness, putting himself in elite company alongside Sir Barton and Burgoo King. Even more historic was the fact that his sire had done the same thing; they were the first father–son duo to achieve the double. His victory was emphatic, demonstrating an ability to be versatile and showing that he could win over a fast track much as he had won over the muddy track at Churchill Downs. Jockey Willie Saunders had ridden the colt masterfully both times, keeping Omaha clear of traffic and in position to make his run when the moment came. William Woodward praised Saunders, saying, "'You rode a fine race, son, and you're going to ride that horse to more victories.'" Looking forward, more victories in Omaha's immediate future possibly included the Withers Stakes and the Belmont Stakes.[44]

Trainer "Sunny Jim" Fitzsimmons agreed. Omaha had come out of the Preakness in fine fettle, and a victory in the Belmont was all but assured provided the colt "continue[d] to stand training and he [stayed] sound as a dollar."[45] Fitzsimmons and Woodward had been down this road before with Gallant Fox, but, with almost a month between the Preakness and the Belmont, Omaha needed one more start to keep him fresh. So the Derby–Preakness winner was shipped home to New York and entered in the Withers Stakes, a one-mile stakes worth $11,250 to the winner. There, he would face his next test after his Derby–Preakness double: fresh horses.

15

The Son Gets His Crown

When Omaha crossed the finish line as the winner of the 1935 Kentucky Derby, Gallant Fox became only the third Derby winner to sire another Derby victor. In the sixty years since the first Kentucky Derby in 1875, only Halma (1895), sire of Alan-a-Dale (1902), and Bubbling Over (1926), sire of Burgoo King (1932), had passed on their legacy at ten furlongs to another generation.[1] With Omaha's Preakness win, the Fox also became the first Derby–Preakness double winner to sire a second Derby–Preakness winner. On top of that, with that win, Omaha looked poised to duplicate another of his sire's deep list of accomplishments: the Triple Crown. First, though, "Sunny Jim" Fitzsimmons took his decades of experience to the entry box and put his charge in the Withers Stakes on May 25, understanding that his horse needed the right fitness to make history. After all, the trainer had been here before, just five short years earlier.

The Withers had amassed a long list of famed winners in its years as part of the New York racing calendar. Inaugurated at Jerome Park Racetrack in 1874, the one-mile test for three-year-olds fell between the Preakness and Belmont Stakes most years, which made it a desirable tune-up in that break between the two races. The month break between those classics meant that Omaha would need a race to keep him on edge before he tried the 1½-mile Belmont Stakes. The Withers had also been added to Sir Barton's list of spring stakes in his pursuit of the first Triple Crown, and its shorter distance posed no trouble for that pioneer. Omaha relished longer tests like the 1¼-mile Kentucky Derby; would a mile be too short for his long stride?[2]

Questions about where the Derby–Preakness winner would run proliferated when Omaha did not appear for training at Belmont Park in the intervening days before the Withers. Perhaps Fitzsimmons would, instead, send him in the ten-furlong Suburban Handicap, to be run five days later. In that race, Omaha would face the 1934 Kentucky Derby winner, Cavalcade; his rival Discovery, who had won the Brooklyn and Whitney Handicaps the year before; and Head Play, who happened to be the horse on the losing end of the famous "Fighting Finish" of the 1933 Kentucky Derby.[3] That race would be more suitable because it was longer than the Withers, and, as a three-year-old, Omaha would carry 110 pounds versus Cavalcade's 127 pounds. Even though he would be facing older horses for the first time, the distance and the weights would set up nicely for Omaha. However, after all of the speculation, Fitzsimmons opted for the Withers, where the Belair colt would face the likes of Plat Eye, Psychic Bid, and Rosemont at equal weights.[4]

With 7–10 favoritism squarely on his shoulders, Omaha joined eight competitors at the post for the Withers. Starting from post two, with only Psychic Bid to his left, Omaha started slowly; Nautch and Special Agent got away fastest, running one and two. Omaha lingered toward the back of the pack, Rosemont just ahead of him. Down the backstretch, Saunders moved Omaha up, but jockey Wayne Wright on Rosemont stayed one step ahead of the Derby–Preakness winner, waiting for Saunders to send his colt for the lead.

At three-quarters of a mile, Plat Eye took the lead from Nautch, who tired and fell out of contention with each stride. Psychic Bid began to fade too as Rosemont and Omaha made their moves for the front. In the stretch, Rosemont turned on the speed, passing Plat Eye with a rush. Omaha was a step slower, gathering momentum to make a run at the new leader. He could only manage to pass Plat Eye, but did not get close enough to Rosemont to truly challenge him for the lead. At the wire, Rosemont held a length and a half advantage over

Omaha; he surprised everyone present with his performance, which was an improvement over his previous start where he had finished third behind Plat Eye.[5] It was the second time that Rosemont had gotten the better of the son of Gallant Fox, dating back to their previous meeting in the Hopeful at Saratoga the previous summer.[6]

For the Belair colt, though, as W. C. Vreeland observed, the Withers demonstrated once again that "Omaha is a distance colt, and is under a serious handicap at less than one mile and a furlong."[7] Rosemont had stayed with Omaha for most of the race, running just ahead of the red-hooded Kentucky Derby–Preakness winner until they hit the stretch. He sprinted away then; and, while Omaha might have had the drive to sustain over a longer distance, he did not demonstrate the same ability to sprint that Rosemont did. Without that quick turn of foot, Omaha would remain at a disadvantage at shorter distances. In the Withers, Omaha "ran a good, honest race, had no excuses, and was beaten because the mile course was too short for him."[8] The pace certainly did not help: Rosemont ran the fastest mile of the Belmont meet to that point, finishing the race in 1:36⅗.[9] Perhaps a turn in the Suburban would be a better fit for Omaha.

Ultimately, though, as May 30 came and went, no Omaha emerged from the Fitzsimmons barn for the call to post for the Suburban. Given the fast pace of the Withers, Saunders had had to ask Omaha to run earlier than he had in previous races and the horse was tired. Both owner and trainer thought it prudent to skip that handicap rather than send him out against Cavalcade, Discovery, and Head Play five days after the Withers. Head Play would win the Suburban in a quick 2:02, confirming that it had been a good decision to skip that race to improve Omaha's chances in the Belmont Stakes on June 8.[10] Despite Omaha's loss to other three-year-olds in the Withers, Fitzsimmons had his colt ready for the Belmont Stakes. A date with history awaited in a matter of days.

Four days before his Thoroughbred namesake was to meet five others for the Belmont Stakes, a wagon horse also named Omaha decided that he needed to show his own propensity for speed—while drawing a cart full of ice down Pacific Street in New York. This other Omaha took the bit between his teeth and dashed toward the *Brooklyn Times Union* building, his spree ended by a run-in with a fence. The result of his escapade? Omaha the wagon horse found himself pinned down by duty, the cart upended by his unceremonious finish. *Times Union* employees and Police Emergency Squad 13 helped free this Omaha from his unfortunate predicament. The horse escaped serious injury. The statement from his owner, Frank Cristallo, about the whole incident was apparently unprintable, but his Omaha, at least, was satisfied with his performance.[11]

No doubt the owner of the Thoroughbred Omaha, William Woodward, would feel the same on Saturday afternoon. The handicappers agreed with him, making the lanky son of Gallant Fox the favorite for the twelve-furlong dash and its purse of $48,230. The total was less than his sire had brought home for his 1930 victory over Whichone, but the victory would be no less meaningful: a Triple Crown was on the line and Omaha was ready for his prize. He looked ready, breezing five furlongs in 1:00⅕ the day before the race.[12]

But his competition did not intend to make it easy for him. Rosemont had followed up his fastest mile of the Belmont meet in the Withers with a five-furlong work in 1:01, the Foxcatcher colt primed for the task ahead. The candidate for the race's dark horse was Cold Shoulder, a son of 1926 Preakness Stakes winner Display, who had worked the 1½-mile distance of the Belmont in 2:29⅗, just four-fifths of a second off Man o' War's record.[13] Cold Shoulder's record to this point did not make competitors quake in their boots, but that workout inspired conversation nonetheless. Firethorn was back for another crack at Omaha after finishing second to him in the Preakness Stakes nearly a month earlier, but few gave him any chance against the favorite. Rounding out the field were long shots Sir Beverley, a Belair stablemate, and Gold Foam, a surprise entry who scratched out the day of the race. Outside of Rosemont and maybe Firethorn, competition for the crown seemed scarce. Forty-five minutes before the race's start, the post positions were drawn: Cold Shoulder, Firethorn, Omaha, Sir Beverley, and Rosemont.

The Belmont Stakes was part of the closing day card for Belmont Park's spring meet, a day marked by the meet's second largest crowd. Nearly thirty thousand jammed roads and trains to make their way to the sprawling racing plant off the Hempstead Turnpike.[14] There, an unwelcome guest greeted them: rain. The deluge started with a cloudburst at the open of the day's card and continued for hours afterward, leaving everyone present feeling some kinship with ducks as they waded through the day's racing.[15]

All of the Woodwards, save for their son Billy, who was away at Groton, were present for the occasion; Mrs. Woodward and the four daughters braved the rain to stand in the paddock to watch the action. They were among the few present to watch the five horses dodge raindrops as they were saddled under Belmont's ancient trees. Willie Saunders came out in the white with red polka dots and dark pants rather than the usual white, wearing the red cap, while Tommy Malley on stablemate Sir Beverley wore the white. In a driving rain, they walked out of the treed enclosure into the tunnel that connected the paddock with the track and emerged onto the big sandy oval, as the soaked fans awaited the day's main event with bated breath.

George Cassidy perched on his starter's stand with his eagle eye on the procession as they entered the Bahr starting gate in good order. Cold Shoulder took a position on the rail, with Firethorn next to him. Rosemont stood on the outside, Sir Beverley to his inside, and, in the middle of them all, the lanky Omaha entered his stall, quiet and focused on his task.[16] At the start, Cold Shoulder sprinted out to the lead, with Firethorn just behind him. Omaha got away to his usual slow start; Saunders allowed him to settle in on the rail, content to wait for his cue. Rosemont and Sir Beverley rounded out the field, trailing behind the Kentucky Derby–Preakness winner.

Cold Shoulder lengthened his lead to five lengths six furlongs into the 1½ miles. Behind him, Sonny Workman and Firethorn were a head in front of Omaha, who was focused on a quiet Willie Saunders. On the turn, Rosemont moved past both, bearing down on Cold Shoulder, who still led the pack. The Vanderbilt colt was running easily on the lead, so much so that for a beat it looked like he might be able to steal the whole thing. But they hit the stretch and Cold Shoulder's confident stride began to shorten, as the grind of that first mile told on the son of Display. In the straightaway, as the distance between the field and the wire grew ever shorter, the onslaught began.

Rosemont made his try for the lead, with Firethorn on the rail. Saunders went to work on Omaha, urging the tall son of Gallant Fox to find his stride and build that same momentum that had carried him to victory so many times before. With a furlong to go, though, Rosemont could not sustain his drive, and Firethorn and Omaha passed him in their rush for the wire. On the rail, Workman urged Firethorn on, the track shrinking before them. Omaha, though, was an undeniable machine: Saunders rode the champion to the wire easily, drawing out to win by a length and a half.[17] Later, Saunders would remember the Belmont as a tough race for the big colt: "He was not a real good 'off-track' horse, being so large," the Triple Crown–winning jockey recalled. "He couldn't get a hold of the racetrack, but he finally got it together and went on and got it."[18] Firethorn finished second, eight lengths in front of Rosemont, with Cold Shoulder and Sir Beverley even farther up the track. The victory sealed, Saunders jogged Omaha back to the full grandstand to the cheers of the thousands who had just witnessed another bit of history as they celebrated the big Belair colt's Triple Crown glory.

"It may have been raining rain and a very wet rain at that to most of the customers, but it was a shower of violets to William Woodward," wrote Nancy Randolph in the society pages of the *Daily News* the following day.[19] The master of Belair, seeming impervious to the weather, borrowed a raincoat and ran down to the track to meet Saunders and Omaha at the judges' stand. While Woodward led his champion into the winner's circle, the soaking rain

William Woodward leads Omaha, with jockey Willie Saunders aboard, into the winner's circle after the 1935 Belmont Stakes. Keeneland Library Cook Collection.

weighed down everything except the owner's jubilation.[20] He even planted a kiss on Mrs. Woodward as he dashed around in the excitement of the moment.[21]

By winning the third Triple Crown, Omaha had duplicated the pioneering feat of Sir Barton's unnamed trio of victories in 1919 and then Gallant Fox's dominant dance around the classics just five years earlier. That alone was historic, but Belair had accomplished two more momentous feats: Gallant Fox was the first and still only Triple Crown winner to sire another Triple Crown winner and Woodward was the first owner and breeder to win the three races twice. Omaha was not close to being done with making history. In the meantime, though, the question was, what was next for the Belair Bullet?

The next day, Omaha contentedly munched hay in his stall while "Sunny Jim" fielded the usual questions about what was next. The famed trainer could only say that the Belair champion came out of the Belmont in fine fettle and that the next race was pending a meeting with the boss.[22] Rumors then swirled about the big horse's next visit: would Omaha go west to seek more fortune? The American Derby? The Detroit Derby? Or would he stay close to home and continue his tour around Gotham? William Woodward chimed in three days after the champion's sweep of the Triple Crown: Omaha would stay in New York and map out a route like his sire's. Woodward named features like the Dwyer, the Travers, and the Jockey Club Gold Cup among Omaha's future starts.[23] "This is a New York horse," Fitzsimmons quoted Woodward, echoing the idea that keeping Omaha in the area rewarded the fans that had supported him throughout his three-year-old campaign.[24] Even better, rather than waiting for the Dwyer, scheduled for three weeks after the Belmont Stakes, Woodward then opted for Omaha to try older horses in the Brooklyn Handicap. The big colt thrived on racing and Fitzsimmons was not one to keep his horses idle.

The Brooklyn, though, would be a different kind of test for the Triple Crown winner. As a three-year-old, he would likely carry less than the older horses in the race, sure, but the Brooklyn was a mile and an eighth, not quite the ten- and twelve-furlong tests that Omaha thrived on. To boot, he would be facing Discovery, who was on the brink of a huge season at age four, and King Saxon, winner of the Metropolitan, Queens County, and Carter Handicaps. Set to carry 114 pounds, nine less than Discovery and thirteen less than King Saxon, Omaha looked like a great bet even at nine furlongs, especially after his last work, where he went a half mile in 0:47 $\frac{2}{5}$, three-quarters of a mile in 1:12 $\frac{4}{5}$, and then the nine furlongs in 1:51. Suddenly Omaha looked to be the favorite for the Brooklyn: his recent wins and workouts made him the bettor's choice. June was early in the year for a three-year-old to face older horses, but Fitzsimmons knew that his colt needed a race before the Dwyer, and this was it.

The Brooklyn Handicap was no small task, but clearly Fitzsimmons and Woodward felt Omaha had something to gain from trying the race. Despite the challenges stacked against a three-year-old winning over older horses at this point in the year, Discovery himself had done it the year before. However, some were skeptical of the big horse's ability in this spot, including the *Brooklyn Times Union*'s John Lewy; he reminded readers that the Triple Crown classics Omaha had just won were his *only* stakes wins and that no three-year-old in recent memory had won the Brooklyn carrying 114 pounds, though Discovery had carried 113 in his victory the previous year.[25] Still, the Aqueduct stretch is long, providing plenty of space for that lengthy stride to wind up and challenge whoever might be on the front end.

As the Brooklyn approached, despite the presence of the previous year's winner, Discovery, in the race, the contest seemed to be down to Omaha versus King Saxon. King Saxon was a consistent miler who had won five of his last six races; his only out-of-the-money finish so far that season was at a mile and a quarter. Omaha had done his best running at ten furlongs and King Saxon at eight and a half furlongs or less, making the nine-furlong Brooklyn a toss-up. The race also had Omaha at a weight advantage, 114 pounds versus 127 for King Saxon. The older horse was a faster starter than Omaha, but even that was not a significant advantage: King Saxon had a history of mixed success at the barrier. Truly, despite the six other horses in the field, the Brooklyn seemed to come down to only two. W. C. Vreeland mentioned one more in passing: "Discovery recently showed improvement and is not altogether 'dead on his feet.'"[26] In the minds of observers of note, Discovery was just an afterthought.

The day before the Brooklyn, news emerged that Willie Saunders would not be the one riding Omaha. The young Saunders was ill with food poisoning and therefore unavailable for this race, so Fitzsimmons tapped Wayne Wright to ride.[27] Wright was about the same age as Saunders and had found great success in his three short years in the saddle. He had already finished second in number of stakes races won in 1933 and was then one of the top five money-winning jockeys.[28] In addition, Wright was available when Woodward's other contract riders Tommy Malley and Jimmy Stout were

committed elsewhere.[29] Would the change of riders make a difference for the three-year-old who was making his first start against
older horses?

On a warm June day, twenty thousand people filled Aqueduct
for the day's racing, which started with news that the field for the
Brooklyn was down to six with the scratches of Kievex and Coequel.
In truth, only three names mattered: King Saxon, with his winning
record; Discovery, the previous year's winner; and Omaha, the Triple Crown winner who was trying something his sire had not
attempted at this same point in his championship year. At the gate,
both King Saxon and Thursday delayed the start with their momen-
tary fractiousness, but the field got away from the gate cleanly. King
Saxon used his post on the rail to zip to the front. He dashed to a fast
first quarter in 0:23⅗, leading Discovery by two lengths. Omaha
was fourth, with Thursday and Good Goods bringing up the rear.[30]

King Saxon maintained his quick pace on the backstretch, running the half mile in 0:46⅕, a remarkably fast pace but not one fast
enough to shake Discovery. Jockey John Bejsack kept him within
striking distance of King Saxon, content to let the leader burn himself out. Behind them, Wright had Omaha in a stalking position
while Somebody held tenuously onto his third-place status. On that
final turn, King Saxon held on to his lead still, but Bejsack had
Discovery on the move. The six-furlong time was 1:11⅖; carrying
127 pounds at that pace, King Saxon could not hold on to that lead
for much longer.[31]

In the stretch, King Saxon's two-length lead shrank with each
stride; Discovery dogged his steps, inching ever forward to take the
lead for himself. With a furlong to go, Discovery was even with King
Saxon and then passed him. Bejsack moved his mount to the rail
with only daylight in front of him. Behind them, King Saxon held
on to his second-place status while Omaha, who had easily passed
Somebody for third place, was too far back to threaten the former
leader. At the wire, Discovery was eight lengths in front of King
Saxon, with Omaha four more lengths back in third.

As Bejsack and Discovery returned triumphant, they were met by the stunned faces of twenty-seven thousand who were left almost silent as they took in the race's result. Not only had Discovery beaten the two favorites soundly, but he had done it in world record time, 1:48⅕ for the mile and an eighth.[32] King Saxon had set the stage for such a time with the record pace he set for the first mile, 1:35⅗, but it was Discovery, who had barely shown the flashes of his 1934 brilliance in 1935, who maintained that pace and set a second world record.[33] Discovery would go on to win eleven of nineteen races in 1935, winning the Whitney Handicap for the second time and then taking home the Merchants and Citizens and the Arlington Handicaps as well.[34]

For his part, Omaha's third-place finish might have been a victory considering the blazing pace of both King Saxon and Discovery on the front end and the shorter distance the long-legged son of Gallant Fox had been asked to run. He gained ground in the stretch, but, beyond that, Omaha had only been a threat on paper. W. C. Vreeland had asked the colt's famed trainer to compare the Belair colt's abilities with those of his sire and of Diavolo, the Wheatley Stable colt that Fitzsimmons had trained to victories in the two-mile Jockey Club Gold Cup and the 2¼-mile Pimlico Cup, among other long-distance wins:

> So you will see that to classify Omaha with his daddy, Gallant Fox, and with Diavolo as a long-distance horse, one is establishing a high standard of merit. Omaha has his pathway to fame open to him. So far he has done remarkably well, particularly over long routes. If he keeps on, maybe he'll reach the heights—which Gallant Fox and Diavolo did. But it's too early to predict this, save in this fashion— Omaha is on his way.[35]

With a focus on the route-running skills of the third Triple Crown winner, his remaining starts for 1935 fit that mold—except one. His next start, the Dwyer Stakes, was another nine-furlong test, but this time he would face other three-year-olds again. Perhaps the turn in the Brooklyn had not been such a risk after all. After running longer races as he skipped from Louisville to Baltimore to New York, that shorter race geared Omaha down for the next challenge in the Dwyer. A week after the Brooklyn and three weeks after Omaha's Belmont Stakes victory, William Woodward sent the son of Gallant Fox after another prized New York stakes. As Omaha trod the same path the Fox had navigated, his owner hoped the horse could duplicate another of his sire's accomplishments: adeptness at shorter distances.

16

The Belair Bullet Rolls On

In 1920, Man o' War came into the nine-furlong Dwyer Stakes with virtually no peer in sight. Of his four starts so far that year, he had set two track records at Belmont Park and carried 135 pounds to an easy victory in the Stuyvesant Handicap. With each start, racing secretaries were running into an absence of competition for the dominant colt, but Harry Payne Whitney had one more trick up his sleeve: John P. Grier. Man o' War dueled with the Whitney colt down the long Aqueduct stretch, neither gaining an advantage and both testing the other in a way that no other had. In the end, it took the rare crack of Kummer's whip on Man o' War's flank to push the immortal to victory over John P. Grier.[1] In 1935, fifteen years after that battle and five years after his sire's win in the same race, Omaha would find little in the way of tough competition in his own Dwyer.

Again, the field he was to face was a small one. With so many good three-year-olds racing elsewhere or on the shelf with injuries, the list was a handful of horses who carried fewer pounds than Omaha, their résumés not deep enough to be weighted at the same 126 pounds. Good Gamble, winner of the one-mile Acorn Stakes, was the most accomplished in the field, but her status as a filly had her carrying 114 pounds. She and Vanderbilt stablemate Cold Shoulder, who had faced Omaha in the Belmont, offered the stoutest competition for the Belair colt. Although both Cheshire and Thorson had been reported as training well prior to the Dwyer, the race was a step up for those two and most turf writers admitted that none of the horses provided anything close to the challenge that John P. Grier had posed all those years ago.[2]

Dwyer Day, June 29, was a sunny summer's day in New York, bringing out a crowd of twenty thousand to Aqueduct to see the day's show. In the fourth race, Boxthorn passed up a chance to face Omaha again in favor of beating Peace Chance, the 1934 Belmont Stakes winner, in the Hornpipe Handicap.[3] The next race was the Dwyer; five horses paraded onto the track to meet the starter. If Good Gamble, a notorious bad actor at the gate, could get off to a good start, could she knock off the favored Omaha? He was carrying twelve pounds more than he had in the Brooklyn, a race that he did not factor in, but he had turned in a fast one-mile workout in 1:37¾ three days earlier.[4] The Triple Crown winner looked ready to take on the shorter distance; and, if he could pull off a victory at a mile and an eighth in the Dwyer, it would give Omaha another stake win and another parallel with his dominant sire.

At the post, Omaha stood next to Good Gamble on his right and Thorson on the rail. The filly was again restless at the start, delaying the proceedings and forcing starter George Cassidy to move her to the outside of the gate. Her new position allowed her to start fast, quickly leading the field by two lengths when they were finally sent away. Thorson followed, but was soon eclipsed by Omaha, who got off to a quicker-than-usual start and sat just back of the filly into the backstretch. With Willie Saunders still absent from the saddle, Wayne Wright was on the Belair colt again; he allowed Omaha to relax into his stride before sending him after the filly. On the final turn, he was within a length of Good Gamble, still winging away on the lead, so Wright gave him a breather before their stretch run.[5] As they swung into the long straightaway, Omaha made his move.

He rushed up alongside the filly and raced on even terms for a furlong. Good Gamble held on valiantly, but the big colt was too much for her after a mile of running on the lead. Omaha powered past her, and Wright moved him to the rail as soon as they were clear. He crossed the wire a length and a half in front of Good Gam-

Omaha leads Good Gamble in the Dwyer Stakes at Aqueduct, June 29, 1935. Keeneland Library Cook Collection.

ble, who was many lengths ahead of third-place Cheshire. Thorson and Cold Shoulder brought up the rear, never a factor in the Dwyer.[6]

The Belair Bullet earned $9,200 and the title "king of the three-year-olds" for his Dwyer victory.[7] His triumph at nine furlongs demonstrated a versatility that previous races had hinted at, though future starts like the Travers Stakes at Saratoga and the Jockey Club Gold Cup at Belmont would ask him to revisit the stamina that he had staked his reputation on to that point. His next start, his next step down the same path his sire had trod, would send him west to Chicago. He had a date with a filly that had already proven she could conquer the colts, and, by all indications, she had the potential to spoil Omaha's try at the Arlington Classic.

La Troienne was a terrible racehorse. Her breeder Marcel Boussac, a French businessman and textile entrepreneur, clearly saw something lovely in the filly; he entered her in stakes events in France and then

England despite her woeful finishes.[8] After all, she was a daughter of the legendary French sire Teddy, who counted Sir Gallahad III among his illustrious progeny. Despite winning only $146 on the racetrack, La Troienne possessed enough quality that Colonel E. R. Bradley paid 1,250 guineas for her when Boussac put her and five others up for sale in England in late 1930.[9] Bradley brought her to the United States, where she became a *reine-de-course,* producing fourteen foals with ten winners, first for Bradley's Idle Hour Farm and later for Greentree Stable. La Troienne might have struck out as a racehorse, but her first foal for Bradley turned out to be a home run.

Black Helen's small stature did not immediately inspire confidence in her owner: at nine hundred pounds and barely fifteen hands, she was not entered for any of the prestigious juvenile stakes, a decision that Colonel Bradley would come to regret. Over the course of her two-year-old season, she won seven of her nine starts, including setting a track record for five furlongs at Arlington Park. While Nellie Flag might have been the best two-year-old filly of 1934, Black Helen was not too far behind her, and she emerged as the better of the two in 1935. But Black Helen's dominance was not limited to her own division; she won the Florida Derby and then the American Derby at Washington Park near Chicago, where she defeated Cold Shoulder, Roman Soldier, and Nellie Flag, all horses Omaha had previously faced and trounced.[10] With the victory at ten furlongs in the American Derby and eleven in the Coaching Club American Oaks, Black Helen had already proven that she was more than capable of meeting Omaha at the Arlington Classic's distance.

And Colonel Bradley was more than willing to put his money where his mouth was. He offered $100,000 to any takers—not necessarily aimed at William Woodward—that his Black Helen could beat Omaha. Bradley had said that Omaha's wins "had been at the expense of cheap three-year-olds."[11] Though he had complete confidence in his filly, by his foundational sire Black Toney, the master of Idle Hour Stock Farm was also a realist. He entered Bloodroot just in case Black Helen might not be up to the task, saying, "If Omaha should happen to catch Black Helen then Blood Root [*sic*] will beat them both."[12] Like John Lewy of the *Brooklyn Times Union,* Bradley was skeptical of the Triple Crown winner, suspicious of his success to that point, and sure of the superiority of his petite "Black Cyclone."[13]

Omaha's workout on the Wednesday before the Classic demonstrated that he was still a formidable foe no matter who was in the field. With the full weight of 126 pounds up, Omaha worked nine furlongs, going a mile in 1:36⅕ and then the full distance in 1:50 flat under restraint, his final time just three-fifths of a second off Arlington's record for 1⅛ miles. The performance astonished the morning crowd of horsemen present.[14] Yet it was not enough to edge the Bradley filly out of the headlines for the coming Classic.

Even though the race was carded with a field of eleven, the inches of newsprint devoted to the Classic in the days leading up to the July 20 race had it down to Black Helen versus Omaha. The race was not without its other challengers, like Roman Soldier, who had been a length and a half back of Omaha in the Kentucky Derby and had won the Detroit Derby in mid-June.[15] John and Fannie Hertz's Count Arthur, whose greatest victories were ahead of him, was also there; this son of Kentucky Derby winner Reigh Count was a winner of four races already in 1935. The *Daily Racing Form* touted St. Bernard as a dark horse on the strength of his quick mile in 1:36 over the fast Arlington surface, a time that suggested he might be one to watch. Certainly, all of these names had an advantage over Omaha: he was giving weight to every horse in the field. The more consistent horses like Black Helen and Roman Soldier had a three-to-five-pound advantage while the longer priced horses like Count Arthur and Bloodroot were the beneficiaries of an eight-to-thirteen-pound break in the weights. The question of weight, though, did not loom over this Arlington Classic; the race shaped up to be less about those factors and more about who would meet Omaha at the start. For all the speculation about the field, most were simply background players to the drama: the eyes of the racing world were upon Black Helen as the last barrier to Omaha's claim to the three-year-old crown.[16]

With up to fifty thousand expected to flock to Arlington for this race, the track prepared to accommodate such an immense crowd within the country's largest racetrack. The weather cooperated and a fast track and a hot, sunny day greeted fans as they flooded in for the day's races.[17] The grandstand and clubhouse overflowed, people spilling out on Arlington's slanting lawns as they craned for a sight of the horses in front of them, much as they had five years earlier. The seventh edition of the Arlington Classic echoed the second one in so many ways: the heat, the crowd, the white and red of Belair. Yet this edition did not have the luxury of the certainty of dominance that had permeated Gallant Fox's edition. Omaha had not found the winner's circle as consistently as his sire had; nevertheless, the bloodlines of Sir Gallahad III and Teddy, Wrack and Flying Fox imbued the Triple Crown winner with the necessary speed and stamina to put on a show.

And put on a show he did. They lined up in the Bahr gate, ten across after the scratch of Blackbirder, with long shot Malbrouk on the rail and Latonia Derby winner Tearout on the outside. Black Helen, St. Bernard, and Omaha stood in the middle of the field in posts five, six, and seven. The ten loaded with little fuss and were away within a minute, with Bloodroot the quickest out of the gate. Jockey Paul Keester hustled St. Bernard to the lead, and Don Meade moved Black Helen a length and a half behind him in second.[18] Wayne Wright moved Omaha to the outside of the pack, running in seventh, to the dismay of the crowd. At the half-mile mark, he was eighth, and Wright kept a tight rein on him as they waited for the leaders to play out their hands. St. Bernard maintained his length and a half advantage over Black Helen, flying on the front end with quick fractions—0:23⅕ for the quarter and 0:47⅖ for the half mile—but unable to separate himself more from Black Helen and the rest of the field. In the backstretch's waning yards, Omaha began his move.[19]

On the outside, he picked off horses one by one as he built momentum for the stretch run. At three-quarters, he was sixth, but he improved his position with each stride, moving past Malbrouk

Omaha and jockey Wayne Wright at the Dwyer Stakes, June 29, 1935.
Keeneland Library Cook Collection.

and Bloodroot, then Chief Cherokee and Black Helen with ease.[20] As they swept out of that final turn and aimed for the wire, Omaha was second: only a length separated him and St. Bernard. As he challenged the front-runner, the crowd roared, echoing a day five years earlier when another Belair bullet came flying down the Arlington stretch.[21]

In the straightaway, Omaha pulled even with St. Bernard. Wright rode his mount hard to pass the challenger and then put daylight between them. With the momentum of his great stride and the heart he needed to dig deep and *go,* Omaha flew past St. Bernard. He sailed out to a length and a half lead amid the wild applause of a crowd in thrall.[22] Behind them, Bloodroot was a scant head back of St. Bernard in third, with Black Helen on her heels in fourth. Colonel Bradley's fillies were no problem for the Belair champion, and, with this win over Black Helen, Omaha clinched the three-year-old championship, even though other starts like the Travers and Jockey Club Gold Cup were still to come.[23] In addition to sealing the championship, he had set a track record for a mile and a quarter: his 2:01⅖ bettered Sun Beau's record by two-fifths of a second. With his share of the race's $36,500 purse, Omaha had amassed $146,105 in winnings; all but $3,850 came from his six victories in 1935.[24]

The sight of the Belair white and red returning to the Arlington winner's circle was a familiar one, 1930 echoed in 1935. This time, the horse was a bronzed chestnut rather than a red bay; his legs were longer and his head higher than his sire's. The continuity of father to son in this race and the others they had in common epitomized the Belair Stud in the 1930s: dominant, consistent, and victorious. At the center of it was the white-haired banker who, in his drive for one elusive prize, had taken down many more along the way. As a sign of the continuity of Belair, his daughter Edith Woodward Bancroft, who was destined to own a champion herself, accepted the Arlington Classic trophy in her father's absence. The elder Woodward was traveling in Europe as his son of Gallant Fox came home victorious.[25]

As for Black Helen and Bloodroot, the two fillies Colonel Bradley had sent to challenge Omaha, their plot to beat the Triple Crown winner had not taken into account St. Bernard, who upended any strategy the Colonel might have laid out for his two jockeys.[26] Though the fillies came home third and fourth, their loss to Omaha did not diminish the greatness they ultimately found as broodmares. Both were dynamic racehorses; Black Helen won fifteen of her twenty-two starts and Bloodroot, who often played second fiddle to her stablemate, won eight of twenty-eight and finished second in races like the Coaching Club American Oaks and the Maryland Handicap.[27] They passed on their talents to the next generation, with twenty-five foals and sixteen winners between them; Bloodroot was also named the first Broodmare of the Year in 1946.[28] These two Idle Hour homebreds carried forward pedigrees that featured La Troienne, Blue Larkspur, and Black Toney, great on both the track and in the breeding shed themselves, to produce winners for both

Colonel Bradley and later Ogden Phipps. Bradley had said that Omaha's wins came against the best of a bad lot of horses.[29] Given the quality of horses like Black Helen and Bloodroot, Bradley's comment might have been a bit off the mark.

With the Classic won, what was next for Omaha? His sire had skipped the Arlington Handicap and instead had been shipped to Saratoga to prepare for the important races to come. Fitzsimmons wanted to keep Omaha in Chicago to race again, possibly in the Arlington Handicap against Discovery if the weights were favorable. All he needed was the word from William Woodward. Even though the weights for the Arlington Handicap had Discovery giving Omaha seventeen pounds, Woodward declined the opportunity and opted to ship Omaha on to Saratoga to prepare for the season at the Spa. His next stop? The Travers Stakes, the same race that had seen Gallant Fox fail in ignominious defeat to the longest of long shots on a muddy track. Would this son of the Fox take down the Midsummer Derby and bring Belair its first Travers? Could he do what his sire had not?

In eight weeks, Omaha had blown through five of the biggest races offered in North America, coming out of it with three wins and two defeats. While he was not quite his sire in the win column, he was proving to be faster; he ran races like the Arlington Classic in track record time and clocked sharper times in all his Triple Crown races. Still, his trainer judged Gallant Fox to be the better of the two, calling the Fox the greatest he had ever trained and "the best ever bred in America."[30] With more races to go, Omaha had more to prove to earn the same place in Fitzsimmons's estimation that Gallant Fox had in his time. As he boarded a train to Saratoga Springs, still a fresh horse after his record-breaking turn at Arlington, the son still had time to step out from his sire's shadow.

17

An Unexpected Stop

As the bugle's call summoned the racing world to the eternal charm of Saratoga Springs, the ghosts of Travers past lingered in the morning mist and the shadow of the next Jim Dandy hung over the coming contest. "It would seem as though," observed New York turf writer W. C. Vreeland, "there were a hoodoo or something—call it what you will—in connection with the Travers."[1] That something had hoodooed Omaha before he had even stepped a hoof on Saratoga's surface. The third Triple Crown winner had gone amiss.

After his triumph in the Classic at Arlington, Omaha was rumored to be starting against the ascendant Discovery in the Arlington Handicap, but, like his sire, Omaha passed up that race and was shipped to Saratoga instead.[2] A few races remained on the lanky son of Gallant Fox's list for 1935, including the chance to avenge his sire's infamous loss in the 1930 Travers Stakes. Since the Kentucky Derby, though, Omaha had grown, gaining almost two hundred pounds; his body was stronger, his quarters and flanks more muscular.[3] The long, lanky colt was a maturing horse, and, with two weeks until the Travers, he had plenty of time to get ready for another meeting with Today and finally bring William Woodward his Travers.

One late July morning, Omaha worked seven furlongs with no trouble, but then returned to the barn sore. Fitzsimmons was concerned, but not enough to count the colt out of the race just yet. After two more workouts produced the same result, the trainer knew that Omaha would not make it to the Travers and that he likely would miss the Saratoga Cup too.[4] After a veterinarian's examination, the trainer ruled the big colt out for the entirety of the Saratoga meet; he shared with W. C. Vreeland that the trouble was a left shoulder injury that likely happened right before the Arlington Classic.[5]

The culprit was something innocuous to the casual eye. When it comes to racing, a dry racetrack is the ideal surface for peak performance. Yet not all dry surfaces are the same. A fast track is "dry, even, and *resilient*."[6] It does not give under the hooves of a horse going at top speed; it bounces back, firm enough to support the impact but not so firm that it will jar bone or muscle. A cuppy track is another story; it is dry as well but is a "loose racing surface that breaks away under a horse's hooves."[7] When a horse runs at top speed over crumbling soil that can become uneven underneath, it creates a prime opportunity for incidental muscle strain that can become a larger problem. In this case, Omaha worked out right before the Arlington Classic over a cuppy surface and, in the process, strained his left shoulder. But the injury did not show up until after his record performance in the Classic, just in time to derail his chances at any of the Saratoga races. No Travers. No rematch with Today. No Saratoga Cup. No chance of mirroring his sire's path further. Omaha was on the shelf until Fitzsimmons was comfortable letting him train again.

After the long shot Gold Foam won the Travers, it was clear that Omaha was still the leading three-year-old of the year. Even though he was sidelined, his Triple Crown and Arlington Classic wins were enough to head the wide-open division. Count Arthur won the Saratoga Cup. Woodward had wanted Omaha to compete for the Cup as his champion sire had, but the strained shoulder kept him from the starting gate.[8] Same with the Belmont meet in September. Firethorn won the two-mile Jockey Club Gold Cup and the 1⅝-mile Lawrence Realization; these were both races that Gallant Fox had won and that had been intended targets for his son.[9] When Fitzsimmons attempted to bring the Belair champion back to training in mid-September, he showed little of the trouble that pesky injury had caused and seemed raring to go after nearly two months off.[10]

Then, despite those promising signs, the strained muscles in his shoulders acted up again when Omaha had difficulty cooling out after his trials. Content to be patient with the colt, Fitzsimmons and Woodward opted to retire Omaha for the season.[11]

"Sunny Jim" Fitzsimmons had nothing more he could do with Omaha, who was unable to train or compete until that shoulder trouble was healed. Instead of keeping him at Aqueduct with the rest of Fitzsimmons's horses, he was shipped back to Maryland to recover at Belair Stud.[12] There, the question became what was next for Omaha. William Woodward already had Gallant Fox at stud so retiring this son to Claiborne Farm seemed a bit premature. Still, if he were not needed in the breeding shed, would he be able to race again? At Belair, after several weeks of recovery time in the care of groom Joe Donellan, Omaha began slow gallops in mid-October, with the intent of both strengthening and testing that tenuous shoulder.[13] That gave way to talk about another possible season, this time in England, where Omaha would compete in 1936 in races like the Ascot Gold Cup. W. C. Vreeland had indulged in just such speculation earlier in 1935, and Omaha's new training regimen seemed to confirm it.[14] The 2½-mile Gold Cup, whose history dated back to 1807, represented another of those traditional prizes that Woodward valued, much like the three-year-old classics of both the English and American Triple Crowns. To win that stakes at Royal Ascot, the most celebrated meet on the English calendar, was to achieve something on par with winning the Epsom Derby. Woodward's childhood ambition to own a racehorse and win a Derby had expanded; it now included winning as many classic races as possible, the Ascot Gold Cup near the top of that list.

If Omaha stood up to this light training at Belair, another year older and months removed from the series of tests that marked his summer campaign, he could do something that neither Sir Barton nor his sire had done: win in England. In the near century since, no other Triple Crown winner has ever traveled overseas to compete against the best that the rest of the world had to offer. This would be an unprecedented journey, but Woodward was determined to follow in James Keene's footsteps and bring the Gold Cup home to America.

With his 1936 decided, Omaha was shipped from Belair back to Fitzsimmons's barn at Aqueduct. There, he would continue to work out and await the arrival of Woodward's English trainer, Captain Cecil Boyd-Rochfort. The Englishman would evaluate Omaha's fitness for a new season of racing, and then, if Boyd-Rochfort felt he were ready, Omaha would accompany the trainer back to England.[15] As 1935 came to a close, Omaha found himself back in a familiar stall facing familiar tasks, unaware of just how singular and historic he was.

Meanwhile, his former jockey, the man who had been tapped as the right pilot for the quirky colt during his Triple Crown run, was making history of his own, trading in fame for infamy over one fateful night in October.

Willie Saunders's illness in June 1935 had prevented him from riding the Belair champion in his remaining starts. Instead, Wayne Wright had inherited the job until that shoulder strain necessitated the end of Omaha's three-year-old season. By mid-July, Saunders was back in the saddle; by fall he was riding under contract for Hal Price Headley.[16] Willie Saunders had gone from his youth in Montana to riding in California, where he studied race riding with George Woolf as his tutor; now, at age twenty, he was riding for the country's biggest stables.[17] His success as a high-profile jockey meant that he had money, a potential recipe for trouble.

On the evening of October 20, Saunders and his friend Walter Schaeffer, an exercise rider, decided to spend their evening at Howard's, a Louisville bar and dance club. The club would not let gentlemen in without dates, so the bouncer asked a regular, Agatha Mackinson, to accompany Saunders and Schaeffer. The men, who introduced themselves as Jimmie and Tommy, still needed a second female companion and suggested that Mackinson invite Evelyn Sliwinski, who appeared to be alone, to join them. After the four danced and drank at Howard's, they decided to move their festivities to two other clubs, Venexia Gardens and then the Cotton Club.[18] The evening's revelries included liberal amounts of both drink and dance, and some friction arose between the newly introduced Saunders and Sliwinski.

As Mackinson related in her statement, Saunders and Sliwinski argued over her approaching another man during their last stop at the Cotton Club. To diffuse the tension, they took the party outside, but the two continued to argue; later, Mackinson accused Saunders of striking Sliwinski. One of the men next suggested the four go for a ride in Schaeffer's car to get some air. As they drove down a dark River Road in Louisville, a drunk Sliwinski vomited; then she either asked to get out of the car or was urged to get out when they stopped on the side of the road. She did, but, still drunk, started to stagger. Mackinson alleged that Sliwinski staggered into the road and that the inebriated Schaeffer hit her with his car, killing her. A local teenager and his date found Sliwinski's body on River Road early the next day.[19] From Mackinson's statement, the police identified Saunders, and he identified Schaeffer as his companion on that fateful evening. The two were arrested for murder. Saunders's charges were later changed to accessory to murder.[20] Their trial was set for January 1936, but the damage was already done.

As his Triple Crown champion slowly recovered from that nagging shoulder strain, William Woodward continued his duties as chairman of the Jockey Club. He was invited to speak at the Thoroughbred Club of America's annual testimonial dinner as their outstanding turfman of the year. Founded in Lexington, Kentucky, by a collection of prominent turfmen, the organization promoted the sport and provided its members with a forum for discussing the issues of breeding, owning, and racing in the United States. As chairman and as the master of Belair, Woodward spent decades of his life focused on building a powerhouse breeding and racing operation and on using his drive and knowledge to win prizes like the Epsom Derby. Also, as he laid out in his speech to the Thoroughbred Club's gathered members, he was invested in the long-term health of the breed and had a particular issue with England's *General Stud Book*: "I am very anxious to see the day, before I shuffle off this mortal coil, when those gentlemen will recognize our American stud book in its entirety."[21] Horses sired by the prolific American stallion Lexington had been excluded from the *General Stud Book* because his pedigree contained a horse of uncertain parentage, so any American-bred sire standing in England could not have their progeny listed in the Stud Book. This did not prevent those horses from racing; however, that "questionable" connection, despite being multiple generations removed, reduced their value at stud considerably.

Woodward had spent time in England as a young man and had befriended such important figures in the country's racing scene as King Edward VII and Lord Derby; since then he had devoted years of his life and chunks of his fortune to building both his American and English stables. To him, it was not only in his own best interest that the English accept American horses but also in the best interest of those in the audience listening to him and of the organization he led. This would become a central goal of Woodward's tenure at the Jockey Club. Its ultimate realization, however, would take another decade and a half.

The Thoroughbred Club of America's annual dinner was just one of the markers of the year's end. As 1935 wound to a close, newspapers engaged in a collective assessment of events across the world of sports. The Detroit Tigers had defeated the Chicago Cubs to win baseball's World Series. College football inaugurated the Heisman Trophy in 1935, crowning Jay Berwanger, a halfback for the University of Chicago, as its first winner. The year was also the last in which the collegiate football championship was decided by entities other than the Associated Press; the winner was anointed by an AP writers' poll starting in 1936. As for awards like Horse of the Year and others, 1935 marked the last year without authoritative voting for such honors. The *Daily Racing Form* and *Morning Telegram* instituted their own poll, and *Turf and Sport Digest* started theirs in 1936. In the end, for the one and only time since the Triple Crown became a part of American horse racing, its winner was not considered the year's best horse. Instead, that honor went to Discovery, who had beaten Omaha in the Brooklyn Handicap. With a record of eleven wins in nineteen starts, Discovery's wins in the Suburban, Brooklyn, and Arlington Handicaps plus the Whitney Stakes and the Narragansett Special made him the Horse of the Year for 1935. Though abbreviated compared to his sire's, Omaha's three-year-old campaign marked him as the year's best three-year-old and the leading money winner. With his four-year-old campaign on the horizon, 1936 promised great things for this son of Gallant Fox.

On another cold December day, Captain Cecil Boyd-Rochfort stepped back onto American soil for his annual sojourn stateside. His agenda included a visit with William Woodward and "Sunny Jim" Fitzsimmons at Aqueduct and an inspection of the newly recovered Omaha. The tall Brit was there to determine whether the third Triple Crown winner was ready to try the English turf and the marathon tests of races like the Ascot Gold Cup. Omaha, already a proven champion, seemed the perfect candidate to make the jump overseas to England and show the Brits that American horses could hold their own and more against their English-bred competition. What better way to convince the Jockey Club in England to open their stud book to American horses than to send the best that the country had to offer across the Atlantic to try the same tests that the English valued?

He would not be the first American classic winner to try. John and Fannie Hertz had sent their Kentucky Derby winner Reigh Count to England to try for the Ascot Gold Cup in his four-year-old season in 1929. At three, Reigh Count had won not only the Derby but also the 1¾-mile Saratoga Cup, the 1⅝-mile Lawrence Realization, and the 2-mile Jockey Club Gold Cup.[22] "We believe Reigh Count the best Thoroughbred in the world," John Hertz said. "He's over there to prove it."[23] When he returned to the United States later

Captain Cecil Boyd-Rochfort, trainer for the English stables of William Woodward, Marshall Field III, and other Americans. National Museum of Racing and Hall of Fame Collection.

that year, Reigh Count had won the Coronation Cup and finished second in the Ascot Gold Cup. The Hertzes, satisfied with Reigh Count's accomplishments both at home and abroad, retired their champion to stud once he was back stateside, opting not to try for Gold Cup glory again. In 1935, as Omaha earned his Triple Crown, Greentree Stables' Twenty Grand, who had won the Kentucky Derby and the Belmont Stakes the year after Gallant Fox did, came out of retirement to try racing in England. Despite the best efforts of trainer Cecil Boyd-Rochfort, he was less successful than Reigh Count; Twenty Grand returned to the United States in late 1935 and subsequently retired for the second time to Greentree Farm.[24] William Woodward was betting that Omaha's sojourn would be more like that of Reigh Count and that it would bring him more of the triumphs he sought each time he sent horses overseas.

First, Omaha had to pass muster with his new trainer. Boyd-Rochfort watched as the Triple Crown winner was put to the test, a breeze over the Aqueduct surface. Although he had been galloping during his convalescence at Belair, he needed to be put to work like any other racehorse. His time at Belair and then at Aqueduct earned the approval of his owner and of Boyd-Rochfort: "Since arriving at Aqueduct he has been working daily under cover. He seems to be in the best of condition and in vigorous health, Woodward observed."[25] Under rider and saddle, Omaha had shown he was ready for another season of racing; this time he was set to do what Reigh Count had been unable to do, what no American horse since Foxhall in 1882 had done: win the Ascot Gold Cup.

On January 2, 1936, William Woodward announced that Omaha would depart for England on January 8, sailing aboard Cunard's RMS *Aquitania*.[26] Six days later, in the dark of predawn, Omaha left his stall at Aqueduct for the last time and boarded a van destined for the *Aquitania*'s dock. With both William Woodward and "Sunny Jim" Fitzsimmons looking on, the tall chestnut champion, his ears poking out of a leather helmet and legs wrapped from fetlock to hip, walked with Bart Sweeney and James Ahearn up the ramp to the deck of the *Aquitania*. There, he would occupy a padded stall with a back window on Passenger Deck C, the same stall in which both Reigh Count and Épinard had traveled, for his week-long voyage from New York to Southampton, England.

As his champion colt started his journey to this next phase of his racing career, William Woodward, already the owner of two Triple Crown winners and an accomplished breeder, kept his eyes on the prizes that had eluded him: wins in races like the Ascot Gold Cup. Omaha had a solid chance at bringing home that prize, provided he could take to the grass as he had to dirt. "I have great hopes for him," Woodward said, "Omaha has always been a favorite with me since the first time I saw him as a gawky yearling."[27] Three years later, that gawky yearling was America's best hope for dominating British race-courses, his long stride and adeptness at running a route of ground promising success.

Fitzsimmons, for his part, understood the challenges the big horse was about to undertake. As the ship moved away from the dock, the legendary trainer ruminated on what was ahead for Wood-ward's horse: "Omaha has one of the toughest assignments ahead of him that ever faced any racehorse, but somehow I have a hunch that he will show the same courage and stamina on the other side that he did in this country."[28]

If he could stay sound, that is.

A week later, the *Aquitania* arrived in Southampton without inci-dent. Omaha was in good health after his transatlantic voyage. Sweeney fitted the horse with a bridle and a halter as he prepared to disembark from the sleek ocean liner. Omaha came down the gang-way and then was loaded onto a van for the drive to Captain Boyd-Rochfort's yard at Freemason Lodge in Newmarket. As he walked up the ramp, Omaha threw his head up and a thick leather piece on the halter caught on the van's door. As he pulled back, the halter and the bridle both came off, leaving the men nearby with no way to catch the loose horse as he backed down the ramp. Suddenly free, Omaha ran free on the Southampton Docks, its open gate his destination.

With men trying to flag him down, he diverted down to the water's edge, but found the footing there too loose for his unshod feet. Omaha backed out of the water and turned around and trotted toward the waiting group of men.[29] Frank Perry, one of Captain Boyd-Rochfort's employees, had been tasked with meeting the *Aquitania* and was on the dock waiting for the American horse. Perry ran after the loose Omaha and lured his new charge with sugar, which was enough of a treat that the horse consented to being caught. Soon, the Ascot hopeful was loaded on a van and sent to Littleton Stud near Winchester for the night.[30] The next day, they continued the journey to Freemason Lodge and a new beginning for this Belair champion.

The day after the *Aquitania* departed for its journey across the Atlantic, a jury acquitted Walter Schaeffer of the murder of Evelyn Sliwinski.[31] As a result, the presiding judge dropped the charges of accessory to murder against Willie Saunders, whose trial had been set to begin shortly after Schaeffer's concluded.[32] The Triple Crown–winning jockey was free, his legal troubles over. No longer connected to Belair or Fitzsimmons, Saunders was able to return to his contract to ride for Hal Price Headley. He was scheduled to ride Headley's Hollyrood in the Kentucky Derby, but his request for a jockey's license in Kentucky was denied that season. Saunders's legal troubles likely contributed to the denial, though the Kentucky Racing Commission did not comment on the refusal publicly.[33] Headley opted to skip the Kentucky Derby after Hollyrood's poor finish in the Wood Memorial.[34] Saunders would not ride in the Derby again; Omaha remained his only mount and his only winner in America's most famous race.

By the time America went to war in 1941, Saunders's battles with weight had made it a challenge to continue riding. He had some successes: he won the Black-Eyed Susan Stakes on Glen Riddle Farm's Sweet Desire, the San Juan Capistrano Handicap with Whopper for Hal Price Headley, and the Santa Margarita Handicap

on Stand Pat for Edward Seagram.[35] Saunders served in the mecha-
nized cavalry in the Pacific Theater of World War II; during his four
years there, he contracted malaria, which resulted in significant
weight loss. When he returned to America in 1946, he was able to
resume riding, going on to win the Louisiana Derby aboard Bovard
and then finishing third in the 1948 Preakness Stakes. In 1950, he
retired from riding and then worked as a racing official at tracks in
Florida, Illinois, and New Jersey for twenty-seven years before fully
retiring.[36] He was inducted into the Canadian Horse Racing Hall of
Fame in 1976.[37] Saunders passed away from cancer on July 30, 1986,
at age seventy-one. He remains one of two Triple Crown–winning
jockeys that have yet to be inducted into the National Museum of
Racing and Hall of Fame.

The new year brought a new start and a new country for the third
Triple Crown winner, another attempt at the American classics for
both Woodward and Fitzsimmons, and an exoneration for the young
man who had ridden Omaha to victory in those American classics.
With the new year, though, came new challenges. The goal was the
twenty-furlong Ascot Gold Cup, a prize valued by horsemen on
both sides of the Atlantic. But Omaha's racing experience had come
on dirt, not grass, and this was just one of the tests that the Belair
champion would have to face. William Woodward had faith in the
brilliant son of Gallant Fox, anticipating that his prized colt would
bring the white with red polka dots the royal victory he sought.

18

Trailblazer

Less than a week after Omaha arrived on the *Aquitania,* England was thrust into a state of national mourning: King George V died after a long battle with chronic bronchitis and other ongoing health issues. With his passing, his son Edward, the Prince of Wales, succeeded him, adopting the regnal name Edward VIII. The new king, suddenly forced into the responsibilities of monarch and head of state, had no taste for his duties; he shirked court protocol and showed disdain for the conventions of ruling. The royal stable continued as did the royal family's pleasure in the sport; mourning, however, would keep them absent from the biggest racing festivals in 1936. Nevertheless, the show went on, and the American champion was a topic of much conversation as the new season began.

Omaha had weathered his transatlantic voyage well, and, despite his dockside adventure in Southampton, arrived at Freemason Lodge without incident. Boyd-Rochfort assigned him to Willie Stephenson, an aspiring jockey; he became Omaha's regular morning rider and worked with the newly arrived colt as they prepared him for the season's racing.[1] Boyd-Rochfort needed the right lad for this job, for Omaha was "a big, powerful horse, in every way, standing sixteen hands, 2½ inches, very deep through the heart, long through the back, and wanting plenty of work."[2] Stephenson, who would later train winners of the Epsom Derby and the Grand National, had his hands full with the "rather crazy, hot-headed horse"; Omaha needed the Englishman's guidance to learn to calm down and settle as he adjusted to his new surroundings.[3] In addition to being a bit erratic,

Omaha had a voracious appetite, not just for corn but also rugs—he ate a couple in the early weeks of his tenure at Freemason Lodge.[4] For the first part of the year, following exercise with others on the Newmarket greens for a couple of hours each day, Omaha would walk back to the barn, part of the slow buildup to racing in the late spring.[5] His ultimate target was Royal Ascot, but Omaha would start his 1936 season with the Victor Wild Stakes at Kempton Park in early May.

Also at Freemason Lodge with Omaha was his full brother Flares. Unlike Omaha, who Woodward had selected to race in the United States at two and three, Flares was sent to England as a yearling, where Boyd-Rochfort was in charge of his training and racing for the whole of his career. Unraced at age two, Flares would begin his career at age three; this son of Gallant Fox needed even more time than his brother to grow into his body and find his racing form.

In late February, as Omaha prepared for his first date with the starter, surprising news came out of Freemason Lodge: no photographers or fans were allowed to observe the Triple Crown winner's training. As twenty of Boyd-Rochfort's horses moved throughout the yard, taking their exercise around Newmarket, the Woodward horse was virtually indistinguishable from his compatriots unless one were especially savvy in picking him out from a crowd.[6] A correspondent from the *Observer* did have a chance to visit Boyd-Rochfort's facility and meet Omaha in the flesh for the first time: "I was considerably impressed with the colt's exceptional length and range. He stands over a great deal of ground and his rare length from hip to hock gives this upstanding horse something of the greyhound appearance."[7] Given Omaha's size and scope, the colt looked like one that "needs some time to settle down to his work," with "an immense stride" best suited for racing longer distances, like that of the Ascot Gold Cup among other English features.[8] Yet, for all of Omaha's advantages in conformation and style, the racing correspondent for the *Observer* still judged that horses like Bobsleigh, Lord Derby's son of Gainsborough, and Lord Astor's Field Trial looked as good as or better than the American invader.[9] While his reputation preceded him and clearly gave him some gravitas on the English racing scene, Omaha needed to race to show where he belonged within the ranks of his new counterparts.

To acclimate his new charge to the demands of racing on the grass in a new country, Boyd-Rochfort regularly sent Omaha out on the Newmarket heath for gallops with his stablemates. A long line of trainees would emerge from the lodge, sometimes sheathed with blankets and other times "stripped" of cover; they would walk to the storied training grounds around Newmarket to gallop or canter, either for a handful of furlongs or longer, sometimes up to two miles. What these gallops could not do, though, was give the Triple Crown winner the experience of racing on an English course, over grass rather than dirt and also going clockwise, with turns to the right unlike his years of turning left on American courses. Omaha would need the right jockey to help him with this transition, and the newest first jockey for the Boyd-Rochfort stable was the perfect candidate for that job.

Patrick Thomas Beasley came from an Irish racing family. His father, Harry Beasley, was the Irish trainer who rode Come Away to victory in the 1891 Grand National. Young Pat began riding as an amateur in 1923 and then turned professional when he shifted his tack to England in 1926. He first rode for Jim Joel, son of Epsom Derby–winning breeder Jack Joel, and then for trainer Victor Gilpin and noted owner Dorothy Paget before signing on with Boyd-Rochfort in 1936.[10] Nicknamed "Rufus" for his blond hair, Beasley would find success with the horses of Freemason Lodge until he joined the Royal Air Force when World War II broke out.[11] In his first years with Boyd-Rochfort, Beasley was aboard several Belair horses for their victories in notable English races. His success and skill earned him a chance to pilot Omaha as he prepared for his turn in the Ascot Gold Cup.

As the Triple Crown winner got closer to his first start, Beasley was regularly seen in the stirrups for his training gallops. The British papers reported on this equine celebrity's movements throughout his preparations. His name had initially appeared in the entries for the April 15 Spring Plate, a nine-furlong stake at Newmarket that also featured Bobsleigh and Plassy, both owned by Lord Derby.[12] However, on the day of the race, when reports emerged that Omaha would not go to the post for the Spring Plate, there was speculation that Boyd-Rochfort was not yet satisfied with the colt's preparations.[13] Instead, the trainer decided to target the March Stakes at Newmarket on April 30, a ten-furlong stakes where he would face Plassy and Quashed, 1935's Epsom Oaks winner.[14] That race came and went, though, with no Omaha. Instead, in early May, the entries for Kempton Park listed Omaha as an entrant for the Victor Wild Stakes, a mile-and-a-half stake named for the Royal Hunt Cup winner and contemporary of 1893 English Triple Crown winner, Isinglass.

Nearly two hours from Newmarket, Kempton Park had started out as an estate whose origins date back to an entry from the Domesday Book in the year 1086; in 1871, businessman Samuel Hyde happened upon the estate on a carriage ride through the countryside and envisioned building a racecourse there.[15] He leased the land and built what is now one of England's premier racetracks. First opened in 1878, Kempton Park got a boost in prestige when the Prince of Wales, Albert Edward, visited in 1889. Now, with the Ascot Gold Cup only six weeks away, the Kempton Park meet was the perfect place for another royal, this one American, to make his first appearance.[16]

He would face a field of five others, including Marshall Field's Enfield, a fellow American entry. Although Omaha had looked good in his gallops at Newmarket, the eight-and-a-half-month layoff since the Triple Crown winner's last start the previous July left many suspecting that he needed a race before he could show his best form. "The American crack is undoubtedly a good horse, but there is the danger that he may not do himself full justice in strange conditions," wrote "Bouverie" in the *Daily Mirror*.[17] The recent ill luck of American stars like Mate and Twenty Grand had not dimmed British enthusiasm for the Belair champion's attempt to race in their

Omaha with jockey Patrick Beasley and groom Bart Sweeney. Keeneland Library Thoroughbred Times.

country, but he was not the pick for the Victor Wild. As the race grew closer, Montrose and Nightcap III prevailed as the picks of many writers, but Omaha remained the odds-on favorite.

Instead, the American challenger surprised them all with his performance at Kempton Park. In front of an eager crowd, Omaha showed why he had been such a champion in his native country the year before, as he won the Victor Wild by a length and a half. The long layoff did not seem to matter. The standing start at the barrier did not faze him. The absence of the same blinkers he ran in at two and three did not matter. He navigated the new surface and right-hand turns like an old pro, running in the same style he always had. Pat Beasley kept Omaha under wraps, lingering at the back of the field for the first part of the race; when they hit the top of the stretch at Kempton Park, the Irish jockey gave Omaha permission to go. The Belair champion's long stride ate up ground as he passed Enfield, Lobau, and Montrose to win comfortably. With that, Omaha demonstrated why he went to the barrier the favorite and the Kempton Park crowd clearly saw the form that Boyd-Rochfort had developed in the American champion.[18]

Beasley counted himself among those impressed by the son of Gallant Fox after that ride. "Omaha is one of the greatest horses I've ever ridden," the Irishman proclaimed after the race. "He was so full of run all the way, but I held him back until we had rounded the last bend. All I had to do was turn him loose."[19] With that performance, Omaha showed himself to be "a worthy contender" for the elusive Ascot Gold Cup, just six weeks hence.[20] To continue his preparations for that iconic race, Boyd-Rochfort targeted the Queen's Plate, also at Kempton Park, three weeks later.

Though the Coronation Cup at Epsom had been another possible landing spot for the Triple Crown winner, the two-mile Queen's Plate was closer to the Gold Cup's distance of two and a half miles. With an abbreviated campaign for Ascot, trainer Boyd-Rochfort needed to get more mileage into his American candidate, and that two-mile race, just under three weeks before Ascot, was a great spot to get it. He was to face Bobsleigh, the Richmond and Newmarket Stakes winner owned by Lord Derby, and three others, Heartbreak, Silverlit, and Crawley Wood. In addition, his victory in the Victor Wild earned him another status: the highest weight in the field. Yet, despite the new impost, observers knew that a repeat performance in the Queen's Plate would make Omaha a formidable challenger for the Ascot Gold Cup.[21]

For his part, Bobsleigh was no rival to be discounted. The year before, he had been touted as one of eventual Triple Crown–winner Bahram's biggest challengers for the Epsom Derby, but Lord Derby had had to scratch his contender after he sustained an injury during training for that classic. By 1936, Bobsleigh had won the Richmond Stakes at age two and the Newmarket Stakes at three; but this son of

Gainsborough, English Triple Crown winner, had not equaled the level of excellence shown on the track by both his sire and his dam, Toboggan, winner of the 1928 Epsom Oaks.[22] Now, a month after his triumph in the Chippenham Stakes and with the Triple Crown winner giving him seven pounds, Bobsleigh could give Omaha a run for his money.

Enhancing Omaha's reputation prior to the Queen's Plate was Montrose's victory in the Durdans Handicap at Epsom. Omaha had beaten Montrose easily in the Victor Wild, impressing skeptical observers in the process. Couple that with Bobsleigh's most recent start, a loss to Taj Akbar in the Chester Vase Stakes at Chester Racecourse, and handicappers were quick to bestow favoritism upon the American challenger. Only three others would join them at Kempton Park, but none would pose a threat, which left "virtually a match race between Omaha and Bobsleigh, in which Omaha should come out the better."[23] The high regard accorded the Belair champion in his second start over the English turf turned out to be much deserved.

As the five horses met the starter on May 30, the skies over Kempton Park opened and soaked the scene but, fortunately for Omaha, not so much the ground. Heartbreak and Silverlit darted out to the lead at the break, with Crawley Wood trailing behind them and Bobsleigh and Omaha bringing up the rear. The pace was slow, which forced jockey Pat Beasley to hold Omaha in check. The big Belair horse resented this, and the legendary rider later remarked that "he [Omaha] does not like that kind of running."[24] With three furlongs to go, Bobsleigh and jockey Richard Perryman made their bid for the lead, but Pat Beasley would not let Lord Derby's horse get too far from them. With just a quarter of a mile to go, Pat Beasley put the Triple Crown winner in gear.[25]

With his great stride swallowing up the ground between the two, Omaha drew level with Bobsleigh, just inches separating the two driving horses. A quarter of a mile from the finish, one and three-quarters of a mile already behind them, the Triple Crown winner pushed his head in front and did not give way, increasing his margin to a neck over Bobsleigh in the race's final yards. With this show of speed and stamina, Omaha demonstrated once again that the American challenger was as at home on the undulating English turf as he had been on the flat dirt tracks of his first two seasons. "What a colt," the wee Irishman said after his ride on the big Belair champion.[26]

After the two duelists came also-rans Silverlit, Crawley Wood, and Heartbreak, bringing up the rear after a fierce battle up front. With less than three weeks to go before the Royal Ascot meet was to commence, that hard-fought victory at Kempton Park stamped Omaha as a serious contender for the Gold Cup, reminiscent of Reigh Count, who had finished second to Invershin in 1929. Though Twenty Grand and Mate had ventured to England to race in the interim, neither had shown what Reigh Count and then Omaha had: the stamina to run such demanding distances and the adaptability necessary to compete on a new surface in a new country.

Royal Ascot and its full slate of iconic races was less than a month away. As the gentlemen collected their tails and top hats and the ladies rushed to find the right dress and headwear for the occasion, Cecil Boyd-Rochfort and Pat Beasley prepared Omaha for his sternest test yet. William Woodward had sent his Triple Crown winner across the sea with this one goal in mind, the Ascot Gold Cup, and with it the chance to strengthen the argument that American horses merited inclusion in the Stud Book. Twenty furlongs stood between Omaha and yet another historic achievement. Would the third Triple Crown winner return to America with one more classic victory on his résumé?

19

The Big Show

In French, *la flêche* means "the arrow," a lethal weapon when shot straight and true. On the racetrack, La Flêche ran straight and true, winning all her races at age two and then the Oaks at Epsom and the St. Leger Stakes against the boys at three. In 1894, at age five, she followed in her sire's footsteps, winning the Ascot Gold Cup by three lengths *while in foal* to Morion, another Gold Cup winner.[1] With her victory, she became the eleventh filly or mare to win the Ascot Gold Cup in its history.[2] Forty-two years later, no other filly or mare had duplicated La Flêche's feat, but, as certainty seemed to anoint Omaha as Gold Cup victor, another filly loomed to challenge him.

At age four, Quashed had already proven herself to be a horse of the highest quality, one with a turn of foot well suited to longer races like the Ascot Gold Cup. As a two-year-old, she ran only three times and finished third in two of those races.[3] The next season, she had won not only the twelve-furlong Oaks at Epsom, much like La Flêche, but also the Jockey Club Cup at Newmarket and the Prince Edward Handicap at Manchester Racecourse, both 2¼ miles.[4] By 1936, the filly had become a stayer of great repute. In the 2¼-mile Great Metropolitan Handicap at Epsom in late April, Quashed carried 130 pounds. She and jockey Richard Perryman made up ground in the stretch to pull even with the leader, the lightly weighted Jack Tar, who carried 104 pounds, and hit the wire in a dead heat.[5] She followed that test with the inaugural Ormonde Stakes, where she carried 123 pounds over the 1⅝ miles plus seventy-five yards, dueled with a staunch Cecil in the stretch, and pushed her head out in front just before the wire. Not only was the filly proven over a route of ground, but she also had demonstrated a fierce determination to finish strong, always willing to push harder in close company. That style would be on full display at the Gold Cup.

Because Britain was in mourning following King George V's passing in January, there would be no royal procession to open each day's festivities at Royal Ascot, but Queen Mary, the future king's mother, absolved race attendees of the need to observe "court mourning." Racegoers could eschew the usual black of bereavement for the colors and fashions synonymous with Royal Ascot.[6] The royal family themselves would not be on hand for the 1936 meet, but King Edward VIII, whose coronation was scheduled for the following year, would be entertaining nearby at Fort Belvedere.[7] The organizers of the summertime meet also faced another concern: a drought. An ongoing dearth of rain left some areas around Ascot parched, but a nearby reservoir provided enough water to keep the turf at the storied racecourse good for the races ahead.[8] The show would go on and what a show it would be.

Quashed and Omaha were the two names on everyone's lips, but the competition for the 1936 edition of the Ascot Gold Cup was absent several horses: Quashed's stablemate Plassy, winner of the Coronation Cup, a race that Omaha had bypassed in favor of the Queen's Plate; Bobsleigh, former Derby hopeful whom Omaha had defeated at Kempton Park; and Cecil, whom both Quashed and Plassy had defeated in earlier races.[9] The field included only seven others alongside Quashed and Omaha. Two were French horses brought over for the Gold Cup, Bokbul and the filly Chaudière, winner of the 2½-mile Prix de Candran; both four-year-old stake winners were owned by financier Baron Edouard de Rothschild.[10] Valerius, owned by Sir Abe Bailey, had won the two-mile Yorkshire Cup in late May.[11] Robin Goodfellow, another of Bailey's horses, had finished second to Bahram in the 1935 Derby and then third in the Coronation Cup behind Plassy and Cecil in late May 1936.[12] Buckleigh had finished second to Bobsleigh in the Chippenham

Stakes and then was an also-ran behind Quashed in the Ormonde. James de Rothschild's Patriot King had won the 1934 Irish Derby in a dead heat with Primero, but had had limited success since then.[13] The other French horse, the filly Samos II, had won the 1935 renewal of the Prix de l'Arc de Triomphe and was that year's champion three-year-old filly for Count Evremond de Saint-Alary.[14] The field might have been only nine horses, but the Gold Cup, the highlight of the Thursday card at Royal Ascot, was deep in classic winners—American, English, and French—with favoritism divided between the American colt and the English filly. The punters all had their picks, and the wise guys and their ostensibly sage takes were splashed across newspapers from one side of the Atlantic to the other.

On the heath near Windsor Castle, with the blessing of the young monarch awaiting his crown, more than a century's worth of tradition went on in earnest. Rich haberdashery and luxurious costumes dotted the timeless landscape of Ascot. The best that the sport of kings had to offer would traverse the undulating greens and put on a show that few would soon forget. On Tuesday, June 16, the meeting opened to glorious sunshine and an upset in the St. James Palace Stakes, in which Rhodes Scholar defeated Epsom Derby winner Mahmoud by five lengths. The weather was perfect again on Wednesday, and the fashionable stood out against the natural green backdrop of the Ascot heath in the warm sunshine. After two lovely summer days, surely the weather would be beautiful again on Thursday, when the Gold Cup was scheduled to go off at 2:30 p.m.

On Gold Cup day, the grounds buzzed with activity as the masses congregated in their finest, some there to see and be seen and others eager just to see the action on the track. The skies opened up around noon, dark clouds expelling a solid sheet of rain that soaked the crowd's expensive costumes and doused Ascot's racing surface with enough water to soften the going.[15] Just two short hours before Omaha's great test against Quashed and others, the grass underneath the feet of the one hundred and fifty thousand men, women, and children present on the third day of the royal meet became soft.

With only two races in England under his belt, Omaha had never run on soft ground. How would he handle this wrinkle?

Another concern was the fact that the son of Gallant Fox had not run at Ascot, not even for a workout, though Boyd-Rochfort had chosen Kempton Park for Omaha's first two starts because of its similar layout.[16] The previous Saturday, he had turned in "a rousing gallop over two miles," a work that the Newmarket representative for the *Yorkshire Observer* called "a grand display," but that gallop was not at Ascot, not around the turns that were part of the running of that twenty furlongs.[17] How close could a gallop over the Newmarket heath or two starts over the Kempton Park turf come to the undulating course, the run uphill in the race's last stages, and that desperate sprint over the straight in front of the Ascot grandstand? The world would soon find out just what the Belair champion was capable of on the Ascot heath.

As the horses were saddled in the paddock, the crowd pressed closer to the nine, eager to get a glimpse of the stars who would run the most anticipated race of the year. The longest shots in the field were the French trio of horses, accomplished in their own country but relegated to afterthoughts at the bookmakers. Instead, the eyes of the crowd were drawn to the tall American chestnut; his wide white blaze was free of the blinkers that had been part of his equipment in his stateside races but absent in his English starts. He carried odds of 11–8, with Quashed at 3–1.[18] The filly, a plain brown package of horse, was leggy and lithe, a contrast to the powerfully built American.[19] In the saddling ring, with the press of people trying to get a glimpse, one horse began to sweat and the other remained cool. As the nine paraded to the barrier, the Ascot crowd saw even more of a show.

Crowds of twenty-five to thirty-five thousand gathered at Belmont Park on Omaha's Triple Crown coronation day and at Arlington Race Course for his last win in America.[20] The 1935 Kentucky Derby crowd would have topped one hundred thousand had the weather cooperated, but in the rains at Churchill Downs, an estimated seventy thousand people were at the track to watch Omaha win the roses.[21] The crowd at Ascot on Gold Cup day was more than *twice* that and they were treated to a spectacle. The Triple Crown winner bucked and shied through the procession, "mistaking our Ascot for a Western rodeo" as one newsreel commentator put it.[22] Pat Beasley found it a challenge to keep his seat with all of Omaha's antics. Was it the immense crowd, the intense pressure of the day's expectations, or could something else be amiss? The experienced jockey calmed his colt enough to get him to the starting line, both ready to face the starter and the 2½ miles ahead.

At the barrier, with the webbing strung across the starting line, they lined up, Quashed on the outside and Omaha in the middle in the sixth position. On the filly's back was Richard Perryman, the contract jockey for Lord Derby, the father of Lord Stanley, in whose colors she ran this day. For the 1936 season, Lord Stanley had leased Quashed from her breeder, Lady Barbara Smith.[23] Perryman had already won the One Thousand Guineas on Pillion and Tide-Way and had been Quashed's regular rider for many of her wins, including her 1936 victories.[24] This could become a marked advantage: he knew his filly well, in contrast with Beasley's shorter relationship with Omaha, whom he had ridden in two races and several gallops over the Newmarket greens. While Beasley had to wrestle Omaha through his antics prior to the race, expending valuable energy, Quashed had been docile under Perryman, prepared for the task in front of them.[25] Regardless, at the starting line, each horse had a chance for an ideal start and a clean trip, a chance to be the right rider and horse on the right day to bring home the famed Ascot Gold Cup. The nine were in line for a beat, facing forward with four feet on the ground, and walking up to the barrier—when the starter Captain Allison pressed the button and away they went.[26]

Unlike most American racetracks, Ascot is not an oval or ellipse, but irregularly shaped, as many English racecourses tend to be. W. C. Vreeland describes the course as being like "a large P," a shape it essentially maintains today. The course has evolved in its three centuries,

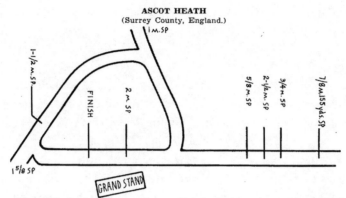

ASCOT HEATH
(Surrey County, England.)

Right hand circular track, one mile, six furlongs, 148 yards. The first half of the course is nearly all on the descent and the last half, which is called the old mile, is uphill the greater part of the way. Twenty-five miles from London.

A diagram of the Ascot course layout, 1936. © 2022 Daily Racing Form LLC and Equibase Company LLC. Republished with permission of the copyright owner.

and the main section is now more of a triangle with a chute, still akin to the "P" shape that Vreeland spoke of in 1936. In the decades since Omaha's Ascot Gold Cup, the course has seen slight changes, especially to that turn at Swinley Bottom; in 1936 it was less of a turn and more of a short straightaway but now is more of a conventional bend.[27] Starting from the short chute to the right of the grandstand, the nine ran three furlongs before they crossed in front of the massive boxy structure that undulated with craning necks. Under the wire for the first time, Chaudière, the French filly who had already won at the Gold Cup distance, led, with Patriot King, Buckleigh, Quashed, and Omaha running behind her. Going around that first turn by the paddock, Buckleigh had taken over the lead, two lengths in front of Chaudière, with Patriot King and Quashed behind them.

For his part, Beasley had orders from Captain Boyd-Rochfort "not to follow Quashed as my colt would be smelling the mare." The Captain was concerned about the potential distraction inherent in Omaha smelling whatever pheromones the filly Quashed might give off.[28] Beasley knew, though, that Quashed was their most likely adversary in the final furlongs and kept his eye on the filly throughout, anxious to keep up with this proven champion of marathon distances.[29] As they approached the final bend into the straight, Perryman and Quashed moved up, taking second behind Buckleigh, prompting Omaha and Beasley to move as well. One of the French horses, Bokbul, was running in fourth, taking that bend wide and carrying Omaha with him.

At last, with two miles down and a half mile to go, they were into the straight, that long stretch from the last turn of the Swinley course to the finish wire in front of the Ascot grandstand. The furious final furlongs saw Quashed take over the lead from Buckleigh, Perryman moving the filly to the rail as they cleared the former leader. Behind her, Beasley had Omaha in a drive, following orders with which he did not wholly agree. William Woodward wrote to his trainer, "reporting that Omaha did his best in America when he started to move up over half a mile out, smothered the opposition, and went clear," advocating for the strategy that Omaha should challenge Quashed earlier in the straight than Beasley thought advisable. The jockey, though, "knowing Omaha's blinding turn of speed," felt it would be better "to wait until the last possible moment and then to pounce on Quashed."[30] For his part, the trainer worried that "Omaha would not pass the mare if he sat on her tail all the way up the Ascot straight" so he agreed with his boss and gave Beasley his marching orders.[31] With a quarter of a mile to go, Omaha had caught the filly and the two were locked in a duel for the ages.

To describe the next two furlongs, the last 440 yards of the Ascot Gold Cup, is best left to the unnamed *Times of London* correspondent who took it all in with his own eyes:

P. Beasley and Omaha came repeatedly at Quashed, who was being beautifully ridden by Perryman. Every time he came at her she found a little more and beat him off. Omaha would not be beaten, and time and after time he challenged

Quashed (left) and Omaha (right) battle to the wire in the 1936 Ascot Gold Cup. ©Alamy Photos.

the filly, but nothing would make her give way an inch. . . . As she got nearer and nearer to the winning-post, the cheering which had greeted her progress died down. After all, it seemed that the great raking American colt would outstride her and that she would be beaten. She went past the winning-post in silence, for only the judge could say which of the two had won.[32]

In the end, without the benefit of a photo finish camera, a somewhat new technology that had yet to reach English shores, the winner of the Ascot Gold Cup was left to the eye of the judge Malcolm Hancock.[33] Which number would hit the board? Would it be Omaha's twelve or Quashed's fifteen? Or would it be a dead heat, Hancock unable to discern a winner?

The numbers were posted, fifteen on top of twelve. Quashed had won by a short head, the result called by Hancock after a few minutes' deliberation. The crowd cheered, rushing toward the unsaddling enclosure to celebrate the triumph of this thoroughly English filly, who ironically was not listed in the *General Stud Book* because of her dam's half-breed pedigree. With an English breeder and owner, Quashed boasted a sire and a dam who were English bred, but counted Tracery, bred by August Belmont II and raced in England, as her grandsire, and the stallion Umpire, descended from the family that produced Lexington, on her dam's side.[34] It was Lexington's indeterminate pedigree that the English objected to, thus rendering Quashed a half-breed. Nonetheless, the crowd cheered her victory, as the prized Gold Cup stayed put rather than going to America with the Belair colt. Later, legendary turf writer John Hervey would say that "everyone who saw the race will, for all time, regard the honors as being equally divided."[35]

As for Omaha, he suffered no loss of clout or caste with his narrow defeat. Captain Boyd-Rochfort, of course, was disappointed, as was Pat Beasley, though both would go on to win the Gold Cup in 1937 with Precipitation.[36] The post-race Monday morning quarter-backing led to thoughtful analysis from the major players. The trainer laid out three factors that, in his judgment, led to Omaha's defeat: the colt had been shipped to England two months later than ideal for the goal laid out before him; Omaha had become uncharacteristically upset and nervous before the race; and Pat Beasley lost his whip in the race's last yards.[37]

In Boyd-Rochfort's mind, had Omaha been shipped to England earlier, he would have had more time to prepare and acclimate to the challenges of racing there after two years of racing on dirt in the United States. Pat Beasley agreed, saying, "I do not think Omaha would ever have been beaten had he always been at Freemason Lodge."[38] The soft going, where the grass was looser and almost slippery under foot, was a new phenomenon for Omaha, who had only had two races over grass prior to the Gold Cup, both on firmer ground. The Swinley Course had inherent challenges that more acclimation could have mitigated. The Ascot Gold Cup is not run over flat ground: the first part of the course is run on a descent and then the last mile of the race is uphill.[39] Not only was Omaha running farther than he ever had in life, but he was running on a decline for the first mile or so and then that final portion of the race, where he was carried wide on the final turn and then dueled with Quashed in the straight, was run over an incline.[40] Even Pat Beasley acknowledged the challenge that the incline presented, saying "I think the hill beat us" after the race.[41] That Omaha lost by such a scant margin, judged a head by Mr. Hancock, is a testament to his stamina and turn of foot, his innate ability born of a pedigree that featured Sir Gallahad III, Gallant Fox, Flambette, and more.

Boyd-Rochfort also pointed out the "Western rodeo" style antics Omaha put on prior to the Gold Cup. Ascot held a crowd larger than any the Belair colt had seen in his prior starts in his native country. In the saddling ring prior to the race, "people pressed around him to get a good look, causing the American horse to break out in a lather of sweat, which he had never done on a racecourse before."[42] Additionally, as Pat Beasley pointed out in his autobiography, Omaha raced in England without the blinkers that he had worn in his two seasons in America. That did not seem to affect him in his two prior starts at Kempton Park, but could that have made a difference on this biggest of stages? "When he came over to us," Beasley reported decades later, "he was excitable and it was all I could do to sit on him in the parade before the race."[43] What could explain Omaha's uncharacteristic antics prior to the Gold Cup? William Woodward, who was not there in person but had one of his daughters there to cheer on the red polka dots, believed something nefarious had happened to his colt:

I am confident that some underworld fellow sprayed Omaha with "high-life." They do this at a distance of three or four feet by using little so-called guns which look like a fountain pen. They use these things in holding up banks in this country.[44]

Omaha's behavior prior to the Ascot Gold Cup might have hinted at such a sensational idea but it was impossible to prove. Omaha's behavior in his next start, though, would signal that this nervousness might not be a singular occurrence.

Boyd-Rochfort's last reason for Omaha's defeat happened at a critical moment in those final seconds of the race. A hundred yards from the finish line, Pat Beasley lost his whip. In *The Captain,* Bill Curling's biography of Cecil Boyd-Rochfort, the author says that Perryman accidentally knocked the stick out of Beasley's hand; in his autobiography, Beasley himself says that he lost it and "that may have made all the difference between victory and defeat."[45] Whether Perryman knocked it out of his hand or Beasley dropped his stick in the fury of their duel, the absence of that tool was potentially enough of a factor in Omaha's defeat that Boyd-Rochfort had to consider it as did the jockey himself.

All of those reasons, however sensational one might have been, could explain the close defeat in the Ascot Gold Cup. Yet, when Omaha returned to the unsaddling enclosure after the race, he was a tired horse who "looked as though he had given all he had to give" in the battle with Quashed.[46] W. C. Vreeland, who had been witness to a number of Omaha's races when the Belair champion was in New York, argued that this defeat, where this champion was "beaten by the margin of his nostrils in a race of two and a half miles, a distance new to him, but almost on the doorstep of Quashed, was no disgrace for Omaha."[47] No one who saw the two dueling down the stretch at Ascot could forget the sight of the handsome American colt and the lithe English filly locked together, looking each other in the eye and never surrendering until well past the wire. In 2002, the 1936 Ascot Gold Cup would be named the greatest race of all time in the *Observer Sport Monthly.*[48] Jack Leach, former jockey turned writer for the *Observer,* wrote, "To see Quashed and Omaha battle out the finish of the Ascot Gold Cup took years off a man's life, though it was well worth it."[49]

Five months after he arrived in England, Omaha had made it to Ascot and attempted to bring home the Gold Cup, which was not a gold cup but a set of gold candlesticks flanking an inkstand decorated with the Royal Arms and engraved with the word "Ascot," a prize selected by King Edward himself.[50] He came within a head of succeeding, held off by the stalwart gameness of Quashed. Seeking another chance at the Gold Cup, William Woodward elected to keep his champion in England one more year, his goal one more try at Gold Cup greatness. Omaha would race on, with Royal Ascot again in his sights.

20

The Adventure's End

With the meet at Newmarket around the corner, Omaha's name appeared in the entries for the Princess of Wales's Stakes, a twelve-furlong try at another big-name contest for the American horse. Two weeks after the longest race of his life, Omaha was attempting a shorter race to find the winner's circle again. Would the same pre-race case of nerves rear its ugly head? Would the son of Gallant Fox be up for battle one more time? The task ahead was titanic for even four-year-old Omaha, who was still recovering from his Ascot Gold Cup trip.

As the most accomplished horse in the short field of six, Omaha would be tasked with carrying 138 pounds, giving thirty pounds to three-year-old Bonspiel and eighteen to the Aga Khan's three-year-old Taj Akbar, who was second to stablemate Mahmoud in the Epsom Derby. No other horse in the field of six carried more than 120 pounds. This heavier burden was made worse when coupled with reports that he had "not been showing his usual dash at exercise during the past week."[1] Thus, as one British writer observed, "one must, in view of this, not be surprised if he is beaten."[2] Yet, if Boyd-Rochfort did not have full confidence in Omaha's condition for the race, a full mile shorter than the Ascot Gold Cup, then he would not send him to Newmarket for the try.

The field for the Princess of Wales's Stakes also included Portfolio, Esquemeling, and Daytona. None received near the consideration that both Taj Akbar and Omaha garnered in the newspapers, although these three-year-olds had had varying degrees of success throughout the classics season. A three-year-old, Fairbairn, had won the Princess of Wales's the year before, so it was not a stretch for the punters to pick Taj Akbar over Omaha. Even given the weight disparity, Taj Akbar and Omaha were cited repeatedly as the choices for the race. But, as correspondent for the *Daily Mirror* "Bouverie" wrote in the July 2 preview for the Princess of Wales's Stakes, "Obviously Omaha is set a very big task, but it is not one I consider beyond his ability to tackle successfully."[3]

At Newmarket, Mary, the Princess Royal, was on hand to watch Omaha in the paddock; she stood with her husband, Lord Harewood, as the American colt walked around the saddling ring. The crowd around the paddock rail was five deep, the spectators on hand eager to see the American challenger once again under tack in England, in his fourth start in the seven weeks since his debut at Kempton Park in early May.[4] Looking fit and "none the worse for his titanic struggle with Quashed in the Ascot Gold Cup," Omaha was not as worked up in the paddock as he had been at Ascot, a promising sign. However, after Pat Beasley took his seat on the back of the Woodward colt and they began the walk to the barrier, the Belair colt began to sweat.[5]

The task ahead for the Triple Crown winner was already a colossal one. He had to face Taj Akbar, who was second behind his record-setting stablemate in the Epsom Derby at a mile and a half and second behind Fairey at a mile at Ascot, and he had to give him eighteen pounds. The three-year-old was carrying less than what weight-for-age scales would have dictated. On an early July day at Newmarket, the sweat was not just because it was a summer's day. Omaha was a nervous horse, so much so that he refused to face the gate for six minutes, which delayed the start to the point that he could have been excused from the race had it been any other horse.[6] Finally, after coaxing from Pat Beasley and the starter's patience with the American star, Omaha faced forward and stood long enough for the six to break.[7]

Bonspiel took the lead early, with Omaha and Portfolio stalking the pace behind him. Conscious of the weight impost, Beasley kept his colt close, poised to make their move for the lead when the time was right. But Bonspiel had not set a fast enough pace for Beasley, who moved Omaha to the lead with a half mile to go.[8] Portfolio went with him, with jockey Charlie Smirke and Taj Akbar moving closer to the front, poised to challenge the front-running Omaha.[9]

With a furlong to go, Taj Akbar took command of the race from Omaha. The Aga Khan's colt was clear of Omaha as the field passed the stands, the wire looming. Not to be denied, the Triple Crown winner dug in and came on again, cutting down the gap between them inch by inch, as Taj Akbar fought to keep his advantage. At the wire, Taj Akbar was a neck in front of the American. Omaha had been beaten again.

"He is a great horse," Pat Beasley said of his mount after the Princess of Wales's Stakes was in the books. "Nine times out of ten, he would have won this race. Unfortunately for him, it was a slowly run race."[10] A slow pace coupled with the spread in weights meant that the American colt was beaten before he left the paddock: "Several [turf writers] declared 'he's greater than either Reigh Count or Twenty Grand, but no horse in the world could win with such a handicap.'"[11] Beasley could not send Omaha too early, but the slow pace Bonspiel put on could not have helped the Belair champion. Move too late and Omaha might not have had enough track to build up to full speed under all that lead. "Omaha's second defeat in this country—by Taj Akbar in the Princess of Wales's Stakes—did nothing to tarnish his reputation," wrote columnist "Amato" in the *Leicester Evening Mail* two days later. Despite losing by a nose to Quashed at Ascot and a neck to Taj Akbar at Newmarket, the Triple Crown winner was still the best of the American horses to invade British racing. In the fifty years since Foxhall's success, Omaha had come the closest to conquering Ascot. He would get one more chance in 1937.

First, though, Captain Boyd-Rochfort had to find a way to keep Omaha from getting anxious in the paddock before races with large crowds like he had seen at Ascot. He brought the Woodward colt to Goodwood in late July, but not to face Quashed in the Goodwood

Cup, where the filly would be making her first start since winning the Ascot Gold Cup. Instead, Boyd-Rochfort would have Omaha school in the paddock there, with the packed crowds for the Goodwood Cup, to acclimate him to future appearances. Indeed, the trainer intended to rest Omaha until September, implying that the big horse might be seen again under colors at the Doncaster Cup.[12] For the moment, though, his time in the Goodwood minor ring, in sight of the horses preparing for the Cup, left him "as cool and composed as could be desired."[13] For her part, Quashed would follow up her Ascot win with a third-place finish in the Goodwood Cup, an indication that even the gamest of fillies, as she had shown herself to be at the Gold Cup finish line, was still feeling the effects of that battle.

If the filly and Omaha crossed paths at all in the ring prior to the Cup, no mention was made of the moment.

Quashed's loss in the Goodwood Cup was met with disappointment. The filly had garnered a following within her native country, her heroic performance in the Gold Cup earning her admiration for her steadfastness in the face of challenges like that of the American champion. After Goodwood, the filly was rested while speculation about Omaha's next start abounded. His name had appeared earlier in the entries for the Burton Plate at Derby, but Omaha did not make the trip.[14] The start at Doncaster was speculation; Boyd-Rochfort had alluded to it but never confirmed Omaha's participation. Instead, the special correspondent to the *Yorkshire Post* shared that the American would "be trained with a view to the Jockey Club Cup," to be run at Newmarket in late October.[15] Quashed was also aimed for the Jockey Club Cup, which she had won the year before, setting up what could become the rematch of the year if Omaha could get to the race in his best condition.[16]

Scheduled for October 29, the Jockey Club Cup was a 2¼-mile stakes race over the Cesarewitch course at Newmarket. Omaha was set to carry 126 pounds, while Quashed was to carry 123 pounds.

Even after the epic Ascot Gold Cup, Omaha still had to give weight to Quashed, who would always carry less when running against colts and geldings because she was a filly. "That every racing enthusiast is anxious to see the pair in opposition again is only to be expected," wrote the racing correspondent for the *Scotsman*. Their rematch was anticipated to inspire record attendance at Newmarket as fans would be out to root not just for Quashed but also for the American champion.[17] "Nothing is more certain than that Omaha will have just as many admirers in the wagering," owing to his previous performances on English tracks and the turn of foot he showed in races like the Victor Wild.[18]

The meeting was not to be. The October 11 edition of the *Observer* brought a report that Omaha had hurt a leg when he was cast in his stall at Freemason Lodge.[19] Horses become cast when they lie down or roll too close to a wall or a stationary object and then do not have enough room to rise. For horses to stand, they need to roll onto their belly and stretch out their front legs to have enough space to push their hind legs up and rise to a standing position.[20] If a horse stays down on one side for too long, it can cause nerve and muscle damage. Omaha came away with only a minor injury, "not a serious matter," but the incident was enough for the *Observer* to report that the American horse's 1936 season was done. A month later, he and Santorin were turned out for the winter.[21] Omaha would return to Freemason Lodge when he was ready to resume training for the new season.

With Omaha absent from the Jockey Club Cup, Quashed went off as the overwhelming favorite, with only one other horse, Penny Royal, meeting her at the barrier. She won easily, of course, her second victory in that Newmarket stakes race. Her only defeat in 1936 came in the Goodwood Cup, after she had won the Great Metropolitan Stakes in a dead heat with Jack Tar and then won the Ormonde Stakes and the Ascot Gold Cup. She would return to racing in 1937 as well, setting up another potential confrontation with Omaha in the Ascot Gold Cup.[22]

As 1936 came to a close, the great experiment of sending Omaha to England to race had yielded two wins in four starts, with two close seconds, an extraordinary feat. For Omaha to have missed months of his three-year-old season with an injury, recovered, and then been shipped to England at all was notable on its own. For him to have done all of that and won twice while also losing the Ascot Gold Cup by a nose was remarkable. No other Triple Crown winner before, or since, had even attempted to race in England; only Sir Barton and Secretariat ventured to Canada to race during their careers. Omaha was already historic as the first horse sired by a Triple Crown winner to win the Triple Crown as well; to that, he added English stakes winner to his résumé, the one and only of this elite club of thirteen horses to do so.

In 1937, he would try for that illustrious prize one more time. He went into winter quarters at Lady Alwayne Compton Vyner's Heath Lodge Stud, with Royal Ascot once again the goal.[23] Would he be able to face Quashed on the Ascot heath and emerge victorious this time around? With a year of racing over the undulating courses of England under his belt, Omaha had acclimated to these surroundings. At age five, he could give William Woodward yet another illustrious title: owner and breeder of an Ascot Gold Cup winner.

All of this was dependent on nothing else going wrong. But horse racing is not a sport known for the absence of hiccups.

In early February 1937, Omaha returned to Freemason Lodge, once again under the watchful tutelage of Captain Cecil Boyd-Rochfort. He and two other Belair horses, Boswell and Flares, Omaha's full brother, were entered for the Ascot Gold Cup in June.[24] William Woodward had his choice of horses to run for that prize, but, for Omaha, other than the Gold Cup, what did he have left to prove? He had competed in and won in several prestigious races, reached the highest of highs in his home country, and come close to the same heights in England. Woodward had already decided that the Gold Cup would be his last race, and, once that was done, win or lose, he would return to America to stand stud with Gallant Fox at Claiborne Farm.[25]

Back in training, Omaha was "thought to be better now than ever" after his winter freshening.[26] His name appeared in the entries for several spring stakes, like the Spring Plate, the March Stakes, and the Chippenham Stakes at Newmarket, but Omaha was not seen under tack for any. He was regularly seen on the gallops at Newmarket, training with the rest of the Freemason Lodge horses, but Boyd-Rochfort did not enter Omaha for his seasonal debut until the Yorkshire Cup on May 26.

At two miles, the Yorkshire Cup was just a half mile shorter than the Ascot Gold Cup; it would give Omaha a chance to race at close to the distance he would be asked to traverse three weeks later. Quashed had been among the nominees, but she did not make the final list of starters. Instead, Omaha was to face a couple of familiar names, including Buckleigh, who had faced Omaha and Quashed in the Ascot Gold Cup, and Penny Royal, who had been the only horse to race Quashed in the Jockey Club Cup the previous year. He was set to carry Pat Beasley and race at 130 pounds, the highest weight in the field, giving anywhere from eight to twenty-three pounds to the field. The *Scotsman* reported that "Omaha gave complete satisfaction when galloped with other members of Captain Boyd-Rochfort's team recently, and is fully expected to make a successful start to his fourth season."[27] The Belair champion looked to be on the verge of victory to open his 1937 campaign.

Rain soaked the York ground for several hours prior to the Yorkshire Cup, scheduled for 3:35 p.m. on Wednesday, May 26. Much to the disappointment of the gathered crowd, Boyd-Rochfort elected to scratch Omaha, citing the soft going.[28] Racegoers were not the only ones who were disappointed: the five-year-old Belair champion was in the paddock with Beasley on his back as they prepared to join the field for the Yorkshire Cup. When the other horses exited the paddock without him, Omaha "seemed quite sad," as though he "would, so it seemed, have loved to be with them."[29] With three weeks left before he was to face the barrier at Royal Ascot, three weeks until his second try at one of his owner's most sought-after accomplishments, Omaha had yet to race in 1937. His last start was in early July 1936, nearly ten months earlier. Judging from his appearance, this "most handsome horse who looks ever better than he did a year ago" was ready to run. How was the trainer going to prepare his horse for his final grand test with no races under his belt?

The answer came at Kempton Park in a race that Omaha had won the year before. Two weeks before the Ascot Gold Cup, Omaha was expected to start in the Queen's Cup, but instead Boyd-Rochfort sent Pat Beasley on Precipitation to the starting line as Omaha was not ready. Next, he was set to race at Royal Ascot, a chance to avenge his defeat by Quashed, on the strength of only training gallops around the Newmarket courses. Although he exercised with the Freemason Lodge contingent, and the reports about his workouts were heaped with praise about his form, he would not face the barrier before Royal Ascot.

On Saturday, June 12, five days before the Ascot Gold Cup, Omaha and Pat Beasley, along with stablemates Flares, Boswell, and Theddingworth, worked thirteen furlongs, a mile and five furlongs, over the Limelkins in Newmarket.[30] A few hours later, Omaha had swelling in a tendon in the left foreleg. By Sunday, the inflammation had set in. Professor Brayley Reynolds, a veterinarian, was called in to examine the Belair champion and judged that further galloping would have "serious results."[31] William Woodward, who had traveled to England for Perifox's try in the Epsom Derby and then Omaha's in the Ascot Gold Cup, was standing with Captain Boyd-Rochfort to watch the Belair horses as they prepared for Royal Ascot. The master of Belair opted to scratch Omaha from the Ascot Gold Cup and send Boswell, his 1936 St. Leger winner, in the Belair white with red polka dots.[32] By Monday, it was official: Omaha would not race again. The Ascot Gold Cup was to have been his last start, and now that was off the table. The risk that came with further galloping, the time required to recover from this setback, and the limited opportunities for a horse of his caliber to add anything to his résumé all led the master of Belair to retire his prized colt.

With that, Omaha's British adventure was over.[33]

On Thursday, June 17, 1937, Pat Beasley rode the Ascot Gold Cup winner into the winner's circle. Leading him in was Captain Cecil Boyd-Rochfort.[34] But the horse that brought home the prized Gold Cup was not named Omaha. It was Precipitation, a chestnut colt owned by Lady Zia Wernher, formerly known as the Countess Anastasia Mikhailovna de Torby, a great-granddaughter of Czar Nicholas I of Russia.[35] Like William Woodward, she was a patron of Boyd-Rochfort, who also trained Persian Gulf for her. She was the first woman to own a Gold Cup winner since 1900. She was also the first to be greeted by the new King of England, George VI, who had been coronated only a month before, after he assumed the crown when his brother Edward abdicated the throne in December.

"I am very thrilled indeed," Lady Wernher said after the race. "It was even more a thrill to me because Precipitation was unable to show his form in the St. Leger. My only disappointment is that Omaha, the American horse, could not run, but if it had it would have been the race of the century."[36] Cecil was second and Quashed third, unable to defend her Ascot Gold Cup crown. The Belair representative Boswell finished out of the money in the field of twelve.[37] The year after that memorable performance, Omaha's absence was as much a story as the winner himself.

In early September, Omaha boarded another transatlantic ship bound for New York; his trip home was not as much of a story as his trip there.[38] He was bound for Paris, Kentucky, and Claiborne Farm, for the quiet life of a Bluegrass stallion, much like his sire and grandsire. After winning two of his four races in England and falling short of his ultimate goal by only a head, had he shown to the British that American horses could compete with their British counterparts? Had he helped his owner, chairman of the Jockey Club, demonstrate that American bloodstock should be included in England's Stud Book?

Woodward would continue that pursuit until his death, sending horses like Flares and Boswell to England even as he kept horses like Granville and Gallant Fox in the United States. Omaha's epic Gold Cup performance certainly left its mark in the minds of the British: "No two horses could ever strive more perfectly than those two did that afternoon. . . . We owe each of them a debt of gratitude."[39]

Omaha returned to his native country a winner over the English turf as he had been a winner over American dirt tracks. In his three years of racing, he had won over grass and dirt, at five furlongs and at two miles, and in two different countries. He had overcome an injury that cut short his three-year-old season to come back at four and win in a new country over a new surface. He was the third horse to win the Kentucky Derby, the Preakness Stakes, and the Belmont Stakes, and the only horse sired by another Triple Crown winner to do so. "In action he was a glorious sight," John Hervey wrote in tribute to the retired champion. "Few Thoroughbreds have exhibited such a magnificent, sweeping, space-annihilating stride, or carried with it such strength and precision. His place is among the titans of the American turf."[40]

As he stepped off that van and into a paddock, as he said goodbye to one phase of his life and entered another, Omaha returned to America singular even among this exclusive club, for he had had a grand English adventure, one that would live on in the memories of racing fans on both sides of the pond.

21

The Road to Omaha

Claiborne Farm lies off scenic Winchester Road in Paris, Kentucky, where the landscape quickly shifts from the sights of a small Southern town to the iconic wooden fences of the Kentucky bluegrass. Turn left off the bend and suddenly the world is not the hustle and bustle of the twenty-first century, but a timeless landscape of lush trees, endless grassy paddocks, and the sights and sounds of horses. Spend five minutes among the rolling grounds that the Hancock family has called home for more than a century and it becomes clear to the observer why this land has nourished a long list of champions since its earliest days.

On Tuesday, September 14, 1937, a horse van drove quietly down the long, shaded lane toward its destination, the stallion barn at Claiborne Farm. On board were Dr. Edward A. Caslick, the veterinarian that had accompanied Gallant Fox on this same trek; David Peel, one of Claiborne's staff; and Omaha, fresh off his ten-day journey home from England.[1] Arthur Hancock, purportedly fond of the distance-loving Belair champion, brought Omaha to Claiborne on a five-year lease, despite already having both his sire and grandsire in the same barn.[2] So Omaha took his place alongside Gallant Fox and Sir Gallahad III, a third generation of greatness among the stallions at the renowned farm.

For his first season at stud, Omaha was listed at a $1,000 fee, with William Woodward already sending his own mares to his champion, son of his other champion. In addition to his sire and grandsire, he stood alongside stallions like Hard Tack, whose son Seabiscuit was

Omaha at Claiborne Farm, May 1939. Courtesy Keeneland Library Thayer Collection.

already enough of a draw that Claiborne mentioned the famed handicapper in their advertisements for the stallion; Blenheim II, who had been imported from England the season before with the hopes that he would duplicate the success of Sir Gallahad III; and Reigh Count, 1928 Kentucky Derby winner who similarly had tried racing in England and also had finished second in the Ascot Gold Cup. The stallion roster at Claiborne was loaded and most of its sires' books were full, including Omaha's. He was off to a promising start, just as Gallant Fox had been just seven years earlier.

On February 2, 1939, without the kind of fanfare that had accompanied the birth of Gallant Prince in 1932, a bay colt greeted the world at Claiborne, just as his sire Omaha had.[3] His dam, Blind Lane, had won the 1930 Beldame Handicap at Aqueduct and finished second in the Latonia Oaks and third in the Arlington Oaks for her owners, Goodestone Stable.[4] After her racing career, Blind Lane was a broodmare at Morven Stud in Virginia, which was part owner of the stallion Pompey, standing at nearby Ellerslie.[5] From the pairing of Omaha and Blind Lane came this first foal, a bay colt later named Wheat.[6] Though he was not a stakes winner, Wheat, who eventually was gelded, raced for ten seasons and logged 142 starts and sixteen wins.

Omaha would stand at Claiborne for the life of his lease; he was advertised at $1,000 per season until 1943, when his stud fee dropped to $250. Each year, Woodward added more stallions to his Claiborne band, including Boswell, Fighting Fox, and Johnstown. From his first two crops, Gallant Fox had produced Omaha and Granville; from Omaha's first two crops came no significant stakes winners. His books were full for his first five seasons; but, though the third Triple Crown winner was advertised at the same $1,000 rate in 1942, he had fewer mares booked that season.[7] By 1943, Woodward had more of his former champions at stud than he could support so he sent several elsewhere. Granville was leased first to Kenneth Gilpin, who stood him in Virginia, and then to John Hay Whitney, who stood the 1936 Horse of the Year at his Mare's Nest Stud near Lexington, Kentucky.[8] Flares was at Ellerslie in Virginia, where he remained until 1944.[9] So, with Omaha's stallion career stalled and a plethora of other Belair-bred bloodstock already available for commercial breeders, the chairman of the Jockey Club decided to send his beloved son of his best horse to serve as part of the Jockey Club's Breeding Bureau in upstate New York.

Those who were invested in horses, whether for their usefulness in military and police work or as companions in the business of sport, pursued the improvement of the breeds necessary for such occupations. Their efforts were evident from the time of the Civil War and into the conflicts and sports that dominated the last part of the nineteenth century and into the twentieth century. In 1906, the Jockey Club established its Breeding Bureau in Avon, New York, where they set up a program akin to that of the United States Army's Remount Service, which provided access to Thoroughbred stallions for small fees.[10] Each stallion was thoroughly vetted before joining the program, going through a series of tests to make sure they passed muster for the programs they were admitted into.[11] This enabled breeders who might want to cross their mares of other sport breeds with Thoroughbreds to produce horses that were even better suited to the tasks they were asked to do, from cavalry work to pleasure riding. A number of prominent breeders, from Joseph Widener to William Woodward, would go on to donate or lease stallions to the Breeding Bureau.[12]

Woodward had donated Spearpoint to the effort in 1924, and, by 1932, the Breeding Bureau had placed upwards of 350 stallions. They were stationed at several farms around New York State, including Ashantee in Avon, later known as the Lookover Stallion Station, originally owned by local horsewoman Martha Wadsworth.[13] Mares covered by Lookover stallions were then placed with members of the Genesee Valley Farmers' and Breeders' Association, for example; each was tasked with the care of both the mares and the resulting foals before they were sold, either at auction or to private buyers. Eventually, the stallions would become part of area horse shows, where Breeding Bureau yearlings and other horses were eligible for prizes.

The term of Hancock's lease done, Omaha finished out the 1943 breeding season at Claiborne and then was shipped north to Avon.[14] In September, he was paraded at the Genesee Valley Colt Show, part of the Thoroughbred stallion class to be shown there.[15] In addition to appearances at local shows, Omaha's time at Lookout saw him stand with stallions like Tourist II, two-time winner of the American Grand National. After a few seasons at Marion duPont Scott's Montpelier Stud in Virginia, Tourist II joined Omaha at Lookover Station.[16] There, the two stallions continued to service mares, and they even produced a few racehorses in their years with the Breeding Bureau.

From 1944 to 1950, Omaha stood for a fee of $15, serving around thirty mares a year. He was still a recognizable name, one of the "22 Favorite Thoroughbreds" in a poll of sportswriters conducted by the Thoroughbred Racing Associations. At age eighteen, his stud services were desirable enough that Grosvenor Porter and J. J. Isaacson proposed bringing Omaha to Nebraska to help energize the state's budding Thoroughbred breeding scene.[17] Porter had been part of the effort to bring racing back to Nebraska a decade earlier, and Isaacson served as general manager of Ak-Sar-Ben Racetrack in Omaha. Both men thought that a horse that shared his name with the state's capital would do wonders for the racing scene in Nebraska. Woodward was reluctant at first, but Porter and Isaacson eventually were able to get the master of Belair to agree to lease the stallion to Porter with provisions: the stallion's fee had to be $25, and he could service no more than fifteen mares a year.[18] After the 1950 breeding season at Lookover, Omaha was put on a train west to one final stop: Omaha, Nebraska.

He arrived at his new home in a railroad baggage car that had a stall specially built for him. When asked to fill out the value of the cargo he was sending, William Woodward valued Omaha at $100,000, a figure well above what he might have been worth but a reflection of the master of Belair's esteem for this son of Gallant Fox.[19] He traveled with Porter's son Morton and enough hay, straw, and oats for the trip from Avon to Omaha. At each stop, Morton Porter would open the car's doors and let the big horse stick his head out to take in the fresh air. As Omaha took in the people who stopped to visit, his young companion would regale passers-by with tales of the stallion's feats on the racetrack.[20] Years removed from his racing career, the old horse still thrilled the people who saw him.

At home in Nebraska, Omaha spent his remaining years at Porter's farm and orchard outside of Nebraska City, land that had originally been part of the estate of the first Secretary of Agriculture, J. Sterling Morton. There, Omaha Thoroughbred Breeders, Inc., which Grove Porter organized after the stallion's arrival, would send

Grosvenor and Morton Porter with Omaha. Courtesy Grosvenor M. "Budge" Porter Personal Collection.

a few mares to Omaha, and then sell the foals at public sale each year.[21] During his time in Nebraska, Morton Porter, who took over Omaha's care after his father died, took the horse to Ak-Sar-Ben for Omaha Gold Cup day. Whenever the starting gate bell sounded, Omaha reacted, pulling hard on the bridle and the shank as though he was still ready to run after all these years. Later in the year, Porter would bring Omaha to the Livestock and Rodeo Show, where he would parade around between events as an announcer read his list of accomplishments.[22] So beloved was the Belair champion that Ak-Sar-Ben erected a triangular granite monument to mark where Omaha would be buried when it was his time. The bronze likeness of their namesake champion would greet Ak-Sar-Ben visitors. Far away from where his life had started, from where his greatest turns around a

OMAHA

Here lies buried, Omaha, one of the immortals of the American turf. The bronze figure is a life-like replica of Omaha's head, fashioned by the Internationally renowned sculptress, Betti Richard Foaled in 1932, Omaha made history in 1935 by winning the Triple Crown, which includes the Kentucky Derby, the Preakness, and the Belmont Stakes. Only eight thoroughbreds in America's entire history have achieved this honor.

Bred by the late William G. Woodward Sr., of New York, Omaha was brought to Nebraska in 1950 by AK·SAR·BEN to contribute to the bloodlines of Nebraska Thoroughbreds. He died in April 1959 at the age of 27

Sign from Omaha's gravesite at Ak-Sar-Ben, Omaha, Nebraska. Courtesy Cynthia Csipkes-Curran.

racing oval had happened, the son of Gallant Fox would spend eternity in his adopted home, a place where he would be celebrated.[23]

Back in Kentucky, Sir Gallahad III and Gallant Fox continued their stud duties at Claiborne Farm alongside Blenheim II, sire of 1941 Triple Crown winner Whirlaway; Fighting Fox, Gallant Fox's full brother; and Princequillo, future damsire of Secretariat.[24] Sir Gallahad III led the general sire list four times and the broodmare sire list twelve times in his twenty-three seasons in the United States, but he was unable to cover the ten mares lined up for him in 1949.

On July 8, as he was turned out into his paddock, he collapsed, his twenty-nine years catching up to him. The sire of Gallant Fox, the grandsire of Omaha, this influential *chef-de-race* was buried at Claiborne Farm, near Marguerite, the mare who had brought him the best of his sons, who had passed away in 1945.[25] The era that had produced Gallant Fox and then Omaha was making its silent march toward an inevitable end, as time claimed the dam, then the sire, and soon the son.

Gallant Fox had limited access to mares in the years since those early crops that had produced Omaha, Granville, and Flares. By 1952, the Fox had been all but retired from stud service and he covered only one mare the following year.[26] In all, from twenty-one crops, he produced 322 registered foals, an average of fifteen foals per season. Of those 322 foals, 172 were winners, eighteen of them stakes winners. Those stakes winners included Calumet Dick, a gelding who won the Dixie Handicap (now the Dinner Party Stakes), the Narragansett Special, and the Southern Maryland and Thanksgiving Handicaps; Olympus, winner of the Merchants and Citizen and Excelsior Handicaps; and Wise Lady, who won the Delaware Oaks and then was second in the Acorn and third in the Coaching Club American Oaks.[27] At age twenty-seven, pensioned from stud duty, Gallant Fox slipped away on the afternoon of November 13, 1954, at Claiborne Farm, just hours before the Gallant Fox Handicap at Jamaica Race Course in New York and the Marguerite Stakes at Pimlico in Baltimore. He was buried near Sir Gallahad III and Marguerite on a hill that overlooked the stallion barns where he had spent his life since those last days on the racetrack, ending his life in the same place where it had begun.[28]

Out in Nebraska, on the same treed land that had inspired Sterling Morton to found Arbor Day, Omaha stood as the oldest of the Triple Crown winners; by 1959, the sport had seven such champions since Sir Barton's crowning forty years earlier. In the years after Omaha's Belmont victory on that rainy day in June 1935, five more horses had added their names to the exclusive fraternity, each one

Gallant Fox's grave at Claiborne Farm. Courtesy Kelly Jecmen.

building the gravitas of the triumvirate of victories to greater and greater heights with their accomplishments. At the age of twenty-seven, though, the stalwart son of Gallant Fox was beginning to show signs that time was catching up to him too. He developed breathing problems, so Morton Porter enclosed the stallion's stall and then set up an oxygen tank to supplement Omaha's own respirations.[29] On April 24, 1959, the Belair champion died in his stall, and then was buried at Ak-Sar-Ben the next day, laid to rest in the spot set aside for him by his Nebraska admirers.[30] With the passing of Omaha, whose dam Flambino, had predeceased him by a dozen years, the era of the Foxes was done.[31]

While Gallant Fox had sired two champions in his early years at stud, Omaha was not able to find such success in his time at stud. His two best foals were geldings, Prevaricator and South Dakota. Prevaricator was part of Omaha's last crop at Claiborne, foaled in 1943. He raced on the West Coast, where he won the San Diego

Omaha's memorial in Stinson Park, Omaha, Nebraska. Courtesy
Cynthia Csipkes-Curran.

Handicap twice and took the Bing Crosby Handicap and the Golden
Gate Mile as well. South Dakota's signature win was the 1945 Louisiana Handicap; he started 115 times and had thirty-four wins over
eight seasons. In seventeen crops, Omaha had 206 registered foals;
144 started a race and eighty-five were winners, seven of them stakes
winners.[32] Later generations, though, would keep Omaha's—and,
by extension Gallant Fox's—name in pedigrees, including one particular champion.

   In 1940, Omaha covered the mare Firetop, producing the filly
Flaming Top in 1941. Flaming Top raced for Arthur Hancock and
then became part of Claiborne's broodmare band; she visited
Menow, Hal Price Headley's good sire at Beaumont Farm, and produced the filly Flaring Top. She raced for E. P. Taylor, the Canadian
businessman, before she became a broodmare for the legendary
owner. He paired Flaring Top with 1951 Canadian Horse of the

Year Bull Page and got Flaming Page. For Taylor and his Windfields Farm, Flaming Page won the Canadian Oaks and the Queen's Plate, the nation's most famous race, and finished second behind Cicada in the 1962 Kentucky Oaks. As a broodmare, Flaming Page continued her on-track success with her three foals, including Fleur, dam of The Minstrel, Epsom Derby winner and Horse of the Year in England in 1977; and Nijinsky II, sired by Northern Dancer, the 1964 Kentucky Derby and Preakness winner for E. P. Taylor. Nijinsky II dominated the English classics of 1970 and became the last winner of the English Triple Crown, to date. When he was retired to stud, this son of Northern Dancer and Flaming Page stood at Claiborne Farm, just like Gallant Fox and Omaha had generations before him.

When Nijinsky II joined the stallion roster at Claiborne in December 1970, that roster also included another famed classic winner, Damascus, winner of the 1967 Preakness, Belmont, and Travers Stakes.[33] The son of Sword Dancer, also a classic winner, Damascus had a legendary performance in the 1967 Woodward Stakes, where he defeated both Dr. Fager and Buckpasser. The win was significant for another reason: the colt wore the familiar white with red polka dots.[34] Damascus raced for Edith Woodward Bancroft, William and Elsie's oldest daughter; his performance in that namesake race echoed the dominance that the Belair silks had over the sport in its heyday, when William Woodward's colors and horses reigned supreme.

Omaha's retirement in 1937 did not spell the end of the white with red polka dots; the famous silks continued to appear in winner's circles for another two decades. In addition to Gallant Fox's and Omaha's Triple Crown wins, Belair earned other American classic wins throughout the 1930s. Between the Fox and Omaha came Faireno's win in the 1932 Belmont Stakes. The year after Omaha's crown, Granville was another classic winner in the famed colors. He lost jockey Jimmy Stout at the start of the 1936 Kentucky Derby, which denied him the chance to wear roses, but he then added the Belmont and Travers Stakes, the Lawrence Realization, and the Saratoga

William Woodward with Granville, jockey Jimmy Stout in the saddle.
National Museum of Racing and Hall of Fame Collection.

Cup. At the end of 1936, Granville was the first horse voted Horse of the Year by the *Daily Racing Form* and *Turf & Sport Digest*. Next, Johnstown, bred by Claiborne Farm and privately purchased by Woodward, won the Kentucky Derby and the Belmont Stakes in 1939, a year dominated by the Maryland-bred Challedon, who was later voted Horse of the Year. While Johnstown ultimately became the last of William Woodward's Triple Crown classic winners, he was not the last of Woodward's champions.

In 1931, the master of Belair purchased Valkyr, a daughter of Man o' War, from the estate of Gifford Cochran, owner of 1925 Kentucky Derby winner Flying Ebony.[35] For Woodward, she produced Vagrancy, a daughter of Sir Gallahad III. At three, Vagrancy won the Beldame and Ladies Handicaps plus the Alabama and Test Stakes at Saratoga and the Coaching Club American Oaks, among her nine stakes wins in 1942. She ended the year as the champion three-year-old filly and champion female handicapper.[36] As a broodmare for

Belair, Vagrancy produced Black Tarquin, a colt by Rhodes Scholar. Woodward sent Black Tarquin to England to Captain Boyd-Rochfort; in the Belair silks, he won the St. Leger Stakes in 1948 and then was second in the Ascot Gold Cup in 1949. In all, Vagrancy produced eight foals, six of whom won on the racetrack, another example of the deep broodmare band that Woodward maintained over his decades as a breeder.

Since he started sending horses to Captain Cecil Boyd-Rochfort's Freemason Lodge in 1928, William Woodward had pursued his childhood goal of winning the Epsom Derby; he started a dozen horses in the English classic over two decades. Among Belair starters, from The Scout in 1930 to Turco II in 1951, the best showings came from Perifox, a son of Gallant Fox who finished fourth in 1937, and then Prince Simon in 1950. In only his third start, Prince Simon, sired by Princequillo, won the Newmarket Stakes, which made him the favorite for the Epsom Derby. He led the field for most of the 1½-mile classic at Epsom but was caught by a fast-closing Galcador in the stretch. Prince Simon rallied to close the gap with the French horse, but could not get by him and finished second by a head.[37] At age seventy-four, the master of Belair had come within a few inches of achieving his dream, but had fallen short, just as he had with Omaha at Royal Ascot in 1936. But that particular goal would not go unmet.

Cecil Boyd-Rochfort continued to train for Americans like William Woodward and Marshall Field, but also for English owners like Lady Zia Wernher and Sir Humphrey de Trafford, with whom he won the St. Leger with Alcide in 1958 and the Epsom Derby with Parthia in 1959.[38] Boyd-Rochfort would become the trainer for King George VI in 1943 and then for Queen Elizabeth II when she took over the royal stables after her father's death and her coronation. When he retired in 1968, Queen Elizabeth II made the legendary trainer a Knight Commander of the Royal Victorian Order. Boyd-Rochfort also named his stepson and assistant trainer Henry Cecil as his successor at Freemason Lodge.[39] Cecil would also go on to become a legendary trainer himself. He won the Epsom Derby and the St. Leger four times each and the Two Thousand Guineas three times; in addition, he conditioned Frankel, the undefeated two-time English Horse of the Year.[40]

Another of Woodward's English successes with Boyd-Rochfort was a horse with a familiar pedigree. Both Gallant Fox and Flambino had shown that they could stay a distance. The Fox had won at distances as long as 1¾ miles and Flambino had finished third in the Belmont Stakes in 1927, only two and a half lengths behind Chance Shot.[41] The combination of the two produced Omaha in 1932, whose long and lanky form equipped him to excel at long distances like the 2½-mile Ascot Gold Cup. Woodward sent Flambino back to Gallant Fox the next year and produced another long and lanky colt, this time a bay that the master of Belair named Flares.

When it came time to select horses to send to England, Flares was sent to Captain Boyd-Rochfort, but, like Omaha, he needed time to develop. Flares won the Newmarket Stakes and Ormonde Plate at three and the Champion Stakes and the Princess of Wales's Stakes at four. At five, he and Boswell, Woodward's St. Leger winner, were sent to the post for the Gold Cup at Royal Ascot. The two were at the back of the pack early, but, with a half mile to go, they began to move up through the field. By the time they reached the final straightaway toward the wire, that same long stretch that had seen the battle between Quashed and Omaha just two years earlier, Flares was mounting a furious bid for the lead. With Marcel Boussac's Senor on the rail and Buckleigh to his outside leading the field down the straight, Flares ranged up on their outside, swerving as he flashed by them to take the lead a furlong from the finish. Buckleigh fought back, coming on to challenge Woodward's horse, but was unable to catch Flares, who won the Ascot Gold Cup by a neck.[42] This full brother to Omaha had achieved what the third Triple Crown winner had been unable to do, and brought home the coveted prize for William Woodward and Belair Stud. Unfortunately, none of the Woodwards were on hand for the win. With that victory, Flares was done; the master of Belair retired his Gold Cup champion and brought him back to the United States to stand stud, first at Ellerslie and then at Claiborne Farm. In 1951, E. P. Taylor purchased the Ascot Gold Cup champion for the Canadian National Stud established in Ontario.[43]

That same year, Segula, a daughter of Belair's dual classic winner Johnstown, foaled a colt by Nasrullah, who had been imported to stand at Claiborne Farm, much like Sir Gallahad III. Nasrullah had been sired by Nearco, the undefeated Italian horse bred by the immortal Federico Tesio, and his success on the racetrack had carried over to the breeding shed.[44] Segula was part of Nasrullah's first book of mares in America, and the resulting colt, whom William Woodward would name Nashua, was tapped by the master of Belair to be sent to Boyd-Rochfort in England. But, before the colt was sent overseas, death intervened.

By 1950, when Prince Simon became Belair's best finisher in the Epsom Derby, William Woodward's health had begun to decline. That year, he gave up his post as chairman of the Jockey Club after two decades of service and he was not on hand to watch Prince Simon come so close to winning at Epsom. That same year he had also been elected an honorary member of England's Jockey Club, after he had successfully lobbied the organization to rescind the Jersey Act and open the Stud Book to families previously considered half-breeds.[45] In June 1949, the Stud Book's policies were amended to state that "any animal claiming admission from now on must be able to prove satisfactorily some eight or nine crosses of pure blood, to track back for at least a century, and to show such performances of its immediate family on the turf as to warrant the belief in the purity of its blood."[46] In 1953, as the yearling Nashua cavorted in his paddock at Belair, Woodward was seriously ill, confined to his Manhattan home. On September 26, the master of Belair, the man who had started a breeding and racing juggernaut with three $100 mares and a $60 stallion, a banker by profession whose passion for horses made him a Pillar of the Turf, died at age seventy-seven. He left behind his wife, Elsie; his four daughters, Edith Woodward Bancroft, Elizabeth Ogden

Woodward Pratt,[47] Sarah Woodward Sewall, and Ethel Woodward DeCroisset; and his only son, William Woodward Jr., or Billy, who inherited the Belair Stud stable, still trained by "Sunny Jim" Fitzsimmons.[48] It would be William Woodward Jr. that would race Nashua, the last of William Woodward's homebred champions.

For the younger Woodward and Fitzsimmons, Nashua would continue the form that had marked the best of the Belair horses of the past. At two, he equaled the track record for six furlongs at Belmont Park and won the Futurity and the Juvenile Stakes at Belmont and the Hopeful and Grand Union Hotel Stakes at Saratoga. He ended 1954 as the year's champion two-year-old colt before going on to win the Preakness and Belmont Stakes at three after losing the Kentucky Derby to Swaps, whom he defeated in a match race later that year. He also won the Dwyer Stakes, the Arlington Classic, and the Jockey Club Gold Cup that year and was recognized as champion three-year-old colt and Horse of the Year for 1954. All in all, it was a season reminiscent of Gallant Fox's own three-year-old season, with high expectations for his four-year-old season. And then tragedy struck.

Billy Woodward had married model turned stage and radio actress Ann Crowell in 1943. The couple then had two sons, William Woodward III and James. Their marriage was turbulent; the couple reportedly argued in private as much as they were seen out in public as part of New York society. They shared a home in Oyster Bay, Long Island, in a neighborhood that had seen a series of burglaries in October 1955. After attending a party for the Duke and Duchess of Windsor the evening of October 29, the couple came home and retired to separate bedrooms. Each kept a weapon nearby in case of a burglary. In the wee hours of the morning, Ann heard movement outside her bedroom door, grabbed her double-barreled shotgun, opened the door, and fired at a shadowy figure standing in the hall. Hearing the shots, the night watchman called the police; when they arrived, they found Ann crying next to her husband's body. Billy's death ended his dreams of revitalizing Belair and returning the estate to a fully functional farm; the Belair horses, including Nashua, were sold in a sealed-bid auction. The colt went to a syndicate headed by Leslie Combs of Spendthrift Farm, in whose colors the last Belair-bred champion raced at age four.[49] After he won a second Jockey Club Gold Cup among his six stakes victories in 1956, Nashua retired to Spendthrift Farm, where he stood stud until his death in 1982.[50] As a stallion, Nashua would produce Shuvee, who won the Triple Tiara at age three and then the Jockey Club Gold Cup twice, just like her sire; and Gold Digger, dam of *chef-de-race* Mr. Prospector.[51] Decades after his death, William Woodward's choice to pair Segula with Nasrullah led to Nashua, Mr. Prospector, and generations of great horses that continued the Belair influence over the sport well into the twenty-first century.

Nashua may not have had continuity in ownership, as he passed from father to son and then to Leslie Combs and partners, but he did have the continuity of care that came from the Sage of Sheepshead Bay. Fitzsimmons trained the Belair horses for the rest of William Woodward's life and then worked with Billy Woodward as he contemplated the future of Belair. After the younger Woodward's death and Nashua's sale, Sunny Jim remained Nashua's trainer. By this point in racing history, what trainer could do better than the man who had conditioned two Triple Crown winners, three Kentucky Derby victors, and numerous other stakes winners and champions? Nashua was in more than capable hands, as were Fitzsimmons's other champions, like Bold Ruler for his longtime clients, the Wheatley Stable.

When James Edward Fitzsimmons retired in 1963, both William Woodward Sr. and Jr. had been gone for the better part of the decade, but he was still actively training for the Wheatley Stable. "I can't get around as well as I used to is all," the renowned conditioner said when asked about his retirement. "These people have a big investment in their stock, and it must be protected. I know I can't do the things I should be doing."[52] His wife, Jennie, had died in 1956 and, at nearly eighty-eight years old, time was catching up to the man who had seen racing evolve from the "frying pan" circuit, where he perfected his trade, to the modern racetracks that were the scenes of many a historic battle. By this time, his six children had given him seventeen grandchildren and forty-three great-grandchildren. His was indeed a sunny life, full of family, friends, and a long list of great horses that had passed through his hands. "The older you get," Fitzsimmons once said, "the more you realize that life itself is a game of luck. The big thing is to wind up with people still liking you. If you can do that, you're a pretty lucky guy."[53]

"Sunny Jim" Fitzsimmons might have been one of the luckiest of them all.

On March 11, 1966, the ninety-one-year-old Fitzsimmons passed away in a Miami, Florida, hospital after a three-week battle with the flu. "His heart just gave out," said his son John. It was a reminder that even the stalwart conditioner, who as a young man had defied a doctor's orders to give up racing after malaria gave him heart palpitations, was also mortal.[54] What he achieved, though, was immortal. Fitzsimmons had been inducted into the National Museum of Racing and Hall of Fame in 1958; he was eventually joined by seven horses that he had conditioned: Gallant Fox, Omaha, Granville, Johnstown, Nashua, Bold Ruler, and Seabiscuit. His 149 stakes winners accounted for 470 stakes wins, including six Belmont Stakes, eight Wood Memorials, and four Preakness Stakes in addition to those Kentucky Derbies with Gallant Fox, Omaha, and Johnstown.[55] When asked which of his horses was the greatest, the Hall of Fame trainer cited Gallant Fox: "He would always battle for you. There were never any excuses with him. The other horse just had to be the best horse if he was to beat him."[56] From 1924 to 1963, James Fitzsimmons, the man who was practically born on a racetrack, the preferred conditioner for two of racing's legendary stables, had made the winner's circle his home on many of the sport's biggest days.

With William Woodward Sr. and Jr. gone, the white and red polka dots had faded from the spotlight, but, in 1967, the classic

Belair silks made a resurgence on racing's biggest stages. The name behind them was not Woodward, but Bancroft: Edith Woodward Bancroft, William and Elsie's oldest daughter, married to Thomas Moore Bancroft. When her brother Billy died, the Belair horses had been dispersed, but Bancroft had retained the Belair silks, though she did not race under that name. She maintained a modest stable, breeding and racing fewer than ten horses at a time.[57] Along with her mother, Elsie, Edith owned shares of a few mares, including Kerala, a daughter of the English sire My Babu.[58] From her pairing with Sword Dancer, 1959 Belmont Stakes winner and Horse of the Year, came a plain bay colt they named Damascus. Damascus was trained by Frank Whiteley, who would later condition both Ruffian and Forego; the colt would win the Preakness and Belmont Stakes in the white with red polka dots. His classic wins echoed an era just three decades earlier, when those same silks had been a fixture in the winner's circles of those classic races. At age three, Damascus would go on to win the Jockey Club Gold Cup, the Travers Stakes, and the Woodward Stakes, ending 1967 as the champion three-year-old colt and Horse of the Year.[59] He would be the last of the champions seen in those familiar silks, though Edith's sons Thomas Jr. and William continued to race in those colors under the *nom de course* Pen-Y-Bryn Farm until they ceased racing in 1995.[60] Dormant since then, the white with red polka dots are still recognized as the emblem of excellence during one of racing's greatest decades.

Damascus retired to a familiar spot for horses with ties to the Belair colors: Claiborne Farm. As part of their stallion band into the 1990s, the son of Sword Dancer eclipsed his sire in terms of production; he sired 438 winners and seventy-two stakes winners, continuing the Teddy sire line that had produced Sir Gallahad III, Gallant Fox, and Omaha.[61] That Edith Woodward Bancroft's champion would wear the Belair colors and then go on to stud at Claiborne Farm was a fitting continuation of the legacy started decades earlier when William Woodward sent his mares to the Paris farm to produce horses sired by their deep list of stallions.

Belair no longer houses young horses. The stables are empty, and the vast acreage was sold off to developers not long after Billy Woodward's death. The house that has stood in various iterations over four centuries is now a museum. This piece of Maryland history is preserved so future generations can experience the resplendent estate, once home to a foundational mare, a colonial governor, and a Pillar of the Turf. Still, Belair remains and Gallant Fox's stall is intact, the famed white with red polka dots a banner that reminds visitors of this celebrated spot in the state's rich racing past. All of this because a young man had a dream and made it his life's work to pursue it, in the process influencing an entire sport for more than a generation.

William Woodward oversaw a transitional moment in the sport, from its contraction in a time of social upheaval to its expansion because of another such moment. In his time, the mechanical starting gate, a technological marvel, was introduced and took the place of the standing start behind a tenuous barrier. Betting, an integral facet of the sport, also changed. Instead of bets being laid with bookmakers, pari-mutuel betting became available in wide swaths of the country. Woodward's work on behalf of American breeders finally opened up England's Stud Book to horses bred here, gaining deserved credibility for the men and women who had, like him, given of their time, their resources, and their passion to the sport. In his time as chairman of the Jockey Club, the sport was modernized but did not forget its roots; while its rules and traditions were solemnized, they were transformed when necessary. As a result, racing continues as a sport that is at once old and new, steadfast amid the ever-changing names at its heart. Last but not least, in his decade of dominance, Woodward helped make the three races that comprise the Triple Crown something more than just purses and trophies, bigger even than the places where they happen.

A quest for a Derby started with a conversation overheard in childhood, and, later, the purchase of three inexpensive mares; by the time he had won a place in the sport's Hall of Fame, William Woodward had turned his quest into gold many times over. From the golden trophies given under Twin Spires to a gold cup won in the presence of royalty, the master of Belair used his time, his fortune, and his determination to turn his dreams into reality. His esteem for the English classics translated to the American ones; he sent his best horses in pursuit of a crown and achieved the extraordinary accomplishment of breeding and owning not one, but *two* such champions, their names immortalized on a short list of the sport's elite. Gallant Fox's record-breaking season and Omaha's status as the lone Triple Crown victor to race in England not only helped make the Kentucky Derby, the Preakness Stakes, and the Belmont Stakes the heart of the American racing calendar but also set a standard for future generations to aspire to: one horse with the right balance of speed, stamina, and heart to outrun and outlast every challenger and emerge victorious on the sport's biggest days. Sir Barton may have done it first, but it was Gallant Fox and Omaha and the men behind them who showed that this was a crown worth pursuing.

Epilogue

The Quest for the Crown

In the twenty-first century, we may take the feat that is the Triple Crown as a given, with importance that seems self-evident. Its presence on the calendar and the attendant series of races that have grown up around it dominate the first half of the racing year. It is a focal point for many a fan, casual or hard core, who looks forward to the first Saturday in May and wonders if this year will be *the* year. "Will we see another one?" we ask ourselves each time the calendar turns to a new year and a new group of names emerges in the countdown to the Triple Crown season. Three-year-old horses, many of them barely that age when the racing season begins, are asked to run distances that range from a mile and a quarter to a mile and a half over a span of five weeks at three different tracks. The pursuit demands more of those who attempt it than even its English counterpart, which spans a much greater nineteen weeks. The test is one that we all want to see passed and we spend hours debating the merits of those who attempt it. But the test is not always one that owners or trainers want their horses to take.

The Triple Crown itself, observed from a purely logistical standpoint, does not make sense. Challenging horses to run what we consider classic distances—a practice culled from our English brothers—is nothing new in racing. However, the choice of those particular locations over that short calendar seems less logical until we realize that these are the places—Kentucky, Maryland, and New York—where the sport has long thrived. With the exception of interruptions due to antigambling movements or war, these three states have played host to the sport and its many facets for more than a century. Several of the earliest breeding operations in the United States date back to Maryland the colony, years before the country declared its independence from the country that has inspired much of our tradition and terminology. New York has long been home to racing; at Saratoga, one of the United States' oldest racetracks, the sport continued even while the country was at war with itself. Racing, which had thrived in the antebellum South, was virtually wiped out by the Civil War, so Kentucky became the focus of breeding and racing in the years after the conflict. That these areas house three American classics that echo English classics like the Epsom Derby is unsurprising. However, that horses are asked to run all three in a matter of weeks rather than months is a uniquely American phenomenon. The English may have inspired American racing, but we have taken pains to make it our own: we prefer dirt to turf and we ask our horses to run in ways that others may not.

When Sir Barton won the Kentucky Derby, the Preakness Stakes, and the Belmont Stakes in 1919, his victories earned him the attendant praise that those victories—and taking the Withers Stakes in between—merited. Cries of "horse of the decade" and the hyperbolic "horse of the century" were bandied about as the chestnut colt stood in the winner's circle at Belmont Park on June 11, but the term "Triple Crown" as we know it did not accompany this triumvirate of stakes wins.[1] In that era, each race stood on its own merits, and certainly the purse money made them all the more attractive. But the idea that these three were connected in any way played no part in the telling of Sir Barton's story until years later. The schedule for the three races between 1920 and 1929 reflects that absence of cohesion; the Derby and Preakness were run *on the same day* in 1922, an unimaginable happenstance a century later.

So, when Man o' War bypassed the Kentucky Derby and started his three-year-old season in the Preakness Stakes, the snub did not carry the same weight that history gives it today. For the modern racing fan, the fact that the twentieth century's greatest horse side-stepped the country's biggest race inspires a level of incredulity not sated by Louis Feustel's recollection of the reasons. "It just so happened that we didn't want to risk the long trip to Kentucky," the trainer recalled. "Besides Man o' War was off his feed then, and I wanted to bring him along for the summer . . . that's the real story."[2] In 1920, though, Kentucky was the West, and Samuel Riddle preferred to stay in the East, where the Preakness and the Belmont Stakes were only a train ride away. Besides, the three races did not yet carry the cachet or the name that would come to signal their significance in the sport. Until 1923, when the *Daily Racing Form* first used the term to refer to the familiar sequence of races, "Triple Crown" referred only to the English classics for three-year-olds: the Epsom Derby, the Two Thousand Guineas, and the St. Leger Stakes, which predated the oldest of the three American races, the Belmont Stakes.[3] That same year, when Zev won the Kentucky Derby and the Belmont Stakes after finishing twelfth in the Preakness, his dual classic wins came without any mention of triple crowns.

By 1930, newspapers were more apt to use the term "triple crown" in reference to Gallant Fox's accomplishment, with various iterations of the term: triple crown, "triple crown," and even Triple Crown. The sport's most famous weekly magazine, the *Blood-Horse,* had not yet adopted the term in its recounting of the Fox's victory in the Belmont, instead saying "that the two [Sir Barton and Gallant Fox] might be called Triple Event winners."[4] Though the term "Triple Crown" did appear occasionally alongside Gallant Fox's list of accomplishments in 1930, it had not yet reached the level of ubiquity that modern fans would expect.

When Omaha won his own Triple Crown in 1935, the third to do so and the first and only one sired by another winner, the *Daily*

Racing Form's headline for June 10, 1935, read "Omaha Becomes Triple Crown Hero."[5] In the article that followed, the son of Gallant Fox was called "a 'triple crown' winner"; the term was still used informally but was nevertheless gaining legitimacy. While newspapers and the *Form* were apt to use the term, the *Blood-Horse* opted to echo its earlier use of "events" to refer to the three races, acknowledging that "Omaha was the third horse to complete the triple."[6] With the addition of Omaha to the list of winners, the sequence of three stakes races had gained not only its sobriquet but also enough prestige to lead one notable owner to pursue the Triple Crown with the best son of his immortal champion.

In 1937, as Captain Boyd-Rochfort was considering when Omaha would make his return to the racetrack before a second try at the Ascot Gold Cup, Samuel Riddle sent his War Admiral to Churchill Downs as his one and only Kentucky Derby starter—and won. Seventeen years after Riddle had declined to run Man o' War in the same race, War Admiral easily beat a field of nineteen horses to bring home the roses. A week later, he would duel with Pompoon down the stretch at Pimlico to take the Preakness. Despite shearing off a portion of his hoof at the start of the Belmont Stakes, War Admiral would complete the fourth Triple Crown in record time, adding his name to the short list of horses that had achieved the feat that was rapidly becoming a clear-cut measure of the merits of a horse's career. With that came a new consideration: how to assess those who had not won the Triple Crown. The year after Sir Barton completed the first one, Man o' War became the first horse to win the Preakness and the Belmont Stakes, but not the Kentucky Derby, adding an asterisk to the career of the twentieth century's greatest horse. Siring a Triple Crown winner would be the closest Man o' War came to wearing the crown himself; but, much like his lone loss to the aptly named Upset, little would ever diminish the fiery juggernaut's reputation.

The Great Depression gave rise to the factors that grew the Triple Crown's prominence in the sport's history. After its virtual death knell at the hands of reformers in the first decade of the twentieth century and then its post–World War I resurgence, racing found an even bigger audience as the Roaring Twenties gave way to the Depression era. When other sports were contracting and losing teams because their spectators could no longer afford to attend, horse racing was growing as states saw the revenues from racing as a chance to improve their bottom line.[7] By 1940, twenty-one states had at least one track, with more in Canada, Mexico, and Cuba. Within another year, Pennsylvania, Virginia, and New Jersey joined the mix. In 1945, the last year of World War II, over nineteen million people attended races at fifty-four racetracks.[8] By 1950, racing had expanded to twenty-four states, with eighty-five racetracks in the United States alone. As the new decade dawned, twenty-nine million visited a racetrack and millions more listened on the radio or watched at home. In 1953, Native Dancer thrilled audiences with his come-from-behind runs on national television; that year the "Gray Ghost" was the second most popular figure on television, behind Ed Sullivan.[9] Racing had entered the American mainstream in a way that August Belmont II could have only dreamed of decades earlier.

With the new tracks came new organizations. The Thoroughbred Racing Associations, a collective of state racing associations across the country, declared the Kentucky Derby, the Preakness Stakes, and the Belmont Stakes to be the Triple Crown—absent quotation marks and officially with capital letters—in 1950. That year, at the TRA's annual banquet dinner, they awarded the first of eight triangular trophies, designed by esteemed jewelers at Cartier, to Sir Barton's owner, Commander John Kenneth Leveson Ross.[10] Each year thereafter, the TRA awarded another trophy to the next winner to be recognized. If no horse won that year, then the trophy would go to a previous winner that had yet to receive one. In 1951, William Woodward received a trophy for Gallant Fox, and, in 1952, for Omaha.

Between War Admiral's Triple Crown in 1937 and the awarding of his trophy in 1953, the list of winners grew by four names, all coming in the same decade: Whirlaway (1941), Count Fleet (1943), Assault (1946), and Citation (1948). In those intervening years, the three races and the pursuit of them grew in stature as the sport spread from sea to shining sea and reached more fans than ever. The proliferation of radios in the 1920s and 1930s and then televisions in the 1950s brought the races into homes everywhere and gave the sport a greater reach than even the increased number of racetracks. With stars like the long-tailed Whirlaway, the club-footed Assault, and Citation, the first millionaire, it was no wonder that the Triple Crown became as much of an institution in the sport as were the individual races that constituted it. With four winners in a decade, the addition of another winner might have seemed a sure bet. Surely, more were to come. Surely, the list would not stop at eight. Events of the 1950s and then the 1960s might have had as much impact on growing the Triple Crown into the dominant force that it is today as did those four winners in the 1940s.

Other horses had won two of the three in the 1930s and 1940s. Helen Hay Whitney's Twenty Grand won the Kentucky Derby and the Belmont Stakes in 1931, and Johnstown, owned by Belair Stud, did the same in 1939, both denied their crowns by losses in the Preakness Stakes. Shut Out lost his chance in the middle jewel as well, running into a troubled trip behind winner Alsab. Bimelech and Capot took the Preakness and Belmont Stakes in 1940 and 1949, but both were denied the Kentucky Derby by long shots. Injury kept Burgoo King and Bold Venture out of the Belmont, denying those Derby–Preakness winners a chance at a crown. Pensive followed in 1944, but he lost his bid for the Triple Crown when he could not outlast a surging Bounding Home in the stretch at Belmont Park. These were all during two decades that saw seven Triple Crown champions. Over a twenty-four-year stretch, from 1949 to 1972, fourteen horses won two of the three, leaving some to wonder whether a change was needed in the calendar or the races in order to welcome another name to the list of eight elites. Their trophies had been awarded and one more sat in a vault, waiting for the right horse to come along and win.

That trophy was waiting for a big red colt named Secretariat.

After twenty-five years of waiting for the next winner, Penny Chenery's Secretariat, bred by her father Christopher, ignited the imaginations of fans across the country with his record-breaking run through the Triple Crown classics in 1973. Setting records in all three races, he broke the two-minute mark in the Kentucky Derby; ran the fastest Preakness ever; and then set the American record for a mile and a half in the Belmont Stakes, where his 2:24 is still the record nearly fifty years later.[11] The big red colt exited the three races as the best to ever win the Crown. He won the Belmont by the largest margin to date, hitting the wire thirty-one lengths in front, an even greater margin than Count Fleet's twenty-five. His dominance at three echoed that of Gallant Fox, but the timing of his moment made him a bright spot in the midst of the tumult of the Vietnam War and ongoing social changes. He was a superstar, beloved by a generation of racing fans who were able to see the flashy chestnut in full color on television.

The 1970s saw two more champions: Seattle Slew and Affirmed took the pursuit to a new level, winning in back-to-back years. Seattle Slew entered his run for the Crown undefeated, the first horse to do so. He met Affirmed the following year in the first-ever meeting of two Triple Crown winners. The four-year-old Seattle Slew beat the three-year-old Affirmed by three lengths in the Marlboro Cup Handicap, three months after Affirmed bested Alydar in all three of the Triple Crown classics. The margins between those two horses were the smallest of any other champions: Affirmed won the Derby by 1½ lengths, the Preakness by a neck, and the Belmont by a head over Alydar, who, in any other year, might have won the Triple Crown himself.

The following year, Spectacular Bid came close to making it three Triple Crowns in a row, giving the decade its fourth dual classic winner and near miss. In 1972, Riva Ridge ran into a muddy track in the Preakness but was successful in the Kentucky Derby and the Belmont Stakes, giving Penny Chenery a preview of the experience just a year before Secretariat. Bold Forbes would do the same in 1976, losing the Preakness after battling Honest Pleasure throughout the race. Little Current ran into traffic in the 1974 Kentucky Derby and finished fifth before winning the Preakness and the Belmont. With three Triple Crown winners and four near-misses in the decade, the 1970s led to the same expectation that followed the multiple winners of the 1940s: that the list would not stop there, that more names would join the eleven already on the board.

Another winner proved elusive over the next three decades, and questions about the series arose once again. Was the schedule too grueling for young horses early in their three-year-old season? Were the requirements for getting into the series too challenging? With the ever-increasing number of horses foaled each year, it became harder for horses to qualify for the three races, to stand out above the rest. In 1927, 4,182 Thoroughbreds were foaled in the United States; by 1975, when Affirmed was foaled, the number was 28,271.[12] The largest foal crop since 1919 was in 1986, when 51,296 horses were foaled. That crop produced Sunday Silence and Easy Goer, who battled through the 1989 Triple Crown series much like Affirmed and Alydar had in 1978, with Sunday Silence coming out on top in the first two and Easy Goer getting the better of his rival in the Belmont Stakes. By 2012, when the number was down to 23,542 foals, a bay colt with a wee star finally became the one.

Trainer Bob Baffert had his share of experience with the Triple Crown series, saddling Silver Charm, Real Quiet, and War Emblem to wins first in the Kentucky Derby and then the Preakness Stakes. All three came into the Belmont Stakes chasing a crown, each year adding another layer of hope at their potential and then disappointment when they were met with defeat. In 2015, Baffert brought American Pharoah to the Kentucky Derby, the race where his sire Pioneerof the Nile had finished second six years earlier. He toughed out a win in the first jewel, his biggest test of the year to that point. In the Preakness, he sloshed through pouring rain and a sloppy surface at Pimlico to set up a run at the Triple Crown. On a picture-perfect June day at Belmont Park, the track was at full capacity—ninety thousand fans—to see American Pharoah win the Triple Crown and end the thirty-seven-year drought. His victory was met with the intense, full-throated adulation of the fans on hand and the racing world as a whole. After years of debate about the schedule, the distances, and the system, American Pharoah came along and showed that it takes an extraordinary horse to do it. Three years later, another Baffert trainee, Justify, would become the thirteenth to win the Crown, doing it in an extraordinarily short career of just 112 days from his first start to his Belmont win.

A few years on from Justify's addition to the list, a century after Sir Barton became the first to win the three races, the Triple Crown remains one of the most elite and elusive achievements in the sport of horse racing in America. Over the course of a century, the three races have come to define the careers of all who achieve them and of those who fall short. The pursuit of the Kentucky Derby, the Preakness Stakes, and the Belmont Stakes comprises the first half of the racing calendar, and the Breeders' Cup, situated at the end of the racing season, dominates the second, creating a series of tests that can make or break a horse's lasting legacy. These races can also make or break a horse's career on and off the track; winning just one of the classics can make a stallion more attractive at stud. From three stakes races, each with its own history and traditions, comes this unified pursuit, which brings even the most casual of racing fans to the television screen or racetrack in the spring of each year. It all began with Sir Barton, who did it first, and then Gallant Fox and Omaha, who made the quest one that others pursued; each brought something special to the history of the Triple Crown, each was there because of the ones who came before them.

William Woodward's passionate pursuit of the goals he set as a young man became a quest for glory at the sport's highest levels, for an excellence that immortalizes the people and the horses who win these races. Woodward threw his time and fortune into his passion, setting a precedent that marked his era and the ones that have followed. He valued and pursued those races steeped in tradition, the ones that had become known as classics; by honoring their traditions, he imbued them with significance that went beyond a purse and a trophy. As the breeder and owner of both Gallant Fox and Omaha, he inspired others, like Warren Wright, whose Calumet Farm bred and owned Whirlaway and Citation. Woodward's role in Sir Gallahad III's journey to the United States inspired similar imports, such as Blenheim II, sire of Whirlaway. Additionally, the master of Belair worked to open the *General Stud Book* to American-bred horses. This made possible America's dominance of international breeding; bloodstock bred in this country are regularly sought out by breeders from Europe to Asia. William Woodward may have valued British bloodstock and British racing, but he cleared the way for America to play a dominant role in the sport on an international scale, expanding racing in ways that perhaps he himself could not have imagined in his time.

With two Triple Crown winners and a long list of other champions, the white with red polka dots dominated a decade and came to symbolize the heights of achievement in the sport of horse racing. While the Belair silks did not grace the winner's circle at Epsom, those colors did flash under the wire first at Royal Ascot, under the Twin Spires, and over the sandy surface at Belmont Park. They were fixtures on many of the sport's biggest days, a legacy of excellence that resonates to this day. Immortalized in the Hall of Fame, conspicuous on the short list of Triple Crown champions, these familiar names, these eternal pursuits—all of this because one young man dared to dream about winning a horse race.

Acknowledgments

Long before I had typed the final words on my first book, *Sir Barton and the Making of the Triple Crown,* I was a fifth grader reading *The Black Stallion* series and falling in love with horse racing. My earliest experiences with the sport were watching the Triple Crown broadcasts on ABC, the welcoming cadences of Charlsie Cantey, Jim McKay, and Dave Johnson intertwined with the memories of Sunday Silence versus Easy Goer and Carl Nafzger narrating Unbridled's Derby victory to owner Frances Gentry. The names on the short list of eleven winners kept me enthralled, wanting to learn more and feeling that all of their stories were richer than the abridged versions in my books on the Triple Crown. It was in that spirit that I wanted to write Sir Barton's story, and then, as I realized that Gallant Fox and Omaha lacked similar treatments, do the same for William Woodward's champions.

To create the book you now hold in your hands is not the work of one person alone. Accompanying me on this journey is a list of people who have helped me find necessary resources, provided both the feedback and the reassurance essential to this kind of undertaking, and invested the same love and affection for the subjects and the craft into this book that I have. Ashley Runyon and Brooke Raby both have made working with the University Press of Kentucky a relationship that I cherish, their focus always on telling the stories that are important to the Bluegrass State and the sport. Patrick O'Dowd and Jamie Nicholson have supported this project with endless emails, texts, revisions, and their confidence that this was a story well told. Having a publisher and editors so willing to give of themselves makes this work that much more fulfilling.

To explore the story of Gallant Fox and Omaha requires not only an ever-shifting pile of books and hours on digital archives but also the knowledgeable and hard-working professionals at the Keeneland Library. Roda Ferraro, Kelly Coffman, and Becky Ryder all fielded my many questions, scanned photos and sources, and aided the searches for elusive facts. Without them, this book and the one that preceded it would not have been possible.

Similar accolades are necessary for Jessica Whitehead at the Kentucky Derby Museum, Susan Proctor and Tiffany Davis at the Belair Stable Museum and Belair Mansion, and Stephanie Luce at the National Museum of Racing and Hall of Fame. Writers may craft the story, but these scholars of information and preservation provide the building blocks.

Grosvenor "Budge" Porter and Cindy Csipkes-Curran made the Nebraska part of Omaha's story come to life. Their enthusiasm for the third Triple Crown winner and his time in Omaha added heart to that unique moment in this book.

Sheila Knight and Kelly Jecmen both gave generously of their time providing their feedback on an early draft of this project. Their comments were an invaluable part of shaping the truly rough draft into a polished adventure through the Belair years.

I owe my family much gratitude for encouraging my interest in horse racing since those early days clutching those Walter Farley books and stealing the television whenever racing was on. My family listened to me talk about this sport and even watched the races with me. My aunt Betty was the first to take me to the Birmingham Race Course to see the sport in person. All of them enabled me to grow this childhood love into a career writing about the sport I love.

Our boys, Jackson and Beckett, have been a touchstone through this writing process, bringing their mother much-needed moments of levity and love through a pandemic, a year of virtual schooling, and another book's worth of long days at the computer. My boys drive me ever forward to the next day and the next thing.

With the story of Gallant Fox and Omaha now complete, after nearly three years of research, drafting, and refining, this book exists only because I have an amazing partner in my corner. My husband, Jamie, has been my rock through two books, from their genesis to their completion, and has encouraged me at every turn. He believed in my potential and my ambition and made all of this possible. For that, I will spend a lifetime sharing my gratitude for the cheerleader, father, and partner that he is.

Appendix

Gallant Fox Pedigree

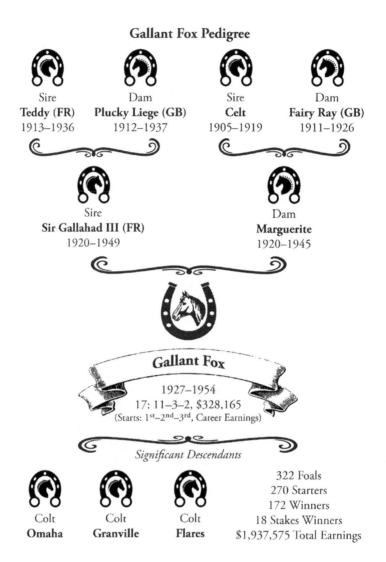

Sire
Teddy (FR)
1913–1936

Dam
Plucky Liege (GB)
1912–1937

Sire
Celt
1905–1919

Dam
Fairy Ray (GB)
1911–1926

Sire
Sir Gallahad III (FR)
1920–1949

Dam
Marguerite
1920–1945

Gallant Fox

1927–1954
17: 11–3–2, $328,165
(Starts: 1st–2nd–3rd, Career Earnings)

Significant Descendants

Colt
Omaha

Colt
Granville

Colt
Flares

322 Foals
270 Starters
172 Winners
18 Stakes Winners
$1,937,575 Total Earnings

Gallant Fox's pedigree. Graphic by Jamie Kelly.

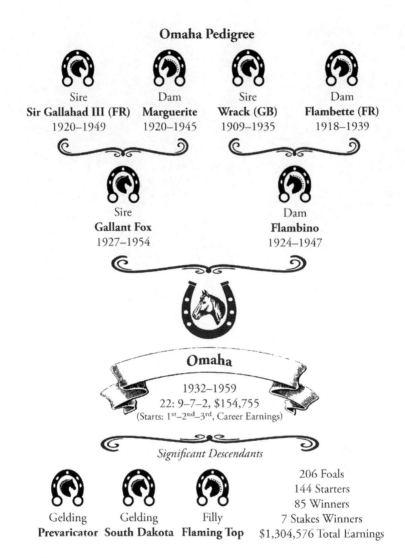

Omaha Pedigree

Sire	Dam	Sire	Dam
Sir Gallahad III (FR)	**Marguerite**	**Wrack (GB)**	**Flambette (FR)**
1920–1949	1920–1945	1909–1935	1918–1939

Sire	Dam
Gallant Fox	**Flambino**
1927–1954	1924–1947

Omaha

1932–1959
22: 9–7–2, $154,755
(Starts: 1st–2nd–3rd, Career Earnings)

Significant Descendants

Gelding	Gelding	Filly	
Prevaricator	**South Dakota**	**Flaming Top**	206 Foals 144 Starters 85 Winners 7 Stakes Winners $1,304,576 Total Earnings

Omaha's pedigree. Graphic by Jamie Kelly.

Notes

1. A New King in Town

1. "Sir Gallahad, French Horse, Arrives in the U.S," *St. Louis Post Dispatch,* December 15, 1925.

2. Épinard was a French stallion who counted English Triple Crown winner Rock Sand as his damsire. Épinard won multiple prestigious stakes races in both England and France before being sent to the United States in 1924. He lost all of his starts in America but was retroactively considered a champion, nevertheless. "Sir Gallahad Arrives," *Thoroughbred Horse,* December 1925, 6.

3. Two horses were already registered under the name "Sir Gallahad" in the Jockey Club records so this Sir Gallahad earned the III to differentiate him from the others.

4. Edward L. Bowen, *Legacies of the Turf,* vol. 1 (Lexington, KY: Eclipse, 2003), 64.

5. Colin went a perfect fifteen for fifteen in his career in 1907 and 1908. He won such prestigious stakes races as the Champagne Stakes, the Withers Stakes, and the Belmont Stakes.

6. Bowen, *Legacies of the Turf,* 22.

7. Bowen, *Legacies of the Turf,* 65.

8. Avalyn Hunter, *American Classic Pedigrees (1914–2000)* (Lexington, KY: Eclipse, 2003), 81; Abram S. Hewitt, *Sire Lines* (Lexington, KY: Eclipse, 2006), 291.

9. Hewitt, *Sire Lines,* 291.

10. Bowen, 66.

11. Bowen, 66.

12. Robert le Diable's sire, Ayrshire, also sired Peep o' Day, who was imported to the United States along with his dam, Sundown, in 1893. Peep o' Day went on to sire Milkmaid, the filly who was a stablemate of Sir Barton during their racing years with Commander J. K. L. Ross's stable.

Thoroughbred Heritage (website): "Ayrshire," accessed March 2019, tbheritage.com/Portraits/Ayrshire.html; "Isinglass," accessed March 2019, tbheritage.com/Portraits/Isinglass.html; "Chelandry," accessed March 2019, tbheritage.com/Portraits/Chelandry.html.

13. Archibald Philip Primrose, Fifth Earl of Rosebery, also happened to be prime minister from March 1894 to June 1895. Avalyn Hunter, "Wrack," American Classic Pedigrees.com, accessed April 8, 2019, http://www .americanclassicpedigrees.com/wrack-gb.html.

14. "Sixteen McKay Racehorses Arrive," *New York Times,* December 17, 1915.

15. Abram S. Hewitt, *The Great Breeders and Their Methods* (Lexington, KY: Thoroughbred, 1982), 126–127.

16. War Cloud was the first horse to traverse what became the Triple Crown trail in 1918; he finished fourth in the Kentucky Derby, won one division of that year's split Preakness Stakes, and then finished second in the Belmont Stakes. He was owned by A. K. Macomber.

17. The Hancock family maintained both Ellerslie and Claiborne Farm until 1946, when the family sold Ellerslie to Robert Schlesinger.

18. Neil Newman, *Famous Horses of the American Turf,* vol. 1 (New York: Derrydale, 1931), 2.

19. The price was reported as 2.5 million francs, between £50,000 and £60,000, or $125,000. In 2022, that would be about $2.025 million. "Sport of the Day," *Leicester Mail,* December 1, 1925; "Sir Gallahad III Sold," *Daily Mail,* December 7, 1925.

20. Sir Gallahad III was initially spelled "Sir Galahad" but was registered as "Sir Gallahad" in France. "Sir Gallahad Arrives," *Thoroughbred Horse* 8, no. 12 (December 1925): 6.

21. Staff of Blood-Horse Publications, *Horse Racing's Top 100 Moments* (Lexington, KY: Eclipse, 2006), 96.

22. Bowen, 66.

23. Avalyn Hunter, "Nimba," American Classic Pedigrees.com, accessed April 10, 2019, http://www.americanclassicpedigrees.com/nimba.html.

24. Kentucky State Fair Board, *Saddle & Sirloin Club Portrait Collection Guidebook* (Louisville, KY: Kentucky State Fair Board, 2013), 71.

25. Bowen, 76.

26. Bowen, 76–77.

27. Marvin Drager, *The Most Glorious Crown* (Chicago, IL: Triumph, 2016), 24.

2. Familial Ambition

1. Marvin Drager with Ed McNamara, *The Most Glorious Crown: The Story of America's Triple Crown Thoroughbreds from Sir Barton to American Pharoah* (Chicago, IL: Triumph, 2016), 24.

2. William H. P. Robertson, *The History of Thoroughbred Racing in America* (New York: Bonanza, 1964), 7.

3. "Longfellow," National Museum of Racing and Hall of Fame, accessed February 2020, https://www.racingmuseum.org/hall-of-fame/horse/longfellow-ky.

4. "Iroquois," Wikipedia, accessed January 2020, https://en.wikipedia.org/wiki/Iroquois_(horse).

5. Wall, Maryjean. *How Kentucky Became Southern: A Tale of Outlaws, Horse Thieves, Gamblers, and Breeders* (Lexington: University Press of Kentucky, 2010), 149.

6. "Iroquois, How Only American Colt Won English Classic," *Chattanooga Daily Times,* January 28, 1906.

7. Bowen, *Legacies of the Turf,* 73.

8. Joshua Dorsey Warfield, *The Founders of Anne Arundel and Howard Counties, Maryland* (Baltimore, MD: Kohn & Pollock, 1905), 124.

9. Warfield, *The Founders of Anne Arundel and Howard Counties, Maryland,* 124.

10. Warfield, 124.

11. "Obituary: William Woodward, Jr.," *New York Tribune,* March 22, 1889.

12. "Obituary: William Woodward, Jr.," *New York Tribune.*

13. Bowen, *Legacies of the Turf,* 73.

14. Apoplexy is a vague medical term, used often in reference to a sudden loss of consciousness, likely due to a stroke or a heart attack. "Death of William Woodward, Jr.," *Charlotte Observer,* March 22, 1889.

15. William Woodward had two other sisters, both of whom died at young ages. "William Woodward," Find a Grave, accessed August 15, 2022, https://www.findagrave.com/memorial/31280174/william-woodward.

16. Warfield, 124; Shirley V. Baltz, *Belair from the Beginning* (Bowie, MD: City of Bowie Museums, 2005), 111.

17. "James Woodward, the Banker, Is Dead," *New York Times,* April 11, 1910.

18. "In the Limelight," *Oakes Times* (Oakes, ND), December 5, 1907.

19. "James Woodward, the Banker, Is Dead."

20. Baltz, *Belair from the Beginning,* 111.

21. "Groton School Alumni," Wikipedia, accessed July 2021, https://en .wikipedia.org/wiki/List_of_Groton_School_alumni.

22. "Harvard Man to Be Private Secretary to Hon. J.H. Choate," *Boston Globe,* March 26, 1901.

23. "Harvard Man to Be Private Secretary to Hon. J.H. Choate," *Boston Globe.*

24. "Joseph Hodges Choate," Wikipedia, July 2021, https://en.wikipedia .org/wiki/Joseph_Hodges_Choate.

25. Edward Sanford Martin, *The Life of Joseph Hodges Choate,* vol. 1 (New York: Charles Scribner's Sons, 1920), 217.

26. Kimberly Gatto, *Belair Stud: The Cradle of Maryland Horse Racing* (Charleston, SC: History Press, 2012), 31.

27. "A Great Victorian" *Blood-Horse,* October 3, 1953, 699.

28. "Big Steamship Docks," *New York Tribune,* April 23, 1903.

29. "Elsie C. Woodward, Philanthropist, Dies Age 98," *New York Times,* July 14, 1981.

30. Lucy Heckman, *Thoroughbred Legends: Damascus* (Lexington, KY: Eclipse, 2004), 12.

31. "Triplets in Society," *St. Louis Post Dispatch,* December 13, 1900.

32. Felicia Warburg Roosevelt, *Doers and Dowagers* (New York: Double-day, 1975), 27.

33. Roosevelt, *Doers and Dowagers,* 27.

34. Hewitt, *The Great Breeders and Their Methods,* 142.

35. Bowen, *Legacies of the Turf,* 74. Governor Bowie was a guest at the famed dinner party at Saratoga Springs that gave rise to the existence of Pimlico Race Course, the Dinner Party Stakes, and, later, the Preakness Stakes.

36. Gatto, *Belair Stud,* 27.

37. Captain Hancock was sired by Eolus, who had also sired Knight of Ellerslie, the 1884 Preakness Stakes winner bred by Captain Richard Hancock. Bowen, *Legacies of the Turf,* 74.

38. William Woodward, *A Memoir of Andrew Jackson, Africanus* (New York: Derrydale, 1938), 42–43.

39. Bowen, *Legacies of the Turf,* 75.

40. "William Woodward," Harvard Class Reports, 1923 (Harvard, Cambridge).

41. "The State Capital," *Baltimore Sun,* January 31, 1898.

42. Baltz, *Belair from the Beginning,* 116.

43. "James T. Woodward, the Banker, Is Dead."

44. "Banker's Public Bequests," *New York Tribune,* April 17, 1910; "J.T. Woodward's Will Filed," *New York Times,* April 17, 1910.

45. "United Incomes Active," *Evening Star,* May 4, 1910.

46. Baltz, 119.

47. "Fanshawe Sale Yields $7,041," *Daily Racing Form,* September 12, 1911.

48. "Notes of the Turf," *Daily Racing Form,* February 9, 1912. Thomas M. Bancroft Jr., *The Red Polka Dots* (Easton, PA: Pinters', 2003), 19.

49. Bancroft, *The Red Polka Dots,* 20.

50. Edward L. Bowen, *Dynasties: Great Thoroughbred Stallions* (Lexington, KY: Eclipse, 2000), 44.

51. Bancroft, *The Red Polka Dots,* 20; Dan Mearns, "A Victorian at Belmont," *Blood-Horse,* June 5, 1972, 1888.

52. Hewitt, *Great Breeders and Their Methods,* 141.

53. "Monthly Meeting of the Jockey Club," *Daily Racing Form,* September 14, 1917.

54. "William Woodward," Harvard Class Reports, 1923.

55. "William Woodward," Harvard Class Reports, 1923.

56. Bancroft, *The Red Polka Dots,* 24–25.

57. Avalyn Hunter, "Nancy Lee," American Classic Pedigrees, accessed July 2021, http://www.americanclassicpedigrees.com/nancy-lee.html; Avalyn Hunter, "Flambette," American Classic Pedigrees, accessed July 2021, http://www.americanclassicpedigrees.com/flambette-fr.html.

58. "Lion d'Or Bought by Commander J.K.L. Ross for $20,000," *Daily Racing Form,* June 5, 1920.

59. "Ambassador Comes to America," *Daily Racing Form,* September 21, 1919.

60. Kent Hollingsworth, *The Kentucky Thoroughbred* (Lexington, KY: University Press of Kentucky, 1976), 139.

61. Bancroft, *The Red Polka Dots,* 26.

62. Gatto, *Belair Stud,* 36–37.

63. Suzanne Wilding and Anthony Del Balso, *The Triple Crown Winners* (New York: Parents' Magazine, 1978), 59; Bancroft, *The Red Polka Dots,* 32.

64. Mearns, "A Victorian at Belmont."

65. Mearns, "A Victorian at Belmont."

3. Here Comes the Sun

1. "James Butler," Wikipedia, accessed December 2021, https://en.wikipedia.org/wiki/James_Butler_(grocer). "Jeff Livingston, Turf Patron, Dies," *New York Times,* February 10, 1931.

2. Avalyn Hunter, "Spur," American Classic Pedigrees, accessed December 2021, http://www.americanclassicpedigrees.com/spur.html; Avalyn Hunter, "Lillian Shaw," American Classic Pedigrees, accessed December 2021, http://www.americanclassicpedigrees.com/lillian-shaw.html.

3. "Assumed Names Registered," *Daily Racing Form,* April 21, 1922.

4. "Success of Belair Stud," *Daily Racing Form*, February 28, 1923.

5. Bancroft, *The Red Polka Dots,* 32.

6. Bancroft, *The Red Polka Dots,* 32.

7. Bancroft, *The Red Polka Dots,* 32.

8. Norris Royden, "Seein' Things," *Lexington Herald,* December 28, 1923.

9. G. F. T. Ryall, "Sunny Jim," *Blood-Horse,* July 13, 1963, 108.

10. Jimmy Breslin, *Sunny Jim: The Life of America's Most Beloved Horseman, James Fitzsimmons* (Garden City, NY: Doubleday, 1962), 77.

11. "They Called Him Mr. Fitz," Kentucky Derby, accessed December 2021, https://www.kentuckyderby.com/horses/news/they-called-him-mr.-fitz -remembering-hall-of-famer-sunny-jim-fitzsimmons. Breslin, *Sunny Jim,* 77.

12. Breslin, *Sunny Jim,* 78.

13. Breslin, 78. "Sheepshead Bay Race Track," Wikipedia, accessed December 2021, https://en.wikipedia.org/wiki/Sheepshead_Bay_Race _Track.

14. Breslin, 78.

15. Breslin, 84–86.

16. Breslin, 87. Ryall, "Sunny Jim," 108.

17. Breslin, *Sunny Jim,* 94.

18. "The Dwyer Brothers," Brisnet, accessed December 2021, http:// brcdn.brisnet.com/content/2017/07/the-dwyer-brothers/. "What's in a Race Name? The Dwyer Brothers," America's Best Racing, accessed December 2021, https://www.americasbestracing.net/the-sport/2017-whats-race-name-the-dwyer-brothers. Robertson, *History of Thoroughbred Racing in America,* 130.

19. "The Dwyer Brothers," Brisnet.

20. "Miss Woodford," Wikipedia, accessed December 2021, https:// en.wikipedia.org/wiki/Miss_Woodford. Avalyn Hunter. "Hindoo," American Classic Pedigrees, accessed December 2021, http://www.americanc lassicpedigrees.com/hindoo.html.

21. Ryall, "Sunny Jim," 109.

22. Ryall, 109.

23. James Roach, "Sport of the Times: Jockey Jim Fitzsimmons," *New York Times,* July 19, 1949.

24. Jim Bolus, "The Happiest Life," *Spur,* November/December 1994, 55.

25. Bolus, "The Happiest Life," 55.

26. Breslin, 129–132.

27. Ryall, 111; Breslin, 141–142.

28. Bolus, "The Happiest Life," 55.

29. Breslin, 143–144.

30. Ryall, 111.

31. Bowen, *Masters of the Turf,* 177.

32. Breslin, 151.

33. Breslin, 151.

34. Breslin, 156.

35. So far, the author has been unable to pinpoint the exact date when Daley first used the moniker "Sunny Jim" for Fitzsimmons. Jimmy Breslin mentions the context of its initial usage in his book, but an actual date for that is elusive. Breslin, 172.

36. Manufactured in Buffalo, New York, Force was the first commercially successful wheat flake cereal, and it remained in production more than a century in the United States and then in the United Kingdom. The character "Sunny Jim" was featured on the cereal box and in advertising; poems and other marketing materials, such as coins, featured his name and likeness. By 1902, this marketing was so successful that "Sunny Jim" was said to be more popular than President Theodore Roosevelt or financier J. Pierpont Morgan. "Sunny Jim," Wikipedia, accessed April 2022, https://en.wikipedia.org/wiki/Sunny_Jim.

37. W. C. Vreeland, "Johnson Said That Hildreth Called Sinclair 'Big Sucker' in the Playfellow Case," *Brooklyn Daily Eagle,* December 14, 1921.

38. Breslin, 188–189.

39. Breslin, 190.

40. James Nicholson, *Racing for America: The Horse Race of the Century and the Redemption of a Sport* (Lexington: University Press of Kentucky, 2021), 69.

41. "Man o' War's Brother Sold," *Daily Racing Form* June 18, 1921.

42. Nicholson, *Racing for America,* 89.

43. Nicholson, 89.

44. Bill Fitzsimmons, "The Playfellow Case: A 100-Year-Old Tale," This Is Horse Racing, accessed December 2021, https://thisishorseracing.com/news/index.php/features/6239-the-playfellow-case-a-100-year-old-tale.

45. Breslin, 192.

46. Fitzsimmons, "The Playfellow Case: a 100-Year-Old Tale."

47. Bowen, *Masters of the Turf,* 177.

48. Breslin, 195.

49. Breslin, 195–196.

50. Breslin, 196.

51. "Fitzsimmons' Stable," *Daily Racing Form,* February 8, 1924.

52. Avalyn Hunter, "Princess Doreen," American Classic Pedigrees, accessed December 2021, http://www.americanclassicpedigrees.com/princess-doreen.html.

53. Bancroft, *The Red Polka Dots,* 33.

54. "Gift to Breeding Bureau," *Daily Racing Form,* April 7, 1924.

55. "The Jockey Club," Wikipedia, accessed December 2021, https://en.wikipedia.org/wiki/Jockey_Club_(United_States).

56. Ryall, "Sunny Jim," 222; Bowen, *Masters of the Turf,* 180–181.

57. Eric J. Ierardi, *Gravesend: The Home of Coney Island* (Mount Pleasant, SC: Arcadia, 2001), 73–74.

58. Breslin, 84; Frank Ortell, "Sunny Jim," *Turf and Sport Digest,* January 1931, 13.

59. "George F. Tappen, Racetrack Aide," *Brooklyn Daily Eagle,* April 9, 1956.

60. "Dallimore, Noted Plater, Passes at 65," *Brooklyn Daily Eagle,* March 28, 1931.

61. Breslin, 197.

4. The Queen Bears an Heir

1. John Eisenburg, "Off to the Races," *Smithsonian,* August 2004, accessed June 13, 2019, https://www.smithsonianmag.com/history/off-to-the-races-2266179/.

2. Eisenberg, "Off to the Races."

3. Johnson owned Omar Khayyam in partnership with C. K. G. Billings. The men purchased the colt from the 1915 Newmarket December sales and then imported him to the United States. After Billings and Johnson decided to dissolve their partnership, Omar Khayyam was sold to Wilfred Viau. Avalyn Hunter, "Omar Khayyam," American Classic Pedigrees.com, accessed June 17, 2019, http://www.americanclassicpedigrees.com/omar-khayyam-gb.html.

4. Neil Newman, *Famous Horses of the Turf,* vol. 1 (New York: Derrydale, 1931), 60.

5. "Radium," Thoroughbred Heritage, accessed June 13, 2019, tbheritage.com/Portraits/Radium.html.

6. Rock Sand won the English Triple Crown in 1903. After Rock Sand's illustrious career, August Belmont II purchased him from the estate of his British owner, James Miller. Belmont imported Rock Sand to the United States, where the stallion went on to sire Mahubah, the dam of the great Man o' War, and many more American horses of note.

7. Newman, *Famous Horses of the Turf,* 61.

8. Newman, *Famous Horses of the Turf,* 61.

9. Salvator, "Horse of the Month," *Horse & Horseman,* March 1939, 40.

10. "Belmont Park Form Chart," *Daily Racing Form,* May 28, 1921.

11. Newman, *Famous Horses of the Turf,* 61.

12. "Belmont Stakes Prospects," *Daily Racing Form,* February 25, 1923.

13. Salvator, "Horse of the Month."

14. Newman, *Famous Horses of the Turf,* 61.

15. Flambette, bred in France, was part of the original consignment of French mares that Woodward had purchased but was unable to bring to the United States until after World War I. Flambette would go on to win the Coaching Club American Oaks in 1921, racing in the colors of P. A. Clark. Avalyn Hunter, "Flambette," American Classic Pedigrees.com, accessed June 19, 2019, http://www.americanclassicpedigrees.com/flambette-fr .html.

16. Reigh Count would later sire Count Fleet, who won the Triple Crown in 1943.

17. Avalyn Hunter, "Petee-Wrack," American Classic Pedigrees.com, accessed June 20, 2019, http://www.americanclassicpedigrees.com/petee-wrack.html. Petee-Wrack can also be found in the pedigree of Fappiano; he sired 1990 Kentucky Derby winner Unbridled, champion Cryptoclearance, and Quiet American, sire of Real Quiet, 1998 Kentucky Derby and Preakness winner.

18. Additionally, the Woodwards hunted foxes at their Belair estate, another tidbit which might have been a part of the naming process for Gallant Fox. "The Kentucky Derby," *Blood-Horse,* May 11, 1935, 612.

19. William Woodward, *Gallant Fox: A Memoir* (New York: Derrydale, 1931), 2.

20. Woodward, *Gallant Fox,* 2.

21. Gatto, *Belair Stud,* 47.

22. Gatto, *Belair Stud,* 47.

23. Mearns, "A Victorian at Belmont."

24. Bill Curling, *The Captain: A Biography of Captain Cecil Boyd-Rochfort Royal Trainer* (London: Barrie and Jenkins, 1970), 28–29.

25. "Sir Cecil Charles Boyd-Rochfort," *Dictionary of Irish Biography*, accessed April 22, 2022, https://www.dib.ie/biography/rochfort-sir-cecil -charles-boyd-a0838.

26. Hewitt, *The Great Breeders and Their Methods*, 148.

27. Gatto, *Belair Stud*, 47; Woodward, *Gallant Fox*, 2–3.

28. Woodward, 3.

29. Woodward, 3.

30. Woodward, 4.

31. Woodward, 4–5.

32. Robert Shoop, *Down to the Wire: The Lives of the Triple Crown Champions* (Everson, WA: Russell Dean, 2004), 59.

5. A Bumpy Road

1. W. C. Vreeland, "'Sunny Jim' May Play Part of 'Bogey Man' on Turf This Year," *Brooklyn Daily Eagle*, February 12, 1929.

2. Vreeland, "'Sunny Jim' May Play Part of 'Bogey Man' on Turf This Year."

3. Woodward, *Gallant Fox*, 5.

4. Woodward, *Gallant Fox*, 5.

5. John Hervey, *Racing in America, 1922–1936* (New York: The Jockey Club, 1936), 151–152.

6. Woodward, *Gallant Fox*, 6.

7. Orlo R. Robertson, "Gallant Fox Scores Upset in Juveniles' Flash Stakes," *Fort Worth Record-Telegram*, July 30, 1929.

8. Woodward, *Gallant Fox*, 7.

9. Woodward, 8.

10. W. C. Vreeland, "Added Starter Winner of Miller Stakes When Blue Larkspur Goes Lame," *Brooklyn Daily Eagle*, August 4, 1929.

11. "Splints and Fractures of the Splint Bones in Horses," Ontario Ministry of Agriculture, Food, and Rural Affairs, accessed May 28, 2020, http://www.omafra.gov.on.ca/english/livestock/horses/facts/89-093.htm.

12. Woodward, 9.

13. Woodward, 9.

14. W. C. Vreeland, "Petee-Wrack Scares Away Six Horses and Wins Twin City Handicap," *Brooklyn Daily Eagle*, September 11, 1929.

15. Woodward, 10.

16. "Belmont Park Past Performances," *Daily Racing Form*, September 14, 1929.

17. "Belmont Park Form Chart," *Daily Racing Form*, September 15, 1929.

18. Orlo L. Robertson, "Whichone Captures Belmont Futurity," *Messenger-Inquirer* (Owensboro, KY), September 15, 1929. "Whichone Winner," *Daily Racing Form,* September 15, 1929.

19. Woodward, 12–13.

20. Woodward, 13.

21. Woodward, 15.

22. "Desert Light Demonstrates Fitness for Junior Champion," *Times Union* (Brooklyn, NY), September 23, 1929,

23. Woodward, 14.

24. "Gallant Fox First in Aqueduct Event," *Philadelphia Inquirer,* September 29, 1929.

25. "Aqueduct Form Chart," *Daily Racing Form,* September 29, 1929.

26. W. C. Vreeland, "Gallant Fox Romps Away with Junior Championship at Aqueduct," *Brooklyn Daily Eagle.* September 29, 1929.

6. The Fox Comes Around

Epigraph: Damon Runyon, *I Got the Horse Right Here: Damon Runyon on Horse Racing,* ed. Jim Reisler (Guilford, CT: Lyons, 2020), 17.

1. Gene Smith, "The Handy Man," *American Heritage,* September 1996, accessed June 2020, https://www.americanheritage.com/handy-man.

2. Jo Baeza, "The Earl Sande Saga Chronicles Legendary Jockey," *White Mountain Independent* (Showlow, AZ), accessed August 22, 2022, https://www.wmicentral.com/news/springerville_eagar/the-earl-sande-saga-chronicles-legendary-jockey/article_43cb81df-8a1b-51aa-8949-82dd74e8e634.html.

3. Joe Hirsch, *The First Century: Daily Racing Form Chronicles 100 Years of Thoroughbred Racing* (New York: Daily Racing Form, 1996), 91.

4. "Sande Badly Hurt, May Ride No More," *New York Times,* August 7, 1924.

5. Hirsch, *The First Century,* 91–92.

6. Hirsch, *The First Century,* 92.

7. Woodward, *Gallant Fox,* 16.

8. Frank G. Menke, "Booting 'Em Home with Sande," *Turf and Sport Digest,* June 1935, 72.

9. Breslin, *Sunny Jim,* 199.

10. Breslin, *Sunny Jim,* 199.

11. Woodward, *Gallant Fox,* 17.

12. Woodward, 17.

13. "Whichone Winter Book Favorite for Derby," *Brooklyn Times Union,* January 30, 1930.

14. Norris Royden, "Whitney Horses in Good Condition," *Lexington Herald,* January 26, 1930.

15. "Star Racers Named in Preakness," *Cincinnati Enquirer,* February 19, 1930.

16. "Gallant Fox Will Like the Derby Route, Records Show," *St. Louis Post-Dispatch,* March 4, 1930.

17. "Where, How Derby Hopes, Wintering," *Owensboro Messenger* (Owensboro, KY), February 25, 1930; "Gallant Fox Is Turf Favorite in a Big Field," *Evening News* (Wilkes-Barre, PA), March 4, 1930.

18. W. C. Vreeland, "Diavolo, Gallant Fox, and Flying Gal in Prime Physical Condition," *Brooklyn Daily Eagle,* March 20, 1930.

19. Drager and McNamara, *The Most Glorious Crown,* 27.

20. "Vanderbilt Horses Appear Strongest of Kentucky Entries," *Rock Island Argus* (Rock Island, IL), April 24, 1930.

21. John H. Lewy, "Kentucky Derby Choices to Match Strides in Wood Stakes," *Brooklyn Daily Times,* April 25, 1930.

22. "Gallant Fox Wins Wood Memorial," *Cincinnati Enquirer,* April 27, 1930.

23. W. C. Vreeland, "Gallant Fox Wins the Wood Memorial and Qualifies for Derby," *Brooklyn Daily Eagle,* April 27, 1930.

24. Vreeland, "Gallant Fox Wins the Wood Memorial and Qualifies for Derby."

25. Norris Royden, "Gallant Fox Easily Beats Crack Brigade in Wood; Desert Light Poor Third," *Louisville Courier-Journal,* April 27, 1930.

26. "Jamaica Form Chart," *Daily Racing Form,* April 27, 1930.

27. Orlo Robertson, "Gallant Fox Now Kentucky Derby Choice," *Morning Call* (Allentown, PA), April 28, 1930.

28. In 1932, the Kentucky Derby settled into its now customary spot on the first Saturday in May, with the Preakness moving to a week later. The two-week gap between the two came along in the 1950s.

29. "New York Turf Notes," *Daily Racing Form,* May 1, 1930.

30. "Gallant Fox at Pimlico," *Daily Racing Form,* May 2, 1930.

31. "Sande Shows Gallant Fox," *Daily Racing Form,* May 3, 1930.

32. "High Foot and Gallant Fox to Be Favorites," *Decatur Herald* (Decatur, IL), May 3, 1930; "Highlights in the Careers of Derby Eligibles: High Foot," *Daily Racing Form,* April 9, 1930.

33. Woodward, 19.

34. Jim Bolus, *Derby Magic* (Gretna, LA: Pelican, 1997), 121.

35. Woodward, 20.

36. "Preakness Stakes Today," *Daily Racing Form,* May 9, 1930.

37. "Pimlico Past Performances," *Daily Racing Form,* May 9, 1930.

38. Woodward, 21.

39. Ben J. Reber, "Earl Sande Rides Gallant Fox to Victory in Preakness," *Atlanta Constitution* (Atlanta, GA), May 10, 1930.

40. Damon Runyon, "Sande Rides Gallant Fox to Preakness Victory," *Evansville Courier* (Evansville, IN), May 10, 1930.

41. "Stall Gate a Success, This Perfect Start Shows," *St. Louis Post-Dispatch,* November 17, 1929.

42. "Buckeye Poet First in Stake Contest at Pimlico Track," *Gazette* (Montreal, Quebec), November 13, 1929.

43. "Preakness to Gallant Fox," *Daily Racing Form,* May 10, 1930.

44. "Preakness to Gallant Fox," *Daily Racing Form.*

45. Woodward, 21.

46. "Preakness to Gallant Fox," *Daily Racing Form.*

47. Woodward, 23.

48. Breslin, *Sunny Jim,* 200.

7. Roses Are Red

1. Debra Ginsburg, "Jim Dandy: 100–1 Colt Pulled Off Greatest Upset in Racing History," *Backstretch,* July/August 2000, 144.

2. J. Keeler Johnson, "What's in a Name? The Man behind the Derby," America's Best Racing, accessed August 2020, https://www.americasbestracing.net/the-sport/2020-whats-race-name-the-man-behind-the-derby.

3. Susan Braudy, *This Crazy Thing Called Love: The Golden World and Fatal Marriage of Ann and Billy Woodward* (New York: Alfred Knopf, 1992), 49.

4. Woodward, *Gallant Fox,* 23–24.

5. "Gallant Fox Arrives for Derby," *Herald-Press* (St. Joseph, MI), May 16, 1930.

6. "Cayuga Sprints to Easy Victory in Feature Event at Churchill," *Cincinnati Enquirer,* May 13, 1930; Ed Danforth, "Two Horses, Two Men Hold Derby Interest," *Atlanta Constitution,* May 16, 1930.

7. Though Gallant Fox and Gallant Knight's names are similar, Gallant Knight was by Bright Knight and, therefore, no relation to Gallant Fox.

8. W. C. Vreeland, "Gallant Fox Favored for Kentucky Derby If the Track Is Dry," *Brooklyn Daily Eagle,* May 15, 1930.

9. Vreeland, "Gallant Fox Favored for Kentucky Derby If the Track Is Dry."

10. "Gallant Fox Runs Poorly in Workout," *Intelligencer Journal* (Lancaster, PA), May 15, 1930.

11. "Sande Pleased with Gallant Fox Workout," *Evening Sentinel* (Carlisle, PA), May 15, 1930.

12. "Experts at Odds as to Whether Gallant Fox Is a Strong Mudder," *Minneapolis Star,* May 15, 1930.

13. Woodward, *Gallant Fox,* 26.

14. "Sixteen to Start," *Daily Racing Form,* May 17, 1930.

15. "Gallant Fox Gets 'Break' in Start Position of Race," *Pittsburgh Post-Gazette,* May 17, 1930.

16. Ray J. Gillespie, "Fairmount to Use Starting Stalls for 49-Day Meet," *St. Louis Star and Times,* April 10, 1930.

17. Charles M. Waite. Stall for starting race horses. US Patent 269,650, filed April 13, 1928, and issued August 16, 1932.

18. Gillespie, "Fairmount to Use Starting Stalls for 49-Day Meet."

19. "American Turf Leaders Plan Lord Derby's Entertainment," *Chicago Tribune,* April 8, 1930.

20. "Today's Radio Programs," *Hartford Courant* (Hartford, CT), May 17, 1930.

21. "Gallant Fox Gets 'Break' in Start Position of Race," *Pittsburgh Post-Gazette.*

22. "Gallant Fox Gets 'Break' in Start Position of Race," *Pittsburgh Post-Gazette.*

23. Frank Getty, "Earl Lauds Reigh Count," *Star-Phoenix* (Saskatoon, Saskatchewan, Canada), May 3, 1930; "Honor Distinguished Guest: Special Plans Made for Entertainment of Lord Derby during Derby Week," *Daily Racing Form,* April 8, 1930.

24. "Earl of Derby Is Improved; Leaves Today," *Lexington Herald,* May 17, 1930.

25. "Derby Day Observations," *Daily Racing Form,* May 19, 1930.

26. "Derby Day Observations," *Daily Racing Form.*

27. "Derby Day Observations," *Daily Racing Form.*

28. "Lord Derby's Impressions," *Daily Racing Form,* May 19, 1930.

29. Woodward, *Gallant Fox,* 26–27.

30. Shoop, *Down to the Wire,* 60.

31. "Gallant Fox Wins the Derby," *Daily Racing Form,* May 19, 1930.

32. Ed Danforth, "Mawnin'," *Atlanta Constitution,* May 18, 1930.

33. John Herchenroeder, "Crowd Braves Rain to see the 56th Derby," *Louisville Courier-Journal,* May 18, 1930.

34. Ed Danforth, "Earl Sande Rides Gallant Fox to Victory in Derby to Write History in Great Race," *Atlanta Constitution,* May 18, 1930.

35. John Herchenroeder, "Crowd Braves Rain to see the 56th Derby," *Louisville Courier-Journal*, May 18, 1930.

36. Herchenroeder, "Crowd Braves Rain to see the 56th Derby."

37. Bruce Dudley, "Gallant Fox, Sande Up, Wins Derby; Gallant Knight, 2d; Ned O. Third," *Louisville Courier-Journal*, May 18, 1930.

38. Woodward, *Gallant Fox*, 26–27.

39. Dudley, "Gallant Fox, Sande Up, Wins Derby."

40. Dudley, "Gallant Fox, Sande Up, Wins Derby.

41. Bill Keefe, "Sande's Master Hands Write New Chapter on Turf, Keefe Says," *Louisville Courier-Journal*, May 18, 1930.

42. Gerald Griffin, "Sande Predicts Derby Victory," *Louisville Courier-Journal*, May 18, 1930.

43. Woodward, *Gallant Fox*, 27.

44. Newman, *Famous Horses of the American Turf*, 68.

45. J. B. Snodgrass, "Lord Derby Says He Doesn't Care for Starting Gate," *Louisville Courier-Journal*, May 18, 1930.

46. Bolus, *Derby Magic*, 127.

47. George Daley, "Gallant Fox, Rider Monopolized Spotlight throughout Classic," *Louisville Courier-Journal*, May 18, 1930.

48. Joe Hart, "Winner Prances Back to Stall," *Louisville Courier-Journal*, May 18, 1930.

49. Hart, "Winner Prances Back to Stall."

50. Griffin, "Sande Predicts Easy Victory."

8. In Pursuit of a Crown

1. "Whichone Appears Sound," *Daily Racing Form*, May 15, 1930.

2. John Lewy, "Suburban and Withers Features at Belmont," *Times Union* (Brooklyn, NY), May 29, 1930.

3. W. C. Vreeland, "H. P. Whitney's Whichone Wins $26,150 Withers Stakes by 4 Lengths," *Brooklyn Daily Eagle*, June 1, 1930.

4. John Lewy, "Whichone Gallops to Victory in Historic Withers Mile," *Brooklyn Daily Times*, June 1, 1930.

5. "Whichone and Gallant Fox Duel May Produce Another Man o' War in Turf World," *St. Louis Post-Dispatch*, June 1, 1930.

6. John Lewy, "Whichone Supporters Confident after Trial," *Brooklyn Daily Times*, June 5, 1930.

7. Frank Getty, "Gallant Fox and Whichone Ready for Acid Test over Mile and a Half Distance," *Dayton Herald* (Dayton, OH), June 5, 1930.

8. "Kentucky Derby Aftermath," *Daily Racing Form,* May 20, 1930.

9. "Belmont Stakes Workouts," *Daily Racing Form,* May 26, 1930.

10. Woodward, *Gallant Fox,* 32–33.

11. "Earl Sande Is Injured in Auto Crash," *Brooklyn Citizen,* June 6, 1930.

12. Woodward, *Gallant Fox,* 33–34.

13. W. C. Vreeland, "Sande's Injuries So Severe He May Never Ride Another Horse," *Brooklyn Daily Eagle,* August 7, 1924.

14. Hirsch, *The First Century,* 92.

15. Woodward, 33.

16. Woodward, 33.

17. Woodward, 34.

18. "Belmont Park Form Chart," *Daily Racing Form,* June 9, 1930.

19. Woodward, 33.

20. Newman, *Famous Horses of the American Turf,* 69.

21. Woodward, 34.

22. Noel Busch, "Gallant Fox and Sande Win," *Daily News* (New York, NY), June 8, 1930.

23. W. C. Vreeland, "Gallant Fox Takes Belmont, 4 Lengths Ahead of Whichone," *Brooklyn Daily Eagle,* June 8, 1930.

24. "Gallant Fox Winner," *Daily Racing Form,* June 9, 1930; John Lewy, "Gallant Fox Beats Whichone Four Lengths to Win Belmont," *Brooklyn Times Union,* June 8, 1930.

25. Lewy, "Gallant Fox Beats Whichone Four Lengths to Win Belmont."

26. Busch, "Gallant Fox and Sande Win"; Vreeland, "Gallant Fox Takes Belmont, 4 Lengths Ahead of Whichone."

27. Vreeland, "Gallant Fox Takes Belmont, 4 Lengths Ahead of Whichone."

28. Vreeland, "Gallant Fox Takes Belmont, 4 Lengths Ahead of Whichone."

29. Al Copland, "$198,730! My, What a Horse," *Daily News* (New York, NY), June 8, 1930; "'Like Zez [sic] against Papyrus.'—Sande," *Brooklyn Daily Eagle,* June 8, 1930; Alan Gould, "Gallant Fox, with Earl Sande Up, Captures Honors in Belmont Stakes," *Morning Call* (Allentown, PA), June 8, 1930.

30. Gould, "Gallant Fox, with Earl Sande Up, Captures Honors in Belmont Stakes."

31. "Belmont Park Form Chart," *Daily Racing Form.*

32. Damon Runyon, "Gallant Fox, with Earl Sande Up, Captures Honors in Belmont Stakes," *Morning Call* (Allentown, PA), June 8, 1930.

33. Woodward, 38.

34. Woodward, 37.

35. Glenn Kendall, "Gallant Fox, Sande Score Smashing Triumph in Belmont," *Louisville Courier-Journal,* June 8, 1930.

36. "Calls Gallant Fox an Exceptional Colt," *Brooklyn Daily Eagle,* June 8, 1930.

37. W. C. Vreeland, "Earl of Derby and J.E. Widener Say Gallant Fox Is an Exceptional Colt," *Brooklyn Daily Eagle,* June 11, 1930.

38. Woodward, 38.

39. Woodward, 38.

40. W. C. Vreeland, "Gallant Fox Likely to Go Down in Turf History as 'Colt of Mystery,'" *Brooklyn Daily Eagle,* June 9, 1930.

9. The Fox Rolls On

1. Jimmy Wood, "Jimmy Wood's Sportopics," *Brooklyn Times Union* (New York, NY), June 17, 1930.

2. Woodward, *Gallant Fox,* 75.

3. Woodward, 38.

4. "Glossary of Horse Racing Terms," Daily Racing Form, accessed April 24, 2022, https://www1.drf.com/help/help_glossary.html#W.

5. Orlo Robertson, "Pony M'Atee to Pilot Whichone," *News Journal* (Wilmington, DE), June 26, 1930.

6. John Lewy, "Make Plans to Handle Huge Crowd at 'Duct," *Brooklyn Times Union,* June 26, 1930.

7. W. C. Vreeland, "Whichone, Suffering 'Quarter-Crack,' Out Till Spa Meeting," *Brooklyn Daily Eagle,* June 28, 1930.

8. John Lewy, "Gallant Fox's Workout Better Than Whichone's," *Brooklyn Times Union,* June 25, 1930.

9. "Brooklyn Handicap to Sortie," *Daily Racing Form,* June 16, 1930.

10. W. C. Vreeland, "Gallant Fox Earns Turf Crown by Winning Dwyer," *Brooklyn Daily Eagle,* June 29, 1930.

11. Woodward, 41–42; "Gallant Fox Canters," *Daily Racing Form,* June 30, 1930.

12. Woodward, 41.

13. "Gallant Fox Canters," *Daily Racing Form.*

14. W. C. Vreeland, "King of Track Makes It 5 Straight Stakes and Garners $210, 220," *Brooklyn Daily Eagle,* June 29, 1930.

15. George Kirksey, "Gallant Fox May Break Zev's Record," *Evening Times* (Sayre, PA), June 30, 1930.

16. Woodward, 42–43.

17. Woodward, 42.

18. Woodward, 44.

19. "Sande and Fox Off Again," *Daily News* (New York, NY), June 29, 1930.

20. "Arlington Park Past Performances," *Daily Racing Form,* July 12, 1930.

21. Woodward, 44–45.

22. French Lane, "50,000 to View Race; Stake is Worth $80,800," *Chicago Tribune,* July 12, 1930.

23. Woodward, 45.

24. Lane, "50,000 to View Race; Stake is Worth $80,800"; "Gallant Fox in Great Shape for Record Try at Arlington; 50,000 Will Watch Wonder Horse," *Brooklyn Citizen,* July 12, 1930.

25. Charles W. Dunkley, "Expect 50,000 People to Witness Classic at Arlington Today," *Morning News* (Wilmington, DE), July 12, 1930.

26. "Arlington Park Form Chart," *Daily Racing Form,* July 14, 1930.

27. Woodward, 45–46.

28. "Gallant Fox Wins Arlington Classic," *Pittsburgh Press,* July 13, 1930; "Sande's Mount Victor by Neck in $80,000 Race," *Indianapolis Star,* July 13, 1930.

29. Woodward, 45–46.

30. French Lane, "Gallant Fox, Sande Win Classic by a Neck," *Chicago Tribune,* July 13, 1930.

31. Lane, "Gallant Fox, Sande Win Classic by a Neck."

32. Lane, "Gallant Fox, Sande Win Classic by a Neck."

33. Orlo Robertson, "Sande Pilots Woodward Colt to Nose Victory in Classic," *New Journal* (Wilmington, DE), July 14, 1930.

34. W. C. Vreeland, "Maybe Gallant Fox Casts a Spell over His Opponents with His 'Wall Eye,'" *Brooklyn Daily Eagle,* July 14, 1930.

35. Woodward, 47.

36. W. C. Vreeland, "Noted Trainer Decides Not to Start Champion in the Arlington Cup," *Brooklyn Daily Eagle,* July 16, 1930.

10. A Dandy Show

Epigraph: Bryan Field, "Jim Dandy, 100 to 1, Beats Gallant Fox, Whichone Is Third," *New York Times,* August 17, 1930.

1. "Gallant Fox is Saratoga Show before Opening," *Post Star* (Glen Falls, NY), July 29, 1930.

2. Woodward, *Gallant Fox,* 49.

3. W. C. Vreeland, "Guards Sit Constantly, Day and Night, at the Door of Gallant Fox," *Brooklyn Daily Eagle,* August 3, 1930.

4. "Gallant Fox Will Race in England," *South Bend Tribune* (South Bend, IN), July 18, 1930.

5. Tom Thorp, "Gallant Fox Will Race in England Soon," *San Francisco Examiner,* July 18, 1930.

6. Woodward, 43.

7. "Fitzsimmons Denies Gallant Fox Will Be Raced in England," *Standard Union* (Brooklyn, NY), July 18, 1930.

8. Max Riddle, "Whichone's Collapse, Defeat Broke Whitney's Heart," *Arizona Republic,* January 20, 1937.

9. John Lewy, "Whichone Returns to the Races as Good as He Ever Was," *Brooklyn Times Union,* August 7, 1930.

10. W. C. Vreeland, "Whichone Serves Notice to Gallant Fox That He Is Ready for Hard Battle," *Brooklyn Daily Eagle,* August 7, 1930.

11. "Harry Payne Whitney's 3-Year-Old Runs an Impressive Race; Jamestown Wins Saratoga Special," *Brooklyn Citizen,* August 10, 1930.

12. Woodward, 49–50.

13. Orlo Robertson, "Gallant Fox, Whichone Square Away Saturday in Rich Travers Stakes," *Lincoln Star* (Lincoln, NE), August 15, 1930.

14. Woodward, 50.

15. "Three Horses Tampered with at Saratoga," *Brooklyn Daily Times,* August 1, 1930.

16. John Lewy, "Whichone Cherry Ripe for Race of His Life," *Brooklyn Daily Times,* August 15, 1930.

17. Riddle, "Whichone's Collapse, Defeat Broke Whitney's Heart."

18. Brien Bouyea and Michael Veitch, *The Travers: 150 Years of Saratoga's Greatest Race* (Saratoga Springs, NY: Four Color Print Group, 2019), 10–14.

19. Bouyea and Veitch, *The Travers,* 10–14.

20. Bill Heller, *Graveyard of Champions: Saratoga's Fallen Favorites* (Lexington, KY: Eclipse, 2003), 60.

21. Newman, *Famous Horses of the American Turf,* 72.

22. "Saratoga Past Performances," *Daily Racing Form,* August 16, 1930.

23. "Saratoga Form Chart," *Daily Racing Form,* August 17, 1930.

24. Newman, *Famous Horses of the American Turf,* 253.

25. Woodward, 52–53.

26. "Saratoga Form Chart," *Daily Racing Form.*

27. Woodward, 52.

28. Woodward, 52.

29. "Saratoga Form Chart," *Daily Racing Form.*

30. Woodward, 53.

31. Riddle, "Whichone's Collapse, Defeat Broke Whitney's Heart."

32. Woodward, 53.

33. Woodward, 54.

34. Damon Runyon, "Jim Dandy Drops out of Clouds to Beat Gallant Fox and Whichone," *Cincinnati Enquirer,* August 17, 1930; J. Keeler Johnson, "The Legend of Jim Dandy," America's Best Racing, accessed August 2020, https://www.americasbestracing.net/the-sport/2016-the-legend-jim-dandy.

35. Heller, *Graveyard of Champions,* 59.

36. Runyon, "Jim Dandy Drops out of Clouds."

37. Woodward, 53.

38. Damon Runyon, "Jim Dandy Drops out of Clouds."

39. Woodward, 59.

40. Edward Hotaling, *They're Off! Horse Racing at Saratoga* (Syracuse, NY: Syracuse University Press, 1995), 232.

41. Woodward, 59.

42. Bancroft, *The Red Polka Dots,* 46.

43. "Whichone Bows Tendon in Race," *Standard Union* (Brooklyn, NY), August 18, 1930.

44. Field, "Jim Dandy, 100 to 1, Beats Gallant Fox; Whichone is Third."

45. W. C. Vreeland, "'Gallant Fox Will Never Start Again on a Muddy Track,'—Sunny Jim," *Brooklyn Daily Eagle,* August 18, 1930.

46. "Sam Rosoff Wins $100,000 By Backing Jim Dandy at Spa," *Brooklyn Times Union,* August 17, 1930.

47. Woodward, 60.

11. Record Breaker

Epigraph: Damon Runyon, "Jim Dandy Drops out of the Clouds to Beat Gallant Fox and Whichone," *Cincinnati Enquirer,* August 17, 1930.

1. "Gallant Fox Not Hurt, Says Owner," *Escanaba Daily Press* (Escanaba, MI), August 20, 1930.

2. Woodward, *Gallant Fox,* 62.

3. "Saratoga Past Performances," *Daily Racing Form,* August 30, 1930.

4. Woodward, 62.

5. "Gallant Fox Wins," *Brooklyn Times Union,* August 31, 1930.

6. Woodward, 62.

7. W. C. Vreeland, "Gallant Fox Captures Cup at the Spa; Winnings Place Him Next to Zev," *Brooklyn Daily Eagle,* August 31, 1930.

8. Orlo Robertson, "Gallant Fox Easy Winner at Saratoga, *"Atlanta Constitution,* August 31, 1930.

9. W. C. Vreeland, "Gallant Fox and Jamestown, Though Beaten at the Spa, Greater Than Ever," *Brooklyn Daily Eagle,* September 1, 1930.

10. Woodward, 63.

11. W. C. Vreeland, "'Gallant Fox Can't Afford to Make Errors or Questionnaire Will Beat Him,'" *Brooklyn Daily Eagle,* September 3, 1930.

12. Woodward, 65.

13. "Gallant Fox Greatness," *Daily Racing Form,* September 3, 1930.

14. W. C. Vreeland, "Gallant Fox Now Tops the Winners of the Turf with $317,865," *Brooklyn Daily Eagle,* September 7, 1930.

15. Vreeland, "Gallant Fox Now Tops the Winners."

16. Vreeland, "Gallant Fox Now Tops the Winners."

17. Woodward, 64–66.

18. Breslin, *Sunny Jim,* 65.

19. Vreeland, "Gallant Fox Now Tops the Winners."

20. "Gallant Fox Surpasses Zev's Record," *Daily Racing Form,* September 8, 1930.

21. Woodward, 65.

22. Woodward, 65.

23. Woodward, 65.

24. W. C. Vreeland, "Will Gallant Fox Beat Sun Beau for Title, 'King of the Turf of 1930'?" *Brooklyn Daily Eagle,* September 15, 1930.

25. Vreeland, "Will Gallant Fox Beat Sun Beau for Title?"

26. Woodward, 68.

27. John Lewy, "Gold Cup Farewell for Gallant Fox Here," *Brooklyn Daily Times,* September 18, 1930; Woodward, 66.

28. W. C. Vreeland, "Gallant Fox Wins Jockey Club Gold Cup and Gleanings Climb to $328,165," *Brooklyn Daily Eagle,* September 18, 1930.

29. Woodward, 70.

30. Woodward, 73.

31. W. C. Vreeland, "'Man o' War Fastest, Gallant Fox Greatest Distance Colt I Ever Rode,'" *Brooklyn Daily Eagle,* May 24, 1931.

32. A hand is four inches, so Gallant Fox stood about sixty-five inches at his withers, the point where his neck meets his torso. Hervey, *Racing in America, 1922–1936,* 157.

33. Newman, *Famous Horses of the American Turf,* 76.

34. Heller, *Graveyard of Champions,* 54.

35. Woodward, 73–74.

36. Woodward, 73–74.

37. "May Recognize Gallant Fox Turf's Greatest Money Winner," *Yonkers Herald*, October 13, 1930.

38. Avalyn Hunter, "Flambino," American Classic Pedigrees, accessed October 5, 2020, http://www.americanclassicpedigrees.com/flambino.html; Hunter, "Flambette"; Hunter, "Omaha," American Classic Pedigrees, accessed October 5, 2020, http://www.americanclassicpedigrees.com/omaha.html.

12. Boys and Girls

Epigraph: Neil Newman, *Famous Horses of the American Turf,* vol. 1 (New York: Derrydale, 1931), 59.

1. "Sires of Winners," *Blood-Horse,* January 17, 1931, 96.

2. "Sires of Dams of Winners during the Year 1930," *Blood-Horse,* January 31, 1931, 180.

3. "The Broodmare Sires," *Blood-Horse,* February 7, 1931, 229.

4. Newman, *Famous Horses of the American Turf,* 80.

5. Salvator, "Horse of the Month," *Horse and Horseman,* March 1939, 41–42.

6. "C.V. Whitney Farm Stallions," *Blood-Horse,* December 26, 1931, 821.

7. "Spinach Winner; Jim Dandy Last in Feature Race," *Elmira Star-Gazette* (Elmira, NY), September 26, 1930.

8. "Jim Dandy's Great Mud-Running Skill Blasted at Bowie," *Evening Sun* (Baltimore, MD), November 18, 1930.

9. "Update: Whatever Happened to Jim Dandy?" Colin's Ghost, accessed September 2021, http://colinsghost.org/2011/08/update-whatever-happened-to-jim-dandy.html.

10. Brien Bouyea, "Travers Shocker! When Jim Dandy Did the Impossible," Saratoga Living, accessed September 2021, https://saratogaliving.com/travers-shocker-when-jim-dandy-did-the-impossible/.

11. "Radio, Talkies Lure Earl Sande as Weight Balks Turf Return," *Lafayette Journal and Courier* (Lafayette, IN); Hirsch, *The First Century,* 92–93.

12. John Lewy, "Earl Sande, Forced Out of the Saddle, Accepts Position as Trainer," *Brooklyn Times Union,* August 24, 1932.

13. Avalyn Hunter, "Stagehand," American Classic Pedigrees, accessed September 2021, http://www.americanclassicpedigrees.com/stagehand.html; Si Burick, "Si-ings," *Dayton Daily News* (Dayton, OH), January 1, 1945.

14. Gene Smith, "The Handy Man," *American Heritage,* September 1996, https://www.americanheritage.com/handy-man#1.

15. Smith, "The Handy Man."

16. Brien Bouyea, "Sande was a Dandy: Hall of Famer Was One of the Most Accomplished Jockeys of All Time," National Museum of Racing and Hall of Fame, accessed September 2021, https://www.racingmuseum.org/blogs/sande-was-dandy-hall-famer-was-one-most-accomplished-jockeys-all-time.

17. "Woodward, Owner of Gallant Fox, Elected Jockey Club Chairman," *Binghamton Press* (Binghamton, NY), November 4, 1930.

18. Bancroft, *The Red Polka Dots,* 63–66.

19. T. B. Macauley, "Sir Andrew Scores in Race at Ascot," *New York Times,* June 17, 1931.

20. Bancroft, 64–65.

21. "Stakes Candidates Train at Aqueduct," *Evening Star* (Washington, DC), February 12, 1931.

22. A $3,000 stud fee in 1931 is roughly the equivalent of $52,000 in 2022, as calculated by the Bureau of Labor Statistics, accessed January 17, 2022, https://www.bls.gov/data/inflation_calculator.htm.

23. Robertson, *The History of Thoroughbred Racing in America,* 7.

24. Robertson, 88.

25. Robertson, 194.

26. "Bookmaker," Wikipedia, accessed September 2021, https://en.wikipedia.org/wiki/Bookmaker.

27. Robertson, 196.

28. Though Jamaica Race Course eventually reopened to racing, it did not conduct any race meets in 1913.

29. Robertson, 275.

30. "Boojum, Whichone Put Whitney on Top for Season," *Brooklyn Daily Eagle,* October 30, 1929.

31. W. C. Vreeland, "Bask and Questionnaire Carry White and Cherry in Front All the Way," *Brooklyn Daily Eagle,* October 29, 1929.

32. "Black Tuesday and the Stock Market Crash," Students of History, accessed September 2021, https://www.studentsofhistory.com/black-tuesday-the-stock-crash.

33. "Wall Street Crash of 1929," Wikipedia, accessed December 2021, https://en.wikipedia.org/wiki/Wall_Street_Crash_of_1929.

34. Ronald Snell, *State Finance in the Great Depression,* National Conference for State Legislatures, March 2009, accessed January 17, 2022, ncsl.org/print/fiscal/statefinancegreatdepression.pdf.

35. Jesse Greenspan, "How the Misery of the Great Depression Helped Vanquish Prohibition," History.com, accessed January 2022, https://www.history.com/news/great-depression-economy-prohibition.

36. Staff of the Daily Racing Form, *The American Racing Manual for 1930* (New York: Daily Racing Form, 1930), 28–126.

37. "Pari-mutuel Betting," Wikipedia, accessed January 2022, https://en.wikipedia.org/wiki/Parimutuel_betting; Alex Gardner, "The History That Preceded Historical Gaming: How Parimutuel Wagering Won its Place in America, as Typified by Kentucky," accessed January 2022, https://www.theiaga.org/assets/docs/Alexander%20Gardner%20Historical%20Gaming%20Paper.pdf.

38. "Purse Distribution," Wikipedia, accessed January 2022, https://en.wikipedia.org/wiki/Purse_distribution.

39. Staff of the Daily Racing Form, *The American Racing Manual for 1930,* 585.

40. Hervey, *Racing in America,* 140.

41. Hervey, *Racing in America,* 142.

42. Staff of the Daily Racing Form, *The American Racing Manual for 1932* (New York: Daily Racing Form, 1932), 588; Staff of the Daily Racing Form, *The American Racing Manual for 1933* (New York: Daily Racing Form, 1933), 582–584.

43. Staff of the Daily Racing Form, *The American Racing Manual for 1933,* 582.

44. "Racing in the Depression," PBS, accessed January 2022, https://www.pbs.org/wgbh/americanexperience/features/seabiscuit-racing-depression/.

45. "The History of Santa Anita Park," Santa Anita Park, accessed January 2022, https://www.santaanita.com/discover/history/; "2021 Media Guide," Del Mar Thoroughbred Club, accessed January 2022, https://www.dmtc.com/data/assets/Static-Pages/Media/Guides/MG2021–2.pdf.

46. "Rockingham Park," Wikipedia, accessed January 2022, https://en.wikipedia.org/wiki/Rockingham_Park; "Narragansett Park," Wikipedia, accessed January 2022, https://en.wikipedia.org/wiki/Narragansett_Park.

47. Staff of the Daily Racing Form, *The American Racing Manual for 1935* (New York: Daily Racing Form, 1936), 493.

48. Staff of the Daily Racing Form, *The American Racing Manual for 1936* (New York: Daily Racing Form, 1937), 530.

49. "Mr. Woodward's Views," *Blood-Horse,* November 23, 1935, 575.

50. "Mr. Woodward's Views," *Blood-Horse,* 575.

51. "Mr. Woodward's Views," *Blood-Horse,* 576.

52. Benjamin Espy DVM, "Equine Reproduction from Conception to Birth," American Association of Equine Practitioners, accessed January 2022, https://aaep.org/horsehealth/equine-reproduction-conception-birth.

53. "Stud News," *Blood-Horse,* March 5, 1932, 413.

13. Second Generation

1. W. C. Vreeland, "Gallant Fox Only Colt in World to Win $308,275 in One Season," *Brooklyn Daily Eagle,* March 3, 1931.

2. Vreeland, "'Man o' War Fastest, Gallant Fox Greatest Distance Colt I Ever Rode.'"

3. Curling, *The Captain: A Biography of Captain Sir Cecil Boyd-Rochfort,* 70.

4. Shoop, *Down to the Wire: The Lives of the Triple Crown Champions,* 80; Fred Glueckstein, *Of Men, Women and Horses,* (Bloomington, IN: Xlibris, 2006), 52.

5. Bancroft, *The Red Polka Dots,* 27.

6. Damon Runyon, "Owner May Send Omaha, Preakness Winner, to England," *Lancaster New Era* (Lancaster, PA), May 13, 1935.

7. Shoop, *Down to the Wire,* 80; Wilding and Del Balso, *The Triple Crown Winners,* 71.

8. Bolus, *Derby Magic,* 134.

9. Edward L. Bowen, *The Lucky Thirteen: The Winners of America's Triple Crown of Horse Racing* (Lanham, MD: Lyons, 2019), 53.

10. Bolus, *Derby Magic,* 134.

11. "1st Aqueduct Past Performances," *Daily Racing Form,* June 18, 1934.

12. "Aqueduct Form Chart," *Daily Racing Form,* June 19, 1934.

13. "1st Aqueduct Past Performances," *Daily Racing Form,* June 23, 1934.

14. John Lewy, "Rose Cross Tops Growler and Singing Wood in Dwyer," *Brooklyn Times Union,* June 24, 1934.

15. "Aqueduct Form Chart," *Daily Racing Form,* June 24, 1934.

16. Al Copland, "Rose Cross 7-Lengths Winner in Dwyer Stakes at Aqueduct," *Daily News* (New York, NY), June 24, 1934.

17. W. C. Vreeland, "Racing Fans Denounce Startling Form Reversal of Back Fence," *Brooklyn Daily Eagle,* June 26, 1934.

18. W. C. Vreeland, "'Racing a Costly Sport for Patrons of Turf,' Says 'Sunny Jim,'" *Brooklyn Daily Eagle,* June 24, 1934.

19. Editors of the *Daily Racing Form, Champions: The Lives, Times, and Past Performances of the 20th Century's Greatest Thoroughbreds* (New York: Daily Racing Form, 2000), 58.

20. "3rd Saratoga Past Performances," *Daily Racing Form,* August 4, 1934.

21. "Cornelius Vanderbilt Whitney," Wikipedia, accessed November 9, 2020, https://en.wikipedia.org/wiki/Cornelius_Vanderbilt_Whitney.

22. James Carroll, "10,000 Fans Attend Opening of Races at Saratoga; Pitter Pat and Black Buddy Win Features," *Post-Star* (Glen Falls, NY), July 31, 1934.

23. Bert E. Collyer, "Collyer's Comment," *Daily News* (New York, NY), August 4, 1934.

24. "Saratoga Form Chart," *Daily Racing Form,* August 6, 1934.

25. W. C. Vreeland, "Balladier Wins $4,050 Stakes for Juveniles," *Brooklyn Daily Eagle,* August 5, 1934.

26. "Saratoga Form Chart," *Daily Racing Form,* August 6, 1934.

27. "Saratoga Form Chart," *Daily Racing Form,* August 13, 1934.

28. "Easily Beats Plat Eye," *Daily Racing Form,* August 13, 1934.

29. "Sanford Stakes," Wikipedia, accessed November 13, 2020, https://en.wikipedia.org/wiki/Sanford_Stakes.

30. "3rd Saratoga Past Performances," *Daily Racing Form,* August 22, 1934.

31. "Saratoga Form Chart," *Daily Racing Form,* August 23, 1934.

32. Damon Runyon, "August 21, 1934," in *I Got the Horse Right Here: Damon Runyon on Horse Racing,* ed. Jim Reisler (Lanham, MD: Lyons, 2020), 303–304.

33. If the name Head Play seems familiar, he and Broker's Tip were dueling down the stretch in the 1933 Kentucky Derby while their jockeys, Bud Fisher and Don Meade, respectively, literally fought each other to the race's finish, which Broker's Tip won by a nose.

34. W. C. Vreeland, "Closing Week at Saratoga to See the Greatest Stake Events Decided," *Brooklyn Daily Eagle,* August 26, 1934.

35. Vreeland, "Closing Week at Saratoga to See the Greatest Stake Events Decided."

36. "Saratoga Form Chart," *Daily Racing Form,* September 2, 1934.

37. "4th Belmont Park," *Daily Racing Form,* September 6, 1934.

38. James Roach, "Belmont Park to Eliminate 32-Year-Old Widener Chute," *New York Times,* December 30, 1958.

39. "Balladier Sparkles," *Daily Racing Form,* September 7, 1934.

40. W. C. Vreeland, "Humphries Overconfidence at Finish Cost Omaha Victory in Stakes," *Brooklyn Daily Eagle,* September 7, 1934.

41. Avalyn Hunter, "Chance Shot," American Classic Pedigrees, accessed November 18, 2020, http://www.americanclassicpedigrees.com/chance

-shot.html; Avalyn Hunter, "Peace Chance," American Classic Pedigrees, accessed November 18, 2020, http://www.americanclassicpedigrees.com /peace-chance.html.

42. "3rd Belmont Park," *Daily Racing Form,* September 15, 1934.

43. John Lewy, "Recent Developments Loom as Possible Victor of Belmont Futurity," *Brooklyn Times Union,* September 10, 1934.

44. "Belmont Park Form Chart," *Daily Racing Form,* September 17, 1934.

45. "Will Rest Chance Sun," *Pittsburgh Sun Telegraph,* September 22, 1934.

46. W. C. Vreeland, "Juveniles Put to the Test at Mile in Running of the Junior Champion," *Brooklyn Daily Eagle,* September 28, 1934.

47. John Lewy, "Aqueduct's Junior Champion to Throw Light on 1935 Three Year Olds," *Brooklyn Times Union,* September 26, 1934.

48. "Aqueduct Form Chart," *Daily Racing Form,* September 30, 1934.

49. W. C. Vreeland, "Sailor Beware Stakes Winner in Nose Finish," *Brooklyn Daily Eagle.* September 30, 1934.

50. Vreeland, "Sailor Beware Stakes Winner in Nose Finish."

51. John H. Lewy, "Omaha at Last Shows Quality Though Beaten," *Brooklyn Times Union,* October 1, 1934.

52. W. C. Vreeland, "Omaha Appears to Have as Good a Chance as Any in Kentucky Derby," *Brooklyn Daily Eagle,* October 7, 1934.

53. Vreeland, "Omaha Appears to Have as Good a Chance as Any in Kentucky Derby."

14. Following the Fox

1. Bancroft, *The Red Polka Dots,* 73–88.

2. Hervey, *Racing in America, 1922–1936,* 234.

3. Bowen, *Legacies of the Turf,* 76.

4. "Latest Kentucky Derby Odds," *Daily Racing Form,* April 23, 1935.

5. Brenda Wahler, *Montana Horse Racing* (Charleston, SC: History Press, 2019), 114–115.

6. Bolus, *Derby Magic,* 131–134.

7. "Jamaica Form Chart," *Daily Racing Form,* April 23, 1935.

8. W. C. Vreeland, "Whitney's Derby Candidate Easily Beats Plat Eye," *Brooklyn Daily Eagle,* April 28, 1935.

9. "Omaha-Chance Sun Now 5–1," *Daily Racing Form,* April 29, 1935.

10. "Beaver Dam and Nellie Flag Downs' Winners," *Daily Racing Form,* April 29, 1935; "Omaha-Chance Sun Now 5–1," *Daily Racing Form.*

11. "Chance Sun Out for Year," *Daily Racing Form,* May 4, 1935; "Whiskolo Captures Preparation Purse," *Owensboro Messenger,* May 1, 1935.

12. Avalyn Hunter, "Nellie Flag," American Classic Pedigrees.com, accessed July 11, 2019, http://www.americanclassicpedigrees.com/nellie -flag.html.

13. Henry McLemore, "Derby Looms as Strictly 6-Horse Race," *Tampa Tribune,* May 2, 1935.

14. Henry McLemore, "Boos and Boosts: Rambles in All Sport Fields," *Daily Chronicle* (DeKalb, IL), May 4, 1935.

15. "Jocky [*sic*] Winner of 2 Derbies Picks Omaha," *Chicago Tribune,* May 4, 1935.

16. Ralph McGill, "Break o'Day!" *Atlanta Constitution,* May 4, 1935.

17. Damon Runyon, *Courier-Post* (Camden, NJ), May 4, 1935.

18. Grantland Rice, "Big Top Raised at Louisville," *Baltimore Sun,* May 4, 1935.

19. Dave Brown, "Derby Crowd Gets Soaked, Doesn't Mind," *Louisville Courier-Journal,* May 5, 1935; "61st Kentucky Derby Form Chart," *Daily Racing Form,* May 6, 1935.

20. Brown, "Derby Crowd Gets Soaked, Doesn't Mind."

21. "61st Kentucky Derby, 6th Churchill Downs," *Daily Racing Form,* May 4, 1935.

22. Brown, "Derby Crowd Gets Soaked, Doesn't Mind."

23. French Lane, "Victor Shows Racing Spirit of His Sire," *Chicago Tribune,* May 5, 1935.

24. "Churchill Downs Form Chart," *Daily Racing Form,* May 6, 1930; "Churchill Downs Form Chart," *Daily Racing Form*, May 19, 1935. Halma (1895) sired Alan-a-Dale (1902); Bubbling Over (1926) sired Burgoo King (1932).

25. Lane, "Victor Shows Racing Spirit of His Sire."

26. Lane, "Victor Shows Racing Spirit of His Sire."

27. Lane, "Victor Shows Racing Spirit of His Sire."

28. "Montana Boy Rides Omaha, Derby Victor," *Montana Standard,* May 5, 1935.

29. "Omaha Will Run in the Preakness, Says Woodward," *Chicago Tribune,* May 5, 1935.

30. "Derby Winner Is to Follow Gallant Fox," *Middlesboro Daily News* (Middlesboro, KY), May 6, 1935.

31. "Derby Winner Is to Follow Gallant Fox," *Middlesboro Daily News* (Middlesboro, KY), May 6, 1935.

32. "Nellie Flag Leaves Louisville, En Route Here for Preakness," *Baltimore Sun,* May 7, 1935.

33. "Preakness Field Big," *Akron Beacon Journal* (Akron, OH), May 8, 1935.

34. "Firethorn New Threat to Omaha in Preakness," *Detroit Free Press,* May 7, 1935.

35. Damon Runyon, "Omaha Ranks Favorite to Capture Preakness," *Courier Post* (Camden, NJ), May 11, 1935.

36. Bruce Copeland, "Preakness Looks Easy for Vindicated Omaha," *Courier Post* (Camden, NJ), May 7, 1935.

37. Copeland, "Preakness Looks Easy for Vindicated Omaha."

38. "Others Given Chance to Win," *Baltimore Sun,* May 11, 1935.

39. "Forty-Fifth Preakness Stakes Today," *Daily Racing Form,* May 11, 1935.

40. Wilding and Del Balso, *The Triple Crown Winners,* 73.

41. "Omaha Wins by Six Lengths," *Chicago Tribune,* May 12, 1935; "Preakness Fans Wager $884,221; Beat 1934 Mark," *Chicago Tribune,* May 12, 1935.

42. "Omaha Wins the Preakness," *Baltimore Sun,* May 12, 1935.

43. "Omaha Wins by Six Lengths," *Chicago Tribune,* May 12, 1935.

44. "Omaha Ready for Belmont," *Huntsville Times* (Huntsville, AL), May 13, 1935.

45. "Omaha Ready for Belmont," *Huntsville Times.*

15. The Son Gets His Crown

1. Nick Costa, "Kentucky Derby: Like Father, Like Son," Horse Racing Nation, accessed December 14, 2020, https://www.horseracingnation.com /blogs/Trackside/Kentucky_Derby_Like_Father_Like_Son_123.

2. John Lewy, "Withers Affords Omaha Chance to Duplicate Sir Barton's Record," *Brooklyn Times Union,* May 20, 1935.

3. "Belmont Park Past Performances," *Daily Racing Form,* May 30, 1935.

4. "Belmont Park Past Performances," *Daily Racing Form,* May 25, 1935.

5. "Belmont Park Form Chart," *Daily Racing Form,* May 27, 1935.

6. Al Copland, "Rosemont Outruns Omaha in Withers," *Daily News* (New York, NY), May 26, 1935.

7. W. C. Vreeland, "Omaha Defeated by Rosemont in Withers," *Brooklyn Daily Eagle,* May 26, 1935.

8. Vreeland, "Omaha Defeated by Rosemont in Withers."

9. "Rosemont Beats Omaha in Withers at Belmont, Returns Backers 8 to 1," *Philadelphia Inquirer,* May 26, 1935.

10. "Here and There on the Turf," *Daily Racing Form,* May 31, 1935.

11. Lester L. Byck, "Omaha, Hot Horse, Runs Away with Load of Ice," *Brooklyn Times Union,* June 5, 1935.

12. "Omaha Favored to Avenge Rosemont in Rich Belmont Stakes Today," *Los Angeles Times,* June 8, 1935.

13. "Sixty-Seventh Belmont Stakes Today," *Daily Racing Form,* June 8, 1935.

14. "Belmont Stakes Draws 30,000; Omaha Favorite," *Brooklyn Times Union,* June 8, 1935.

15. Nancy Randolph, "Society Finds Omaha Belmont's Best Duck," *Daily News* (New York, NY), June 9, 1935.

16. "Omaha Becomes Triple Crown Hero," *Daily Racing Form,* June 10, 1935.

17. "Omaha Becomes Triple Crown Hero," *Daily Racing Form.*

18. Bolus, *Derby Magic,* 140.

19. Randolph, "Society Finds Omaha Belmont's Best Duck."

20. Damon Runyon, "Omaha Turns On Speed in Stretch to Win Belmont Stakes," *Cincinnati Enquirer,* June 9, 1935.

21. Randolph, "Society Finds Omaha Belmont's Best Duck."

22. "Omaha's Trainer Uncertain as to Next Race for Colt," *Cincinnati Enquirer,* June 10, 1935.

23. "Omaha's Campaign Follows That of Sire," *Lexington Leader,* June 11, 1935.

24. John H. Lewy, "Omaha Will Continue Racing in New York Instead of Going West," *Brooklyn Times Union,* June 12, 1935.

25. John H. Lewy, "Fast Trial Likely to Make Omaha Favorite in Brooklyn Handicap," *Brooklyn Times Union,* June 19, 1935.

26. W. C. Vreeland, "Omaha and King Saxon Ready to Fight It Out in Brooklyn Handicap," *Brooklyn Daily Eagle,* June 19, 1935.

27. "Omaha and King Saxon Outstanding Horses of Year Meet Today in the Brooklyn Handicap," *Daily Racing Form,* June 22, 1935.

28. "Historic Review Committee Elects Jockey Wayne Wright, Preakness Winner Tom Ochiltree to Hall of Fame," Paulick Report, accessed January 4, 2021, https://www.paulickreport.com/news/people/historic-review-committee-elects-jockey-wayne-wright-preakness-winner-tom-ochiltree-hall-fame/.

29. John Lewy, "Wright Likely Pilot of Omaha in Brooklyn 'Cap," *Brooklyn Times Union,* June 21, 1935.

30. "Discovery at His Best," *Daily Racing Form,* June 24, 1935.

31. "Discovery at His Best," *Daily Racing Form.*

32. W. C. Vreeland, "Vanderbilt Horse Soundly Trounces King Saxon, Omaha," *Brooklyn Daily Eagle,* June 23, 1935.

33. "Discovery at His Best," *Daily Racing Form.*

34. "Discovery," Wikipedia, accessed January 5, 2021, https://en.wikipedia .org/wiki/Discovery_(horse).

35. W. C. Vreeland, "Omaha Kept Home So Fans Could See First Class Horses Run," *Brooklyn Daily Eagle,* June 23, 1935.

16. The Belair Bullet Rolls On

1. Tom Hall, "John P. Grier Made Mighty Man o' War Work in Dwyer," Bloodhorse.com, accessed January 6, 2021, https://www.bloodhorse.com /horse-racing/articles/242354/john-p-grier-made-mighty-man-o-war-work -in-dwyer.

2. "Small Field for Dwyer," *Daily Racing Form,* June 28, 1935.

3. "Aqueduct Form Chart," *Daily Racing Form,* July 1, 1935.

4. John H. Lewy, "Aqueduct Form," *Brooklyn Times Union,* June 29, 1935.

5. W. C. Vreeland, "Omaha Easily Wins $9,200 Dwyer Stakes," *Brooklyn Daily Eagle,* June 30, 1935.

6. Vreeland, "Omaha Easily Wins $9,200 Dwyer Stakes."

7. Vreeland, "Omaha Easily Wins $9,200 Dwyer Stakes."

8. "Marcel Boussac," Wikipedia, last modified December 19, 2019, accessed January 18, 2021, https://en.wikipedia.org/wiki/Marcel_Boussac.

9. Avalyn Hunter, "La Troienne," American Classic Pedigrees, accessed January 18, 2021, http://www.americanclassicpedigrees.com/la-troienne-fr. html. That amount in 2022 would equate to about $6,562.50. La Troienne's selling price of 1,250 guineas in 1930 converts to ~$113,568 in 2022. Alan Eliasen, "Historical Currency Conversions," Future Boy.us, accessed January 18, 2022, https://futureboy.us/fsp/dollar.fsp?quanti-ty=1737&currency=florins&fromYear=1445.

10. "Washington Park Form Chart," *Daily Racing Form,* June 24, 1935.

11. Walter H. Pearce, "Bradley Offers $100,000 on Helen," *Collyer's Eye,* July 13, 1935.

12. Pearce, "Bradley Offers $100,000 on Helen."

13. Pearce, "Bradley Offers $100,000 on Helen."

14. Hervey, *American Race Horses 1936,* 179–180.

15. "Arlington Park Past Performances," *Daily Racing Form,* July 20, 1935.

16. "Expect Over 50,000 for Rich Classic," *Daily Racing Form,* July 20, 1935.

17. French Lane, "Omaha Wins $36,500 Classic; Sets Record," *Chicago Tribune,* July 21, 1935.

18. "Woodward Colt Runs Greatest Race of Career," *Brooklyn Times Union,* July 21, 1935.

19. "Woodward Colt Runs Greatest Race of Career," *Brooklyn Times Union.*

20. "Arlington Park Form Chart," *Daily Racing Form,* July 22, 1935.

21. "Woodward Colt Runs Greatest Race of Career," *Brooklyn Times Union.*

22. Lane, "Omaha Wins $36,500 Classic; Sets Record."

23. "Omaha Easily Wins the Classic Stakes," *Daily Racing Form,* July 21, 1935.

24. Lane, "Omaha Wins $36,500 Classic; Sets Record."

25. Lane, "Omaha Wins $36,500 Classic; Sets Record."

26. John H. Lewy, "St. Bernard's Presence in Classic Foiled Carefully Made Plans of Bradley," *Brooklyn Times Union,* July 22, 1935.

27. Avalyn Hunter, "Black Helen," American Classic Pedigrees, accessed November 11, 2020, http://www.americanclassicpedigrees.com/black -helen.html; Avalyn Hunter, "Bloodroot," American Classic Pedigrees, accessed November 12, 2020, http://www.americanclassicpedigrees.com /bloodroot.html.

28. Ellen Parker, "Bloodroot," Reines-de-Course, accessed January 22, 2021, http://reines-de-course.com/bloodroot/.

29. Walter H. Pearce, "Bradley Offers $100,000 on Helen."

30. Max Riddle, "Omaha Still Has a Long Way to Go to Equal Dad's Famous Record," *Muncie Evening Press* (Muncie, IN), July 24, 1935.

17. An Unexpected Stop

1. W. C. Vreeland, "1935 Travers Stakes Living Up to Reputation of Hoodoo Horse Race," *Brooklyn Daily Eagle,* August 14, 1935.

2. "Discovery Will Run at Arlington; Omaha Shipped to Saratoga," *Press and Sun Bulletin* (Binghamton, NY), July 24, 1935.

3. W. C. Vreeland, "Omaha Gaining Strength Every Day and Developing Muscle," *Brooklyn Daily Eagle,* August 4, 1935.

4. John H. Lewy, "Travers Jinx Hits Omaha; Colt May Be Out of Stake," *Brooklyn Times Union,* August 10, 1935.

5. W. C. Vreeland, "Omaha, in a Bad Way Physically, Won't Go to Post in Travers," *Brooklyn Daily Eagle,* August 13, 1935.

6. "Glossary of Racing Terms: F," SaratogaRaceTrack.com, accessed February 9, 2021, https://www.saratogaracetrack.com/about-horse-racing/glossary-racing-terms/f/. Emphasis mine.

7. "Glossary of Racing Terms: C," SaratogaRaceTrack.com, accessed February 9, 2021, https://www.saratogaracetrack.com/about-horse-racing/glossary-racing-terms/c/.

8. Vreeland, "Omaha, in a Bad Way Physically, Won't Go to Post in Travers"; "Saratoga Cup," Wikipedia, accessed September 2022, https://en.wikipedia.org/wiki/Saratoga_Cup.

9. "Jockey Club Gold Cup," Wikipedia, accessed February 2021, https://en.wikipedia.org/wiki/Jockey_Club_Gold_Cup; "Lawrence Realization Stakes," Wikipedia, accessed February 2021, https://en.wikipedia.org/wiki/Lawrence_Realization_Stakes.

10. John H. Lewy, "Trainer May Start Colt a Week Later in Gold Cup Race," *Brooklyn Times Union,* September 17, 1935; John H. Lewy, "King to Be Fit for Test in Realization," *Brooklyn Daily News,* September 21, 1935.

11. "Omaha Retired for the Season," *Brooklyn Daily Eagle,* September 26, 1935.

12. W. C. Vreeland, "Omaha May Go to England to Try for Ascot Cup in 1936," *Brooklyn Daily Eagle,* September 8, 1935; "Omaha Will Return to the Races, But Plans Remain Indefinite," *Evening Sun* (Baltimore, MD), November 22, 1935.

13. Vreeland, "Omaha May Go to England to Try for Ascot Cup in 1936"; "Omaha Will Campaign in England Next Year," *Brooklyn Times Union,* December 4, 1935.

14. Vreeland, "Omaha May Go to England to Try for Ascot Cup in 1936."

15. "Omaha Will Campaign in England Next Year," *Brooklyn Times Union.*

16. "Bozeman Lad Loses Inverness Gallop," *Billings Gazette,* July 17, 1935.

17. "Willie Saunders," Wikipedia, accessed February 2021, https://en.wikipedia.org/wiki/Willie_Saunders.

18. Jessie Oswald, "Triple Crown? Murder? It Was 1935," *Louisville Courier-Journal,* April 25, 2014, https://www.courier-journal.com/story/sports/horses/2014/04/25/kentucky-derby/8168917/.

19. Jessie Oswald, "Triple Crown? Murder? It Was 1935," *Louisville Courier-Journal.*

20. "'35 Derby Winner Charged with Murder," *Sandusky Register* (Sandusky, OH), October 24, 1935.

21. "Text of Address as Delivered by William Woodward at Testimonial Dinner," *Lexington Herald,* January 30, 1936.

22. Avalyn Hunter, "Reigh Count," American Classic Pedigrees, accessed March 23, 2021, http://www.americanclassicpedigrees.com/reigh-count.html.

23. "Vedette," Notes and Comments, *Evening Post* (Wellington, NZ), April 12, 1929. https://paperspast.natlib.govt.nz/newspapers /EP19290412.2.30.1.

24. Avalyn Hunter, "Twenty Grand," American Classic Pedigrees, accessed March 23, 2021, http://www.americanclassicpedigrees.com/twen-ty-grand.html.

25. "Omaha to Bid for Ascot Racing Cup," *Nebraska State Journal,* January 3, 1936.

26. "Omaha to Be Shipped to England," *St. Louis Star and Times,* January 3, 1936.

27. George Kirksey, "Omaha on Boat," *Evening Sun,* January 9, 1936.

28. Kirksey, "Omaha on Boat."

29. Bancroft, *The Red Polka Dots,* 134.

30. Curling, *The Captain: A Biography of Captain Sir Cecil Boyd-Rochfort,* 74–75.

31. "Jury Acquits Schaeffer of Woman Murder," *Kenosha News* (Kenosha, WI), January 9, 1936.

32. "Willie Saunders Freed on Count of Accessory in Kentucky Death Ride," *Montana Standard* (Butte, MT), January 10, 1936.

33. "Willie Saunders Refused License by Racing Group," *Des Moines Register,* April 26, 1936.

34. "Hollyrood Out of Derby," *Daily Racing Form,* April 28, 1936.

35. "Triple Crown 1935: The Colt, the Kid . . . and the Murder of Evelyn Sliwinski," The Vault, accessed February 2021, https://thevaulthorserac-ing.wordpress.com/2015/04/13/triple-crown-1935-the-colt-the-kid-and -the-murder-of-evelyn-sliwinski/.

36. "William (Smokey) Saunders," Canadian Horse Racing Hall of Fame, accessed February 2021, https://www.canadianhorseracinghall offame.com/1976/12/02/william-smokey-saunders/.

37. "William (Smokey) Saunders," Canadian Horse Racing Hall of Fame.

18. Trailblazer

1. British newspapers listed Omaha's assigned groom at Freemason Lodge as one E. Challice, but research did not yield more information about this person.

2. Curling, *The Captain: A Biography of Captain Sir Cecil Boyd-Rochfort,* 75.

3. "Willie Stephenson, Royston Hertfordshire," Waymarking.com, accessed February 2021, https://www.waymarking.com/waymarks/WMAYF0_Willie_Stephenson_Royston_Hertfordshire.

4. "U.S. Champion Colt at Newmarket," *Belfast Telegraph* (Belfast, Northern Ireland), March 5, 1936.

5. Curling, *The Captain: A Biography of Captain Sir Cecil Boyd-Rochfort,* 75.

6. "English Fans Banned as Omaha Trains for Ascot Gold Cup Race," *Baltimore Sun,* February 23, 1936.

7. "The Turf," *Observer* (London, England), February 23, 1936.

8. "The Turf," *Observer.*

9. "The Turf," *Observer.*

10. "Jack Barnato Joel," Wikipedia, accessed February 2021, https://en.wikipedia.org/wiki/Jack_Barnato_Joel.

11. "Patrick Beasley," Jockeypedia, accessed February 2021, https://sites.google.com/site/jockeypediayeareight2/beasley-pat.

12. "Newmarket Programme and Probable Starters," *Leeds Mercury* (Leeds, Yorkshire, England), April 15, 1936.

13. "White Knight," "Bobsleigh Test," *Leeds Mercury* (Leeds, Yorkshire, England), April 15, 1936.

14. "Newmarket Debut?" *Leeds Mercury* (Leeds, Yorkshire, England), April 4, 1936.

15. The Domesday Book is a 1086 survey commissioned by England's King William I to assess the land within the boundaries of his new kingdom to determine the owners of each parcel and the value of the land so that the government could determine taxes owed. "Domesday Book," *Encyclopedia Britannica,* accessed April 24, 2022, https://www.britannica.com/topic/Domesday-Book.

16. "Kempton Park Racecourse," Wikipedia, accessed February 2021, https://en.wikipedia.org/wiki/Kempton_Park_Racecourse; "The History of Kempton Park Racecourse," The Jockey Club, accessed April 5, 2021, https://www.thejockeyclub.co.uk/kempton/about/history/.

17. "Bouviere," "Derby Second May Be First in Jubilee," *Daily Mirror* (London, England), May 9, 1936.

18. Gayle Talbot, "Omaha Romps to Win in Victor Wild Stakes" *Democrat and Chronicle* (Rochester, NY), May 11, 1936.

19. Talbot, "Omaha Romps to Win in Victor Wild Stakes."

20. "'Jubilee' Surprise," *Western Morning News and Daily Gazette* (London, England), May 11, 1936.

21. "Amato," "Taj Akbar the Form Horse for the Derby," *Gloucestershire Echo,* May 23, 1936.

22. "Toboggan," Wikipedia, accessed April 2021, https://en.wikipedia .org/wiki/Toboggan_(horse); "Gainsborough," Wikipedia, accessed April 2021, https://en.wikipedia.org/wiki/Gainsborough_(horse).

23. "Kempton Races," *Western Morning News,* May 30, 1936.

24. "Omaha Captures Queen's Plate in Thrilling Finish at Kempton Park," *Democrat and Chronicle* (Rochester, NY), May 31, 1936.

25. "Omaha Captures Queen's Plate in Thrilling Finish at Kempton Park."

26. "Omaha Captures Queen's Plate in Thrilling Finish at Kempton Park."

19. The Big Show

1. "La Flêche," Wikipedia, accessed April 2021, https://en.wikipedia. org/wiki/La_Fleche_(horse).

2. "Ascot Gold Cup," Thoroughbred Heritage, accessed April 2021, https://www.tbheritage.com/TurfHallmarks/racecharts/UK/ascotgoldcup .html.

3. "The Turf: Oaks Winner from Half-Bred Mare," *Sydney Morning Herald* (Sydney, Australia), June 10, 1935.

4. "U.S. Horses Defeated," *Salt Lake Tribune,* November 1, 1935; "Quashed," Wikipedia, accessed May 2021, https://en.wikipedia.org/wiki /Quashed.

5. "Dead Heat in Metropolitan," *Province* (Vancouver, BC), April 21, 1936.

6. "No Royal Parade," *Detroit Free Press,* June 14, 1936.

7. "World's Greatest Race Meet Opens," *Ottawa Journal* (Ottawa, ON), June 16, 1936.

8. "The Turf: Royal Ascot," *Observer* (London, England), June 14, 1936.

9. W. C. Vreeland, "Omaha Carries Hopes of U.S. in Race for Ascot Gold Cup," *Brooklyn Daily Eagle,* June 14, 1936.

10. "Ascot Gold Cup," *Sunderland Daily Echo and Shipping Gazette* (Sunderland, England), June 13, 1936.

11. "The Yorkshire Cup: Valerius Wins by Short Head," *Scotsman* (Edinburgh, Scotland), May 21, 1936.

12. "Coronation Cup for Lord Derby," *Yorkshire Post* (Yorkshire, England), May 29, 1936.

13. "Topics of the Turf," *Green 'Un* (Sheffield, England), April 11, 1936.

14. Spot White, "Quashed to Outstay Gold Cup Challengers?" *Sunderland Daily Echo and Shipping Gazette* (Sunderland, England), June 17, 1936; "Evremond de Saint-Alary," Wikipedia, Accessed April 2021, https://en.wikipedia.org/wiki/Evremond_de_Saint-Alary.

15. "Thunderstorm at Ascot," *Evening Telegraph* (Dundee, Scotland), June 19, 1936.

16. Sean Magee with Sally Aird, *Ascot: The History* (London: Methuen, 2002), 187.

17. "Great Gallop," *Yorkshire Observer,* June 15, 1936.

18. "Omaha Beaten in Ascot Race," *Baltimore Sun,* June 19, 1936.

19. Magee and Aird, *Ascot: The History,* 187.

20. W. C. Vreeland, "Omaha Gallops to Victory in Belmont," *Brooklyn Daily Eagle,* June 9, 1935; French Lane, "Omaha Wins $36,500 Classic; Sets Record," *Chicago Tribune,* July 21, 1935.

21. "Gallant Fox's Son, Omaha, Wins Derby," *Daily Racing Form,* May 6, 1935.

22. "Ascot Gold Cup horse race," YouTube video, 1:35, posted by British Pathé, November 12, 2020, https://www.youtube.com/watch?v=Fm4D3OnHSO4.

23. Curling, *The Captain: A Biography of Captain Cecil Boyd-Rochfort,* 76.

24. "Richard Perryman," Jockeypedia, accessed April 2021, https://sites.google.com/site/jockeypedia/perryman-rica.

25. Gayle Talbot, "Quashed, an English Filly, Noses Out American Favorite," *Morning Call* (Allentown, PA), June 19, 1936.

26. Magee and Aird, *Ascot,* 188.

27. Vreeland, "Omaha Carries Hope of U.S. In Race for Ascot Gold Cup"; Magee and Aird, *Ascot,* 412.

28. Patrick Thomas "Rufus" Beasley, *Pillow to Post: The Life and Times of Rufus Beasley* (York, England: Westminster, 1981), 43.

29. Beasley, *Pillow to Post,* 43.

30. Curling, *The Captain,* 77.

31. Curling, *The Captain,* 77.

32. "Racing: The Gold Cup," *Times of London,* June 19, 1936.

33. "Jan. 16, 1936: Day at the Races, and Your Nag in a Photo Finish," *Wired,* accessed April 2021, https://www.wired.com/2013/01/jan-16–1936-day-at-the-races-and-your-nag-in-a-photo-finish/#:~:text=Modern%20digital%20cameras%20can%20take,reading%20on%20a%20single%20image; "Racing: The Gold Cup," *Times of London.*

34. John Hervey, *American Race Horses 1936* (New York: Sagamore, 1936), 182.

35. Bowen, *The Lucky Thirteen,* 66.

36. "Ascot Gold Cup," Wikipedia, accessed April 2021, https://en .wikipedia.org/wiki/Ascot_Gold_Cup.

37. Curling, *The Captain,* 77.

38. Beasley, *Pillow to Post,* 43.

39. Gayle Talbot, "Quashed, an English Filly, Noses Out American Favorite"; Vreeland, "Omaha Carries Hope of U.S. In Race for Ascot Gold Cup."

40. Vreeland, "Omaha Carries Hope of U.S. In Race for Ascot Gold Cup."

41. "150,000 See Turf Thriller," *Windsor Star* (Windsor, ON), June 18, 1936.

42. Curling, *The Captain,* 76.

43. Beasley, *Pillow to Post,* 43.

44. William Woodward, "Letter to Cecil Boyd-Rochfort, 1949," quoted in Magee and Aird, *Ascot,* 190.

45. Curling, *The Captain,* 77; Beasley, *Pillow to Post,* 43.

46. Curling, *The Captain,* 77.

47. W. C. Vreeland, "Omaha, Despite Defeat, Rates Recognition in Britain's Stud Book," *Brooklyn Daily Eagle,* June 20, 1936.

48. Sean Magee, "The 10 Greatest Horse Races of All Time," *Guardian,* accessed May 2021, https://www.theguardian.com/observer/toptens/story /0,,1079224,00.html.

49. Quoted in Magee and Aird, *Ascot,* 191.

50. "Clattering Hoofs," *York Dispatch* (York, PA), June 18, 1936.

20. The Adventure's End

1. "Omaha's Challenge at Newmarket," *Yorkshire Post,* July 2, 1936.

2. "Omaha's Challenge at Newmarket," *Yorkshire Post.*

3. "Bouverie," "Classic Colts to Meet Omaha at Newmarket To-Day," *Daily Mirror,* July 2, 1936.

4. "Stable Boy," "American Crack Racehorse Beaten Again," *Birmingham Gazette,* July 3, 1936.

5. "White Knight," "Gallant American." *Leeds Mercury,* July 3, 1936.

6. "Omaha Beaten Again by Inches in England," *Evening Sun,* July 3, 1936.

7. Curling, *The Captain,* 77.

8. "Bouverie," "Taj Akbar Home by a Neck," *Daily Mirror,* July 3, 1936.

9. "Omaha Beaten Again by Inches in England," *Evening Sun.*

10. "Stable Boy," "American Crack Racehorse Beaten Again."

11. "Woodward's Omaha Loses by Neck to Taj Akbar in Newmarket Race," *New York Times,* July 3, 1936.

12. "The Boaster for Next Week's Bibury Cup," *Gloucestershire Echo,* July 4, 1936.

13. "Omaha On View," *Leeds Mercury,* July 31, 1936; M.C., "Ex-Pools Players," *Northern Daily Mail,* July 31, 1936.

14. "Derby Programme and Possible Starters," *Leeds Mercury,* September 3, 1936.

15. "Newmarket Teams at Work," *Yorkshire Post,* September 21, 1936.

16. "Old Rivals," *Sunday Dispatch,* October 4, 1936.

17. "Quashed and Omaha to Renew Gold Cup Rivalry," *Scotsman,* October 5, 1936.

18. "Quashed and Omaha to Renew Gold Cup Rivalry," *Scotsman.*

19. "The Turf," *Observer* (London, England), October 11, 1936.

20. Denise Steffanus, "Cast Horses: What to Do (And Not to Do) to Help," Paulick Report, accessed August 18, 2021, https://www.paulickreport.com/horse-care-category/cast-horses-what-to-do-and-what-not-to-do-to-help/.

21. "White Knight," "A Gamble Landed," *Leeds Mercury,* November 11, 1936.

22. "Racing Notes," *Times of London,* November 30, 1936.

23. Bowen, *The Lucky Thirteen,* 67.

24. "Ascot Gold Cup," *Belfast Telegraph,* December 18, 1936.

25. "Injury Ends Omaha's Racing Career," *Daily Racing Form,* June 15, 1937.

26. "Prospect for Flat Racing Season," *Scotsman,* March 8, 1937.

27. "Reappearance of Omaha," *Scotsman,* May 26, 1937.

28. "Why Omaha Did Not Run," *Belfast News-Letter,* May 27, 1937.

29. "Rapier on Racing," *Illustrated Sporting and Dramatic News,* June 4, 1937.

30. "Horses to Note for Ascot," *Yorkshire Observer,* June 14, 1937.

31. "Omaha Withdrawn," *Scotsman,* June 14, 1937.

32. "Omaha Withdrawn," *Scotsman.*

33. "Here and There on the Turf," *Daily Racing Form,* June 16, 1937.

34. "Glamorous Gold Cup Day at Ascot," *Western Morning News and Daily Gazette,* June 18, 1937.

35. "Anastasia de Torby," Wikipedia, accessed May 2021, https://en.wikipedia.org/wiki/Anastasia_de_Torby.

36. "Glamorous Gold Cup Day at Ascot," *Western Morning News and Daily Gazette*.

37. "Favorite Wins Ascot Gold Cup," *Baltimore Sun,* June 18, 1937.

38. "Omaha Goes Home," *Birmingham Gazette,* September 2, 1937.

39. "Brighton Meeting," *Times of London,* September 2, 1937.

40. Hervey, *Racing in America,* 234.

21. The Road to Omaha

1. "Omaha at Claiborne," *Blood-Horse,* September 18, 1937, 363.

2. Frank Jennings, *From Here to the Bugle* (Lexington, KY: Host Communications, 1949), 290.

3. Nina Carter Tabb, "Omaha's First Son Is Foaled in Kentucky; Blind Lane Dam," *Richmond Times-Dispatch* (Richmond, VA), February 16, 1939.

4. "Blind Lane," Equibase, accessed May 2021, https://www.equibase.com/profiles/Results.cfm?type=Horse&refno=48206&registry=T.

5. "Morven Stud Consignment to Sales Is Best Offered by Virginia Nursery," *Collyer's Eye and The Baseball World,* August 3, 1940.

6. "Gallant Fox," *Equineline,* accessed January 2022.

7. "Claiborne-Ellerslie Stallions," *Blood-Horse,* February 7, 1942, 249.

8. Avalyn Hunter, "Granville," American Classic Pedigrees, accessed January 2022, http://www.americanclassicpedigrees.com/granville.html.

9. Avalyn Hunter, "Flares," American Classic Pedigrees, accessed January 2022, http://www.americanclassicpedigrees.com/flares.html.

10. "Jockey Club's Plan for Improving Breed of Horses," *Buffalo Evening Times* (Buffalo, NY), May 28, 1906.

11. "War Department Believes in 'Improving the Breed,'" *Daily Press* (Newport News, VA), January 19, 1945.

12. "Hurryoff," Wikipedia, accessed January 2022, https://en.wikipedia.org/wiki/Hurryoff.

13. "Jockey Club Bureau Aids Horse Breeding," *New York Times,* December 26, 1932.

14. "Omaha Presented to Belmont's Stud," *Windsor Star* (Windsor, Ontario), May 26, 1943.

15. "Derby Winner to Appear at Genesee Valley Show," *Rochester Democrat and Chronicle* (Rochester, NY), September 19, 1943.

16. "Tourist," Thoroughbred Heritage, accessed January 2022, https://www.tbheritage.com/Portraits/Tourist.html.

17. L. D. Gasser, "Here and There in Sports," *Owensboro Messenger* (Owensboro, KY), March 31, 1945; Steve Haskin, "The Story of Mort and Omaha," Bloodhorse.com, accessed January 2022, http://cs.bloodhorse .com/blogs/horse-racing-steve-haskin/archive/2013/07/17/the-story-of -mort-and-omaha.aspx.

18. Haskin, "The Story of Mort and Omaha."

19. "Triple Crown Winner Omaha Could Spin Fabulous Tale," *Lincoln Star* (Lincoln, NE), June 23, 1957.

20. Haskin, "The Story of Mort and Omaha."

21. Dan M. Bowmar III, "Thoroughbreds in Nebraska," *Blood-Horse,* November 27, 1954, 1262.

22. Haskin, "The Story of Mort and Omaha."

23. "Triple Crown Winner Omaha Could Spin Fabulous Tale," *Lincoln Star.*

24. "Standing at Claiborne Farm," *Blood-Horse,* January 1, 1949, 4; Avalyn Hunter, "Fighting Fox," American Classic Pedigrees, accessed January 2022, http://www.americanclassicpedigrees.com/fighting-fox.html; Avalyn Hunter, "Princequillo," American Classic Pedigrees, accessed January 2022, http://www.americanclassicpedigrees.com/princequillo-ire.html; Avalyn Hunter, "Blenheim II," American Classic Pedigrees, accessed January 2022, http://www.americanclassicpedigrees.com/blenheim-ii-gb.html.

25. A *chef-de-race,* or chief of racing, is an influential sire in Thoroughbred pedigrees as defined by the Dosage Index, a mathematical formula used in breeding and sometimes in handicapping. The five categories include Brilliant, Intermediate, Classic, Solid, and Professional. Sir Gallahad III is a Classic *chef-de-race.* Wikipedia, accessed August 31, 2022, https://en.wikipedia.org/wiki/Dosage_Index.

26. "Gallant Fox Dies at 27," *Blood-Horse,* November 20, 1954, 1187.

27. "Gallant Fox," *Equineline,* accessed January 2022.

28. "Gallant Fox Dies at 27," *Blood-Horse.*

29. Haskin, "The Story of Mort and Omaha."

30. "Famed Omaha Horse Is Dead," *Hastings Daily Tribune* (Hasting, NE), April 25, 1959.

31. Avalyn Hunter, "Flambino," American Classic Pedigrees, accessed January 2022, http://www.americanclassicpedigrees.com/flambino.html.

32. "Omaha," *Equineline,* accessed January 2022.

33. "Famed Sire Nijinsky II Destroyed," *Chicago Tribune,* April 16, 1992, accessed January 2022, https://www.chicagotribune.com/news/ct -xpm-1992-04-16-9202040132-story.html.

34. Avalyn Hunter, "Damascus," *American Classic Pedigrees,* accessed January 2022, http://www.americanclassicpedigrees.com/damascus.html; Bob Ehalt, "Damascus: An Unforgettable Champion," *America's Best Racing,* accessed January 2022, https://www.americasbestracing.net/the-sport/2020-damascus-unforgettable-champion.

35. Avalyn Hunter, "Valkyr," *American Classic Pedigrees,* accessed January 2022, http://www.americanclassicpedigrees.com/valkyr.html.

36. Avalyn Hunter, "Vagrancy," *American Classic Pedigrees,* accessed January 2022, http://www.americanclassicpedigrees.com/vagrancy.html.

37. Bancroft, *The Red Polka Dots,* 278.

38. "Sir Humphrey de Trafford, 4th Baronet," Wikipedia, accessed January 2022, https://en.wikipedia.org/wiki/Sir_Humphrey_de_Trafford,_4th_Baronet.

39. Curling, *The Captain,* 277–279.

40. "Henry Cecil," Wikipedia, accessed January 2022, https://en.wikipedia.org/wiki/Henry_Cecil.

41. "Belmont Park Form Chart," *Daily Racing Form,* June 12, 1927.

42. Bancroft, *The Red Polka Dots,* 159–160.

43. Mary Jane Gallaher, "First Call," *Lexington Leader* (Lexington, KY), February 27, 1951.

44. Avalyn Hunter, "Nasrullah," *American Classic Pedigrees,* accessed January 2022, http://www.americanclassicpedigrees.com/nasrullah-ire.html.

45. Curling, *The Captain,* 168.

46. Staff of Blood-Horse Publications, *Horse Racing's Top 100 Moments,* 125.

47. Elizabeth would marry Alexander Cushing in 1971, two years after the death of John Teele Pratt Jr.

48. "William Woodward, 77, Dies; Famous Breeder of Horses," *Boston Globe,* September 27, 1953.

49. Gatto, *Belair Stud.*

50. Editors and Writers of the *Daily Racing Form, Champions: The Lives, the Times, and Past Performances of America's Greatest Thoroughbreds* (New York: Daily Racing Form, 2016), 166.

51. Edward L. Bowen, *Nashua: Thoroughbred Legends* (Lexington, KY: Eclipse, 2001), 45–50, 120–121.

52. Bolus, "The Happiest Life," *Spur,* November & December 1994, 59.

53. Bolus, "The Happiest Life," 59.

54. Bolus, "The Happiest Life," 59; Edward L. Bowen, *Masters of the Turf: Ten Trainers Who Dominated Horse Racing's Golden Age* (Lexington, KY: Eclipse, 2007) 175.

55. "James E. 'Sunny Jim' Fitzsimmons," National Museum of Racing and Hall of Fame, accessed January 2022, https://www.racingmuseum.org/hall-of-fame/trainer/james-e-sunny-jim-fitzsimmons.

56. Quoted in Shoop, *Down to the Wire: The Lives of the Triple Crown Champions*, 55.

57. Whitney Tower, "Rushing out of the Barn and Into the Picture," *Sports Illustrated,* April 3, 1967.

58. "Edith Woodward Bancroft Dies; Damascus Owned by Her Stable," *New York Times,* accessed January 2022, https://www.nytimes.com/1971/11/05/archives/edith-woodward-bancroft-dies-damascus-owned-by-her-stable.html; Bowen, *Legacies of the Turf,* 86.

59. Avalyn Hunter, "Damascus," American Classic Pedigrees, accessed January 2022, http://www.americanclassicpedigrees.com/damascus.html.

60. Heckman, *Thoroughbred Legends: Damascus,* 147.

61. Hunter, "Damascus."

Epilogue

1. "American Record Lowered by Sir Barton in Belmont," *Louisville Courier-Journal,* June 12, 1919.

2. Quoted in Dorothy Ours, *Man o' War: A Legend Like Lightning* (New York: St. Martin's, 2008), 142.

3. Jennifer S. Kelly, *Sir Barton and the Making of the Triple Crown* (Lexington: University Press of Kentucky 2019), 205.

4. "Gallant Fox the Champion," *Blood-Horse,* June 14, 1930, 734.

5. "Omaha Becomes Triple Crown Hero," *Daily Racing Form,* June 10, 1935.

6. "Omaha's Belmont Victory," *Blood-Horse,* June 15, 1935, 723.

7. Jonathan Williams, "Sports Economics: NFL, MLB, NHL, and the Effects of the Depression," Bleacher Report, accessed February 2022, https://bleacherreport.com/articles/131212-sports-economics-nfl-mlb-and-nhl-and-the-effects-of-the-depression.

8. Staff of the *Daily Racing Form, American Racing Manual, 1946* (New York: Daily Racing Form, 1946), 569.

9. Tom Ferry, "Native Dancer's Sagamore," All About the Race, accessed January 2022, http://allabouttherace.com/nativedancer.

10. Commander Ross did not attend the banquet as he had relocated to Jamaica in the intervening years between his bankruptcy in 1927 and the TRA's recognition of Sir Barton's achievement in 1950.

11. "North American Records," Equibase, accessed January 2022, https:// www.equibase.com/about/northamericanrecords.cfm; Secretariat's Preakness record was not official until 2012. Chenery maintained that Secretariat had run faster than Pimlico's official time on the day, but the track could not confirm the time "due to extenuating circumstances." A Maryland Racing Commission hearing heard testimony and ruled that 1:53 was the official time for the 1973 Preakness Stakes. Bloodhorse, accessed August 31, 2022, https://www.bloodhorse.com/horse-racing/articles/128636/secretariats -preakness-time-changed.

12. "Annual North American Foal Crop By Decade," Jockey Club, accessed January 2022, https://www.jockeyclub.com/factbook/foalcrop -nabd.html.

Selected Bibliography

Baltz, Shirley V. *Belair from the Beginning.* Bowie, MD: City of Bowie Museums, 2005.

Bancroft, Thomas M., Jr. *The Red Polka Dots.* Easton, PA: Pinters', 2003.

Bolus, Jim. *Derby Magic.* Gretna, LA: Pelican, 1997.

Bowen, Edward L. *Legacies of the Turf: A Century of Great Thoroughbred Breeders,* vol. 1. Lexington, KY: Eclipse, 2005.

————. *The Lucky Thirteen: The Winners of America's Triple Crown of Horse Racing.* Lanham, MD: Lyons, 2019.

————. *Masters of the Turf: Ten Trainers Who Dominated Horse Racing's Golden Age.* Lexington, KY: Eclipse, 2007.

————. *Matriarchs: Great Mares of the 20th Century.* Lexington, KY: Blood Horse, 2000.

Breslin, Jimmy. *Sunny Jim: The Life of America's Most Beloved Horseman, James Fitzsimmons.* Garden City, NY: Doubleday, 1962.

Curling, Bill. *The Captain: A Biography of Captain Sir Cecil Boyd-Rochfort, Royal Trainer.* London: Barrie & Jenkins, 1970.

Drager, Marvin, with Ed McNamara. *The Most Glorious Crown: The Story of America's Triple Crown Thoroughbreds from Sir Barton to American Pharoah.* Chicago, IL: Triumph, 2016.

Gatto, Kimberly. *Belair Stud: The Cradle of Maryland Horse Racing.* Charleston, SC: History Press, 2012.

Hirsch, Joe. *The First Century: Daily Racing Form Chronicles 100 Years of the Thoroughbred Racing.* New York: Daily Racing Form, 1996.

Magee, Sean, and Sally Aird. *Ascot: The History.* London: Methuen, 2002.

Robertson, William H. P. *The History of Thoroughbred Racing in America.* New York: Bonanza, 1964.

Runyon, Damon. *I Got the Horse Right Here: Damon Runyon on Horse Racing.* Edited by Jim Reisler. Lanham, MD: Lyons, 2020.

Shoop, Robert. *Down to the Wire: The Lives of the Triple Crown Champions.* Everson, WA: Russell Dean, 2004.

Index

Ballot Handicap, 82

Bancroft, Edith Woodward, 188,
242, 246, 250

Bancroft, Thomas M., Jr., 29,
250

Bancroft, William Woodward,
250

Bannerette, 95

Barbee, George, 68, 70

Barnes, Eddie, 85

Bask, 133

Beasley, Harry, 204

Beasley, Patrick Thomas "Pat" (aka
"Rufus"), 204, 206, 208–209,
214–216, 218–220, 223–224,
228–230, 307

Bejsack, John, 178

Belair (estate), 10, 12, 17, 20–27,
39, 41–44, 47, 49, 52, 63, 66,
140, 141, 164, 166, 192–193,
198, 246, 247, 251; Benjamin
Tasker Jr. as caretaker, 43;
James T. Woodward purchases,
17; Omaha recuperates at,
192–193; Selima, 43–44;
weanlings at, 10, 42, 47;
William Woodward inherits, 21

Belair Stud, 10, 12, 20, 22–25, 47,
49, 54, 63, 66, 140, 148, 164,
166, 192

Belair Stud stable, 27, 28, 39, 131,
151, 156, 157, 164, 188, 245,
247, 250

Beldame, 113

Beldame Handicap, 233, 243

Belmont, August, II, 10, 19,
25–26, 29, 31, 35, 90, 218, 257,
279n6

Belmont, Mrs. August, II, 90

Belmont, Beau, 153

Belmont Park, 24, 29, 45, 54, 75,
82–87, 92–93, 112, 118,
121–123, 133, 149–151,
170–173, 181, 183, 191, 213,
247, 254, 258, 261–262

Belmont Stakes, 16, 27, 40, 46, 54,
60, 66, 73, 81–86, 88–94, 98,
105, 108, 114, 117, 125, 133,
139–140, 148, 151, 154–156,
164, 168–169, 171, 173,
174–176, 180–182, 198, 231,
239, 242–243, 245, 247,
249–250, 252, 254–261, 271n5,
272n16; 1930 race, 86–90;
1935 race, 173–175

Ben Machree, 114

Berwanger, Jay, 195

Billings, C. K. G., 278n3

Billy Kelly, 147

Bimelech, 258

Blackbirder, 186

Black Cyclone, 185

Black-Eyed Susan Stakes, 200

Black Gift, 150

Black Helen, 184–189

Black Majesty, 82–83

Black Monday, 101, 134

Black Tarquin, 244

Black Toney, 145, 184, 188

Black Tuesday, 133

Blazes, 46

Blenheim II, 233, 238, 262

Blind Lane, 233–234

Blinkers, 78, 115, 125, 206, 213,
219

Blood-Horse, The, 138, 255–256

Bloodroot, 184–189

Blue Larkspur, 99, 122, 146, 163,
166, 188

Bobashela, 107

Horses in History

Series Editor: James C. Nicholson

For thousands of years, humans have utilized horses for transportation, recreation, war, agriculture, and sport. Arguably, no animal has had a greater influence on human history. Horses in History explores this special human-equine relationship, encompassing a broad range of topics, from ancient Chinese polo to modern Thoroughbred racing. From biographies of influential equestrians to studies of horses in literature, television, and film, this series profiles racehorses, warhorses, sport horses, and plow horses in novel and compelling ways.